BY **MATT**
WITH **PA**

MW00479696

HATING JESUS

THE AMERICAN LEFT'S
WAR ON CHRISTIANITY

barbwire
BOOKS

Endorsements:

"*In Hating Jesus: The American Left's War on Christianity,* Matt Barber delivers a masterful blow-by-blow investigation of how the Left sucker-punched people of faith. His book is filled with truth bombs that are guaranteed to send liberals scampering to their safe spaces."

Todd Starnes, Fox News Radio

"In his 'must read' book, *Hating Jesus,* my friend Matt Barber persuasively argues that anti-Christian facets of the organized Left have placed the Christian faithful squarely in their crosshairs. Though Christ foretold this would happen and Scripture instructs us to 'count it all joy,' we must still defend our Savior and fight tirelessly for our religious liberty. Accordingly, Matt calls on the body of Christ to unite in the effort and provides a realistic and effective action plan. A timely and inspirational clarion call."

David Limbaugh, attorney, best-selling author
and brother of talk-radio host Rush Limbaugh

"Matt Barber is very plain spoken and with *Hating Jesus* he proves for any skeptics that there is a full blown attack on Christianity and explains how we can fight back."

Tim Wildmon, president of the American Family Association
and American Family Radio

"In his terrific new book, *Hating Jesus,* Matt Barber exposes the shameful secret agenda underlying what the Left euphemistically calls its 'fundamental transformation of America' – and that is, the relentless elimination of Christian values, morals and institutions in this once-Christian nation. In particular, Matt documents how the Left has unleashed the full fury of its money, power and political influence to advance the ever-more-bizarre LGBT agenda, which has effectively became the 'point of the Left's spear' for attacking Christians. Fortunately, Matt, a former undefeated heavyweight boxer and now a heavyweight attorney and culture warrior, shows Christians not only how to effectively defend themselves, but how they can breathe new life into America's besieged Christian culture and demonstrate God's love and power at the same time."

David Kupelian, best-selling author of
***The Marketing of Evil* and WND.com managing editor**

"With one compelling example after another, Matt Barber hits us between the eyes with the reality that war has been declared on Christians and the Christian faith in the very nation that was founded on Christian principles. What will you tell your kids and grandkids when they ask you what you were doing when their most fundamental rights were taken away?"

Michael L. Brown, Ph.D., host of the national Line of Fire radio broadcast

"Matt Barber lays bare the true goal of progressivism, which is the vanquishing of a Biblical worldview from American public life. The reason being is that throughout history the most effective antidote to tyranny has been the resolve and courage of conviction of God's covenant people. Whether that tyranny takes the face of Antiochus Epiphanes, wannabe Roman god-emperors, or King George III, it is the church that defiantly reminds the state only God is God and the state is not. Thank God we still have a remnant of men in America like Matt willing to kick Baal in the groin instead of bowing the knee."

Steve Deace, Salem Radio Network/Conservative Review

About the Book:

The new pagan gods of the late, great USA are self-worshipping men and women who, realize it or not, spend every waking hour doing evil. You know them as American leftists. They are waging a War on Christianity and, for now at least, are winning.

Just a few short decades ago a church-going man who publicly supported the right to life, backed laws protecting marriage, and spoke freely of Christ's love for fallen man, would be universally recognized as a fine and upstanding citizen. He would be welcomed anywhere, including at the highest levels of power. But things have changed. In today's America, the "progressive" left destroys such a man.

Secular leftists don't merely have a disagreement with Christianity. They demand nothing less than the abolition of the biblical worldview, and the destruction of Christ's followers right along with it.

In *Hating Jesus* Matt Barber first documents how successful the American left has been in its War on Christianity and then concludes by providing both hope and a simple plan on how the body of Christ can fight back against the enemies of God.

About the Authors

Matt Barber

Matt Barber is founder and editor-in chief of BarbWire.com. He serves as Associate Dean with Liberty University School of Law, is an attorney concentrating in constitutional law, and holds both a Master of Arts in Public Policy and Juris Doctor from Regent University.

Matt is an author and a popular columnist. He's known for a unique writing style (an entertaining blend of thoughtful analysis and Swiftian satire, delivered with a rapier wit). Many newspapers and online publications run Matt's columns, including *WND, TheBlaze, The Washington Times, TownHall* and many more. Author of the book, *The Right Hook: From the Ring to the Culture War*, Matt is also penning his first novel.

In addition to frequent public speaking engagements, Matt has appeared as a cultural analyst on the Fox News Channel, MSNBC and CNN and is a regular guest on dozens of talk radio programs and networks including Michael Savage, American Family Radio, Dennis Prager, the Michael Medved Show, the Janet Mefferd Show and others. Matt also co-hosts "Faith and Freedom," a daily legal and cultural issues talk radio program hosted by Mat Staver, provided by Liberty Counsel and heard on dozens of radio stations across the country.

Matt served twelve years in the Army National Guard, was a law enforcement officer for three years and a corporate fraud investigator for five years.

Setting him apart from others in his various fields, Matt was an undefeated heavyweight professional boxer retiring in 2004. Prior to turning pro, he was a several time state and regional Golden Gloves champion, competing in the 1992 Western Olympic Trials and winning a Gold Medal in the 1993 Police and Fire World Games.

Paul Hair

Paul Hair writes fiction and nonfiction. He writes under his own name and he ghostwrites for other authors and personalities.

He is a creator at Liberty Island, a webzine dedicated to promoting authors of novels and short stories. *Mortal Gods: Ignition* and *Winning through Losing*, two short story collections, are available at Amazon.com.

His nonfiction writings have appeared at BarbWire.com, *Breitbart, The Daily Caller, WND,* and other nationally recognized outlets.

Paul also is a veteran intelligence analyst who consults for a variety of clients. He provides them with professional intelligence analysis and other national security insights for strategic planning, geopolitical and economic analysis, forecasting and risk management solutions, and other related uses. He also writes open-source intelligence assessments and policy solutions.

Connect with him at www.liberateliberty.com. Contact him at paul@liberate-liberty.com if you are interested in hiring him for writing, ghostwriting, or intelligence consulting.

Hating Jesus

The American Left's War on Christianity

By Matt Barber

with Paul Hair

Dedication

This book is dedicated to my wife and best friend, Sarah Barber. I'm so blessed to do life with you, baby. You are the most beautiful and godly woman I know.

Contents

Acknowledgements

First, a note on the Bible verses I cite throughout the book. I cite many Bible verses and use various translations in doing so. Where appropriate, I note the translation I used. In other cases, I do not list a translation because the excerpted verse is so short and because multiple translations render that excerpt exactly the same.

And now for the acknowledgements.

Special thanks to my co-laborer on this project, Paul Hair, for his many hours of painstaking research and editing. I'd likewise like to thank our terrific copy editor, Janna Madsen, who also happens to be my younger sister. Paul and I are responsible for any mistakes left in the book.

Thank you also goes to BarbWire Books CFO and Managing Publisher Tristan Emmanuel who oversaw this project and ensured its completion. The book wouldn't have happened without him.

Finally, thank you Jesus for loving the world and saving a wretch like me.

Introduction

"If the world hates you, keep in mind that it hated me first. If you belonged to the world, it would love you as its own. As it is, you do not belong to the world, but I have chosen you out of the world. That is why the world hates you. Remember what I told you: 'A servant is not greater than his master.' If they persecuted me, they will persecute you also. If they obeyed my teaching, they will obey yours also. They will treat you this way because of my name, for they do not know the one who sent me."

– John 15:18-21 (New International Version)

Christians are under attack in America.

The owner of a popular fast food restaurant chain is a Christian who supports protecting marriage. Homosexual activists and their supporters target him and his business for destruction.

An extremist, anti-Christian "law center" targets a well-respected, mainstream Christian organization on a "hate group" map on its website. As a result, a homosexual terrorist and anti-Christian acolyte targets the headquarters of the Christian group for mass murder, only to be stopped by a heroic security guard.

American troops attempt to follow their Christian faith, and anti-Christian activists respond by attempting to ruin their careers and lives, all while the U.S. actively fights for Christian-killing Muslims in nations across the globe— including nations where the U.S. helped officially establish Islamic theocracies.

A bakery politely declines to help homosexuals celebrating the desecration of the institution of marriage. The homosexuals sue the Christian owners for discrimination—and win.

1

An American pastor encourages the nation of Uganda to resist the homosexual agenda. The United States government responds by allowing a nongovernmental extremist organization to charge him in court with "crimes against humanity."

Christian parents don't want their children to engage in sexual deviancy and try to help them determine the cause of their unwanted same-sex attractions. A homosexual lawmaker threatens to take their children away from them by claiming the parents are "abusing" their children. Meanwhile, doctors sexually mutilate gender-confused children and pump them full of dangerous hormones in an attempt to make them cosmetically appear as the opposite sex, all while politicians and cultural leaders applaud.

Are these travesties things you thought never you'd witness in a free America? If so, you aren't alone. Many Americans never imagined the day when their countrymen would increasingly deny the Christian heritage of our nation. Many more never thought they'd see an America that would openly despise and persecute Christians for their unwavering faith in Jesus Christ, the one true God and Savior of the world.

Yet that day has arrived.

American Christians are now struggling for basic human rights and living under daily threat of legal, reputational and even physical abuse, simply for exercising their faith. On top of this, the U.S. has become a global force for evil, evangelizing against Christianity, and aggressively pushing for sexual deviancy and other sins. Immorality has become our chief export and pride our chief import.

How did this once great nation fall so far, so fast? How did this hatred of Christianity and Christ's followers come about, and is it possible to defeat it, put the U.S. back on the right track and avoid God's well-deserved wrath? Can we ever, once again, receive the great favor He bestowed upon us some time ago?

In order to answer these questions we must examine several items, including:

1. The history of Christianity and the United States of America.

2. Specific examples of anti-Christians attacking Christianity in America.

3. How the specific examples of anti-Christian attacks in America are part of a larger war in America meant to destroy Christianity and all liberty.

4. The point in recent history when the anti-Christians organized and developed a strategy to wipe out Christianity in America, taking us to where we are today.

Examining these four major areas will then help us to better understand how we might fight back and win—how we can undo the damage the enemies of

Christ have wreaked, while setting the nation back on a path to repentance, peace, prosperity and, most importantly, a deep love for God, both individually and corporately.

To be sure, while there are many persons and groups in the U.S. who hate Christ, perhaps the chief extremists leading the War on Christianity are the "LGBT" special interests; or, as I prefer, the "Big Sin" lobby. They are tremendously well-funded, organized and highly influential. For this reason, you will see multiple examples in the coming pages of homosexuals attacking Christianity in general, and Christians in particular, even as there remain myriad more anti-Christians and other "progressive" extremist groups (some of which we will detail) who, likewise, hate authentic Christianity in America.

Among other things, I've written about these issues in my columns for years now. If you've followed my writing, you'll see that, for the purposes of this book, I've adapted, expanded and expounded upon the cultural, political and spiritual issues in my columns that matter so much to the lives, faith and freedom of every American citizen.

PART 1

Chapter 1

Yes, America Did Begin as a Christian Nation

"America is neither now, nor has it ever been a 'Christian nation.'"

This statement is something you're as likely to hear from conservatives as from progressives—from Christians, as from atheists. Those who repeat this line seem to take solace in imagining that our nation has *never* been Christian.

One of the reasons Christ-haters are so bold in attacking Christianity in America is that they've long been successful in rewriting history with the above disinformation, convincing others with relentless propaganda that their secularist revisionism is historical reality, while, at one go, suggesting that those actually tethered to reality are the ones guilty of historical revisionism. It's progressivism 101. Call up down, an apple an orange and then ridicule those who disagree. It's important to acknowledge this historical fallacy and to understand why it's wrong. Therefore let's take time to examine Christianity in America before we move on to the more present war being waged against American Christians.

It is true that America was not founded as a Christian theocracy. Yet because the federal government of the United States of America was never a theocracy, many people, including those who acknowledge that God, Christianity and Christians played a fundamental role in the history and founding of the U.S., argue that this means that America was not founded as a Christian nation.

For instance, the Heritage Foundation published an adaptation of a lecture that Dr. Mark David Hall, distinguished professor of politics at George Fox University, delivered in 2011.

Hall makes it clear in the body of "Did America Have a Christian Foundation?" that Christianity was a fundamental part of foundational America:

The Founders were also informed by the Anglo-American political-legal tradition and their own political experience, and like all humans, they were motivated to varying degrees by self, class, or state interests. My contention is merely that orthodox Christianity had a very significant influence on America's Founders and that this influence is often over-looked by students of the American Founding.[1]

At the same time, an excerpt from the abstract of the lecture adaptation says this about America having a Christian Founding:

Did America have a Christian Founding? This disputed question, far from being only of historical interest, has important implications for how we conceive of the role of religion in the American republic. Mark David Hall begins by considering two popular answers to the query—"Of course not!" and "Absolutely!"—both of which distort the Founders' views.

American history buffs might enjoy reading the entire lecture adaptation and are encouraged to do so. Decide for yourself exactly what Hall and the Heritage Foundation have concluded about the role Christianity played in the foundation of America; decide whether you agree.

However, it is wrong to posit that America was never a Christian nation merely because the federal government was never a Christian theocracy. There are three reasons why.

1 – A Christian Nation Doesn't Have to Be a Christian Theocracy

First, if the definition of what constitutes a Christian nation is that a nation must be a theocracy, then we have a very narrow definition indeed. And if that's the case, then such a definition should apply to all countries and religions. Still, it's hard to imagine people applying such a strict definition to any other nation denoted by some non-Christian religious majority.

For instance, are nations we think of as Islamic truly Islamic if their governing documents do not explicitly say they are? The Turkish constitution expressly says that this Muslim majority nation is a secular nation (repeatedly), so does this mean that Turkey is not an Islamic nation? "Yes!" some might say. Well, try living in this 99.8 percent Islamic nation before denying its Islamic heritage and Islamic influence.[2] Go there and proclaim on any street corner that because Turkey's constitution purports to be secular, Turkey is therefore not Islamic. But do so at your own risk. You may just lose your head in the process.

Many naysayers will also argue, disingenuously so, that America's treaties with the Barbary States in the late eighteenth and early nineteenth centuries firmly establish the U.S. as a secular nation. But this argument falls flat too. Specifically, anti-Christians frequently cite the Treaty of Peace and Friendship between the U.S. and Tripoli, signed in 1796, as "proof" the U.S. is not a Christian nation.

ARTICLE 11.

As the government of the United States of America is not in any sense founded on the Christian Religion, -as it has in itself no character of enmity against the laws, religion or tranquility of Musselmen, -and as the said States never have entered into any war or act of hostility against any Mehomitan nation, it is declared by the parties that no pretext arising from religious opinions shall ever produce an interruption of the harmony existing between the two countries.[3]

All the normal rules of academic and intellectual honesty seem to disappear when people cite this one passage from a little-known, late-eighteenth-century treaty as their proof that America was never a Christian nation. For instance, the above cited passage only appears in the English version of the treaty—not the Arabic one. People attempt to get around this by saying the English version is the one the Senate ratified, and therefore that's all that matters. That might be true, but reverse the situation for a moment: if a hypothetical secular nation, filled with secular documents and writings, had a single document—a treaty attempting to appease an enemy—that stated (in its English version only) that the notional secular nation had never been secular, would anyone argue that notional document "proved" the notional secular nation wasn't secular?

And appeasing the Musselmen (Muslims) of Tripoli was indeed what the United States was attempting to do in the Treaty of Peace and Friendship. The official Department of State website provides context into why the U.S. signed this treaty with Tripoli, and also shows how the treaty essentially became irrelevant once Tripoli violated it:

Prior to independence, American colonists had enjoyed the protection of the British Navy. However, once the United States declared independence, British diplomats were quick to inform the Barbary States that U.S. ships were open to attack. In 1785, Dey Muhammad of Algiers declared war on the United States and captured several American ships. The financially troubled Confederation Government of the United States was unable to raise a navy or the tribute that would protect U.S. ships. ...

In 1793 a brief Portuguese-Algerian truce exposed American merchant ships to capture, forcing the United States, which had thus far only managed to conclude a treaty with Morocco, to engage in negotiations with

9

the other Barbary States. In 1795, The U.S. Government dispatched diplomats Joel Barlow, Joseph Donaldson, and Richard O'Brien to North Africa and successfully concluded treaties with the states of Algiers, Tunis, and Tripoli. Under the terms of these treaties, the United States agreed to pay tribute to these states. The treaty with Algiers freed 83 American sailors.

The adoption of the Constitution in 1789 gave the U.S. Government the power to levy taxes and to raise and maintain armed forces, powers which had been lacking under the Articles of Confederation. In 1794, in response to Algerian seizures of American ships, Congress authorized construction of the first 6 ships of the U.S. Navy. In 1801, the Pasha of Tripoli, Yusuf Qaramanli, citing late payments of tribute, demanded additional tribute and declared war on the United States. The United States successfully defeated Qaramanli's forces with a combined naval and land assault by the United States Marine Corps. The U.S. treaty with Tripoli concluded in 1805 included a ransom for American prisoners in Tripoli, but no provisions for tribute.[4]

So, the U.S. ratified the Treaty of Peace and Friendship because it couldn't adequately defend itself at that early point in its history, and it was forced to use conciliatory language at that time with the Muslims of Tripoli. The U.S. wasn't truly able to begin projecting global power and influence until after 1800.

Moreover, the U.S. Department of State history page notes that Tripoli broke the treaty when it declared war on the United States. The U.S. sent in the Marines and put an end to that war and the U.S. and Tripoli signed a new treaty. Not only did this subsequent Treaty of Peace and Amity omit any conciliatory language about not being "founded on the Christian Religion," but, instead, it now added language demanding that the Muslims of Tripoli respect the religion of the American people. That, of course, was, and is, Christianity:

As the Government of the United States of America, has in itself no character of enmity against the Laws, Religion or Tranquility of Musselmen, and as the said States never have entered into any voluntary war or act of hostility against any Mahometan Nation, except in the defence of their just rights to freely navigate the High Seas: It is declared by the contracting parties that no pretext arising from Religious Opinions, shall ever produce an interruption of the Harmony existing between the two Nations; And the Consuls and Agents of both Nations respectively, shall have liberty to exercise his Religion in his own house; all slaves of the same Religion shall not be Impeded in going to said Consuls house at hours of Prayer. The Consuls shall have liberty and personal security given them to travel within the Territories of each other, both by land and sea, and shall not be prevented from going on board any Vessel that they may think proper to visit; they shall have likewise the liberty to appoint their own Drogoman and Brokers.[5]

Sounds a bit different from the Treaty of Peace and Friendship, doesn't it?

So, when someone attempts to cite this broken, obsolete treaty as "proof" that the U.S. was never a Christian nation, remind them of what those words in Article 11 actually mean. And remind them that it is an utterly irrelevant document that was trumped by the Treaty of Peace and Amity—that the latter document takes a completely different tone with the Musselmen of Tripoli and that, not only does it not deny the fact of Christianity's profound influence on America, it directly bolsters it.

Still, many anti-Christians refuse to give up after citing the Treaty of Peace and Friendship in asserting that the U.S. was never a Christian nation; they sometimes point to our founding documents as well. For instance, Jeff Schweitzer, identified as a "Scientist and former White House Senior Policy Analyst; Ph.D. in marine biology/neurophysiology," argued in a 2015 *Huffington Post* opinion piece that the Constitution and other foundational documents define the U.S. as secular:

> *Let us be perfectly clear: We are not now, nor have we ever been, a Christian nation. Our founding fathers explicitly and clearly excluded any reference to "God" or "the Almighty" or any euphemism for a higher power in the Constitution. Not one time is the word "god" mentioned in our founding document. Not one time.*
>
> *The facts of our history are easy enough to verify. Anybody who ignorantly insists that our nation is founded on Christian ideals need only look at the four most important documents from our early history—the Declaration of Independence, the Articles of Confederation, the Federalist Papers and the Constitution—to disprove that ridiculous religious bias. All four documents unambiguously prove our secular origins.*[6]

These statements by the good doctor are demonstrably false. Not only is his assertion that the U.S. is "secular" inaccurate, since "secular" never appears anywhere in any of the foundational documents he cites, but his proclamations about God not appearing in them are equally wrongheaded. In fact, Schweitzer later undercuts his own arguments by pointing out where three of the documents do refer to God—often with synonyms—only to attempt to argue that they don't say what they say.

So what do they say?

The Declaration of Independence begins by openly acknowledging that "our Creator" (aka, "God") gives us our rights. That is to say, our rights come from God—not from secularism, not from mankind. Meanwhile, the U.S. Constitution ends by referring to "the Year of Our Lord" (more on the significance of this phrase later). And the Federalist Papers at one point reference "Providence" (again, a synonym for God's hand in our lives and the life of a nation). They deliberately include the word "God" in at least one instance as well. Finally, the Articles of Confederation talk about the "Great Governor of the World," which Schweitzer notes in one of the many instances that serve to undercut his own arguments. Additionally, like the U.S. Constitution, the Federalist Papers end with the phrase, "the Year of Our Lord."

The Declaration's explicit affirmation that our rights come from our Creator is particularly difficult to overcome for those wishing that the U.S. had never been a Christian nation. In fact, they can't. Yet they try. They try to get around this by arguing that the Declaration isn't part of U.S. law—that the Founders essentially rejected it when they created the Constitution.

Schweitzer attempts this in the aforementioned article, "Remember, too," he asserts, "that this document was not written to form or found a government but was stating intent in a way that was meant to appeal to an audience with European sensibilities."

Mark Edwards, a progressive history professor at Spring Arbor University in Michigan, makes a similar, and equally erroneous, suggestion in a CNN. com opinion piece. "To be sure, the Declaration of Independence appealed to 'the laws of Nature and Nature's God' and asserted that all men had basic rights 'endowed by their Creator,'" he writes. "But the Constitution—the document that actually enumerated and enshrined those rights—lacked even those vaguely drawn references to a deity."[7]

Both men's arguments are invalid and demonstrably so. While not addressing these men directly, Alabama Chief Justice Roy Moore, for instance, demonstrated the baselessness of their historical interpretations—interpretations shared by many progressives—while appearing on CNN's *New Day* on February 12, 2015, and utterly humiliated host Chris Cuomo after Cuomo tried to argue with the Chief Justice during a debate over the actual definition of marriage.

> MOORE: *No, I believe that's a matter of law because our rights contained in the bill of rights do not come from the Constitution; they come from God. It's clearly stated.*

> CUOMO: *Our laws do not come from God, Your Honor, and you know that. They come from man.*

MOORE: Well, let me ask you one question. Let me ask you one question, Chris. Is the Declaration of Independence law?

CUOMO: You would call it organic law as a basis for future laws off of it?

MOORE: I would call it the organic law because the United States code calls it organic law. It is organic law because the law of this country calls it the organic law of our country means where our rights come from. And if they come from there, men can't take them away.

CUOMO: Our rights do not come from God. That's your faith. That's my faith. But that's not our country. Our laws come from collective agreement and compromise.

MOORE: It's not a matter of faith, sir; it's a matter of organic law, which states we hold these truths to be self-evident that all men are held equal and endowed by their Creator with certain inalienable rights, that among these are life, liberty, and the pursuit of happiness. And the only role of government is stated in the next sentence, is to secure those rights for us. When government starts taking those rights away from us, then it's not securing it for us; it is violating the whole purpose of government.[8]

The argument that the Constitution fails to reference God, or a deity, is likewise erroneous. But let's first look at another misrepresentation about the federal Constitution— one that claims it requires "separation of Church and State."

The words, "separation of Church and State" appear nowhere in the U.S. Constitution. Neither does the Constitution require Church-State separation in a way those hostile to Christianity insist that it does.

And they know it.

Anti-Christians have intentionally created confusion about what the Constitution says about God and religion through activist liberal (or "progressive") historical and judicial revisionism. They accomplished this through a decades-long religious cleansing campaign designed to, as Barack Obama calls it, "fundamentally transform America." Progressives have misused and abused the Establishment Clause of the First Amendment—just ten words in length—as their primary tool in achieving this fundamental transformation. Nevertheless, and despite their success in misrepresenting the Establishment Clause, its true meaning remains abundantly clear. So let's break down what, "Congress shall make no law respecting an establishment of religion…." actually means.

First, what do you suppose the framers of the U.S. Constitution—a document specifically designed to limit the powers of the federal government—intended with the word "Congress"? Were they referring to state governments? Municipal governments? Or what about your local school board or even third grade teacher?

Obviously they were not referring to any of these. They were referring to exactly what they said: Congress—as in, the United States Congress.

Next, what did they mean by, "…shall make no law respecting an establishment of religion"? Thomas Jefferson (often touted by progressives as the great Church-State separationist) answered this question through a letter to Benjamin Rush, a fellow signer of the Declaration of Independence. "[T]he clause of the constitution" covering "freedom of religion" was intended to necessarily preclude "an establishment of a particular form of Christianity thro' the US," Jefferson wrote to Rush.[9]

So Jefferson assured Rush that the Establishment Clause of the First Amendment was simply intended to restrict Congress from affirmatively establishing, through federal legislation, a national Christian denomination (similar to how the Anglican Church of England is the official denomination of England).

Now, with this understood, let's go back to the claim that the Constitution makes no reference to Christ, God or deity of any kind.

The Constitution closes by declaring that it was "done in Convention by the Unanimous Consent of the States present the Seventeenth Day of September in the Year of our Lord one thousand seven hundred and Eighty seven…" As mentioned above, this is a significant phrase. It is a specific reference to Jesus Christ—an explicit acknowledgement of His Divinity and Leadership. The rationalizing secularist might immediately object to pointing to this language as evidence that America was indeed founded as a Christian nation: "Oh, that was just the language of the time. It would be no different than saying, 'July Fourth, Seventeen Seventy-six' today," they might say. Or, "It's simply archaic language that is no longer used today but also didn't mean that Christ or Christianity had any special significance back then either."

Such a counterargument might have worked at one time but is fast becoming increasingly weak. In fact, paradoxically, it is often anti-Christian overreach that unintentionally ends up making the strongest case that, based upon the Constitution's unambiguous language, America was indeed founded as a Christian nation.

Here's why.

Even as people might currently argue that the use of "in the Year of Our Lord" is an archaic phrase that didn't mean what it actually says it means, even in 1776, there is a sustained, modern effort to eliminate use of the terms "B.C."

("Before Christ") and "A.D." ("Anno Domini"—Latin for, "Year of Our Lord") when referring to dates. Those warring against B.C. and A.D. want to replace those terms with "C.E." and "B.C.E."—"Common Era" and "Before Common Era."

This is how passionate many progressive Church-State separatists and religious segregationists are in their hatred of Christ and Christianity. They want to wipe out every vestige of Jesus from history and even everyday life—including when referencing dates.[10] In bellowing that Western Civilization's centuries-old practice for recording dates based upon the birth of our Savior offends them, they inadvertently reveal that the phrase, "in the Year of Our Lord" truly does have timeless historical, spiritual and cultural significance—not just in 1776, but today as well.

So, since the term, "in the Year of Our Lord" is acknowledged by secularists to mean what it truly means—in the year of our Lord Jesus—then the argument that the Constitution makes no reference to Christ, or God the Father, and, thusly, that America is not now, nor has it ever been, a Christian nation, simply doesn't hold water. This will become more and more evident as progressives and other anti-Christians ramp up efforts to codify their hatred of "B.C." and "A.D." by manipulating state and federal governments in the U.S. to ban the use of these transcendent date stamps in official government business. This is already being done in a number of other anti-Christ nations.[11]

2 – The Federal Government Was Never a Christian Theocracy, but Many Individual States Essentially Were

The second reason we must reject the argument that America was never a Christian nation because it was never a Christian theocracy is that such reasoning depends on either a willfully ignorant, or purposefully skewed understanding of the federal government's primary purpose.

The correct, the original, understanding of how the Framers intended the federal government to operate can be derived from our nation's very name: the United States of America. The U.S.A. was, in essence, meant to be an organization of multiple independent nations (note that the term "state" regularly refers to an independent country) that granted certain and very limited authorities to an umbrella governmental body (the federal government) for the common good.

Therefore, while it's true that the United States of America was never a Christian theocracy at the federal level, it's equally true that there were many individual Christian "theocracies," if you will, at the state level, something Hall notes in his Heritage lecture:

It is true that the last state church was disestablished in 1832, but many states retained religious tests for public office, had laws aimed at restricting vice, required prayer in schools, and so forth. Because the federal government was not to be concerned with these issues, they were not addressed in the Constitution. The First Amendment merely reinforced this understanding with respect to the faith—i.e., Congress has no power to establish a national church or restrict the free exercise of religion.[12]

Notice, as Hall points out, that "the last state church was disestablished in 1832."[13] So what does this mean? It means that, throughout our nation's nearly first half-century, there were official state churches (exclusively Christian denominations) in multiple states, even after the ratification of the U.S. Constitution, and, thus, it means—it proves—that the Founding Fathers allowed for Christian "theocracies" at the state level. There's no denying it. So-called "separation of Church and State" is nothing more than an anti-Christian myth. It's wishful thinking on the part of those progressives endeavoring to "fundamentally transform" America to reflect their own secular humanist self-image.

The argument that America was not, and is not, a Christian nation proves even more derisory when one considers each state's individual constitution. You might be amazed to learn that all fifty state constitutions explicitly and unequivocally thank God—the God of Christianity—for His benevolence, and further acknowledge that we as a nation are wholly dependent upon Him—that He is the sole source of our freedoms. This is true, not just for the so-called red states, but for the bluest of the blue.

For instance, let's look at Massachusetts (home of "the last state church" referenced above by Hall). It is perhaps the most progressive state in the Union. Yet here is what the third paragraph of its constitutional Preamble declares:

We, therefore, the people of Massachusetts, acknowledging, with grateful hearts, the goodness of the great Legislator of the universe, in affording us, in the course of His providence, an opportunity, deliberately and peaceably, without fraud, violence or surprise, of entering into an original, explicit, and solemn compact with each other; and of forming a new constitution of civil government, for ourselves and posterity; and devoutly imploring His direction in so interesting a design, do agree upon, ordain and establish the following Declaration of Rights, and Frame of Government, as the Constitution of the Commonwealth of Massachusetts.

Part I, Article 2 of the same constitution invokes God again:

It is the right as well as the duty of all men in society, publicly, and at stated seasons to worship the Supreme Being, the great Creator and Preserver of the universe. And no subject shall be hurt, molested, or restrained, in his person, liberty, or estate, for worshipping God in the manner and season most agreeable to the dictates of his own conscience; or for his religious profession or sentiments; provided he doth not disturb the public peace, or obstruct others in their religious worship.

Did you know that, people of Massachusetts? According to your own constitution it's not just your absolute right, but your "duty"—your constitutional duty—to publicly worship God. And if the ACLU, People for the American Way (PFAW), the Freedom From Religion Foundation or some other band of anti-Christian segregationists comes along and tries to "hurt," "molest" or "restrain" you in so doing, you can tell them to go straight to—well, they can hurry along to where they're already headed (of course we hope and pray they don't).

Later still in Chapter V, Section 1, Article 1 the constitution talks about God and education:

Whereas our wise and pious ancestors, so early as the year one thousand six hundred and thirty-six, laid the foundation of Harvard College, in which university many persons of great eminence have, by the blessing of God, been initiated in those arts and sciences, which qualified them for public employments, both in church and state: and whereas the encouragement of arts and sciences, and all good literature, tends to the honor of God, the advantage of the Christian religion, and the great benefit of this and the other United States of America...

Oh, but how hard has fallen the once great Harvard.

So, from the original text of the Constitution of the Commonwealth of Massachusetts alone, you can again see that the claim that the U.S. Constitution has a Church-State separation requirement is a lie. But also, again, the Massachusetts constitution isn't alone in demonstrating this. All the other states invoke God in their constitutions as well—even the ones that never had an official state religion. I won't go through them all but I'll provide you with a sample of how such constitutions read.

The Preamble of the Constitution of the State of Illinois expresses its gratitude towards God: "We, the People of the State of Illinois—grateful to Almighty God for the civil, political and religious liberty which He has permitted us to enjoy and seeking His blessing upon our endeavors...do ordain and establish this Constitution for the State of Illinois."

And the Preamble of the California Constitution also gives thanks to God: "We, the People of the State of California, grateful to Almighty God for our freedom, in order to secure and perpetuate its blessings, do establish this Constitution."

New York does the same thing with its constitutional Preamble: "We The People of the State of New York, grateful to Almighty God for our Freedom, in order to secure its blessings, DO ESTABLISH THIS CONSTITUTION" (emphasis in the original).

The Constitution of the Commonwealth of Pennsylvania mentions God too. It invokes Him in its Preamble. And it invokes God again in Article I, Section 3 when it declares, "All men have a natural and indefeasible right to worship Almighty God according to the dictates of their own consciences." But it explicitly mentions Him for a third time in Article I, Section 3 when it says, "No person who acknowledges the being of a God and a future state of rewards and punishments shall, on account of his religious sentiments, be disqualified to hold any office or place of trust or profit under this Commonwealth."

The bottom line is this: it's true that the federal government of the United States of America was never intended to be a Christian theocracy (nor should it be), but it's just as true that the original states enjoyed the constitutional right, in their own right, to officially set themselves up as Christian states, which most did.

Even the states that weren't officially identified as Christian states did, nonetheless, with their many references in their respective state constitutions to the God of Christianity (references that remain to this day), effectively identify as Christian states.

And so, when one becomes aware of the historical facts detailed above, it becomes increasingly difficult—nay, impossible—to argue, or believe, with any level of seriousness, that the United States of America was not, and is not, a Christian nation.

Unless one is a Christ-hater.

3 – The Founding Fathers Extended a Courtesy to Non-Christians—and Now Anti-Christians are Using It to Attack Christianity

The third reason we must reject the notion that America was never a Christian nation because it was never a Christian theocracy, is that the argument itself casts courtesy in the faces of the very God-fearing men who established the United States—our Founding Fathers, whom, by vast majority, were devout, self-professing Christians. The historical record is unequivocal and irrefutable on this fact.

The Founders, and the colonists before them, were quite familiar with various kinds of persecution, especially religious persecution. So when they immigrated to the New World and established towns and cities (then, territories and colonies) out of the wilderness, and, finally, independent states with a federal government, they desired to treat others better than they themselves had been treated. And so, even as nearly 100 percent of the European-Americans in the nation at the time of the founding—an overwhelming majority of the country—were Christian, the Founding Fathers extended a courtesy to the extreme minority in America by allowing for anyone, non-Christians included, to follow the faith of their choosing and, therefore, ultimately opted to forego an official, federal religion (more accurately, an official federal Christian denomination).[14] Moreover, and as previously mentioned, since the U.S. Constitution already allowed for our nation's robust Christian heritage to be reflected through the establishment of official Christian states, it would have been extraneous to have done so at the federal level.

Still, this federal courtesy that extended to the tiny minority of non-Christians, was likewise applied at the state level, where, even those states with official state denominations nonetheless granted those who did not adhere to that state religion the freedom to practice their own faith, and the general ability to live free.

Consider the total lack of religious liberty in Muslim-majority and Communist nations. One would think that we as a once free nation would forever remember this courtesy that our majority Christian Founders extended to practitioners of all faith traditions, including secular humanists. You would think that American citizens, particularly non-Christians, would be eternally grateful to the Christians who granted them these freedoms. Instead, this courtesy has been scoffed at, denied and even thrown in the faces of our Founding Fathers. Moreover, it's been used as a hammer over the head of contemporary Christian Americans, with organized and well-funded anti-Christians misrepresenting and abusing this courtesy to disingenuously insist that America is a fundamentally secular nation. They now demand that all public professions of Christianity be restricted, under force of law, and further push to have all historical reminders of America's Christian heritage scrubbed from the history books. Such religious cleansing is as unconstitutional as it is un-American.

*****

Indeed, we must reject all arguments that America is not, and has never been, a Christian nation for the revisionist lies they are. And we most certainly must reject the current and fashionable argument that any public expression or acknowledgment of Christianity must now be purged from all public fora.

Yet, regrettably, and due in large part to the willful silence of an apathetic Christian majority, the secularists and Islamist enemies of Christ who make up the tyrannical American minority, are having a great deal of success in manipulating many to acquiesce to their American "fundamental transformation." This provides ammunition in the escalating War on Christianity by making it seem as if we Christians, who actually argue from a position of truth, compassion, liberty and historical accuracy, are the ones trying to "fundamentally transform America"—that we're somehow intent on reshaping our "secular" nation into a Christian theocracy—an absurd proposition on both counts, by any objective standard.

Again, it's critical to understand the true history of our Christian nation and how those who hate Christ—those who hate us, His followers—have whitewashed and rewritten it. We must fully grasp this in order to better understand the unprecedented extent to which Christ and Christianity are under attack in today's America, and why we, those commanded by Christ to be salt and light in a world that loves darkness, must take a stand, push back, speak truth, in love, and fearlessly and boldly proclaim the full counsel of God, no matter what the temporal consequences may be.

PART 2

Chapter 2

The Attacks on American Christians

The overwhelming weight of the evidence has established beyond any reasonable doubt to the contrary, that America was originally a Christian nation, expressly founded upon biblical principles. But this does not mean that many have not tried, even from the moment of our nation's inception—nor that they will not continue to try, to undermine our irreversible Christian heritage. Christianity, which is absolute truth revealed by God, has always been under attack in America—indeed, in every corner of the world—due to both the malefactions of the spiritual powers and principalities, as well as to the fallen nature of the world and every human being who ever graced its surface. It's rebellion. It's pride. And it's idolatrous self-worship. Satan wants to be like God, and so does mankind. Evil has tried to undermine good from before the question was asked, "Did God really say?" in a garden long ago. America is no exception. That same battle between good and evil, light and darkness, rages on in today's America.

And it will continue to rage until Christ's return.

Still, many may wonder when this serious escalation—the American left's fevered and well-organized War on Christianity—really began. While the exact moment is debatable, most Christian cultural analysts agree that, in the past fifty years or so, several landmark instances of abject evil triumphing over good—secular humanism triumphing over revealed truth and the natural created order—can be identified. These "transformative" moments in time have shaken, and cracked to her core, America's Christian foundations. Now they're trying to finish the job. While the following items in no way represent a comprehensive list, they do, very generally, provide for some of the primary catalysts.

23

In the 1960s, leftist attorneys on the U.S. Supreme Court removed God, the Bible and prayer from our schools. In the 1970s the Court presumed to divine a phantom "constitutional right" to infanticide. Meanwhile, secular humanism, America's emerging new state religion—complete with its high priests of psychology—arbitrarily declared that homosexual conduct and same-sex attraction were, somehow, magically, and due to political pressure alone, no longer the behavioral manifestations of a mental disorder, but, rather, had morphed into a benign "sexual orientation"—a "civil right"—that must not only be "tolerated," but celebrated. By the late 1970s and into the '80s the anti-Christians had become so emboldened, brazen and hostile to our religious liberties and transcendent, founding national principles, that Bible-believing Christians began to unify and fight back, organizing what had, theretofore, been a relatively silent "Moral Majority." This movement proved to be extremely successful, for a time, helping to usher in an era that provided resistance to the mounting attacks on foundational America and Christianity, even as it fell short of reversing, or stopping, the metastasizing cancer that is progressive secular humanism.

Yet something changed in the 1990s, and that change has led us to where we are today. The Jesus-haters began moving from merely harassing, to overtly persecuting American Christians, pining for the day that public professions of fidelity to the biblical moral code would be, effectively, criminalized. We'll examine exactly what happened in the 1990s later. But first, let's look at just how bad these progressive attacks on Christians and Christianity in America are now. A great place to start is by unpacking events in 2008, when Christians were supporting a ballot measure in California known as Proposition 8. The measure was intended to protect marriage in the Golden State and, ultimately, proved successful until five extremist attorneys on the U.S. Supreme Court presumed to deconstruct and redefine marriage nationwide in June of 2015.

While the debate over Proposition 8 was underway, the hostility the enemies of God directed toward Christians in support of the ballot initiative reached a fever pitch. "We have boys dying...protecting our freedom in Iraq," Pastor Jim Garlow told the Christian news site *OneNewsNow.com*, "while we have our freedom being taken as people rip signs out and destroy them and deface them. It's quite an amazing venue to find ourselves in [here] in America."[15]

Animosity and physical assaults like that—and far worse—have only increased since then. Rising reports of once unimaginable assaults on American Christians are increasing daily. We will document some in coming pages. Until then, what follows are shocking, and broad-based, examples of how hateful and serious the attacks in the War on Christianity in America are, and why Christians must, and will, reorganize and renew our resistance. Such peaceful resistance, obedience to God and civil disobedience to man, can, and I believe will—God-willing and with the help of the Holy Spirit—spur much-needed spiritual revival in an America in freefall.

Chapter 3

God Expelled from the Democratic Party

"But whoever disowns me before others, I will disown before my Father in heaven."

(Matthew 10:33 – New International Version)

Are you a believer? I'm not asking if you're a Democrat, a Republican or an independent. I'm asking if you believe in God. The God of Abraham, Isaac and Jacob. The God of the living, not the dead. The great "I Am." If so, here's something to seriously consider in the voting booth from now on. In its official 2012 version, the Democratic Party finally scrubbed all recognition of God from its party platform. This was intentional. It was by design. No one should have been surprised. It was a long time coming.

In just the last fifteen years or so, extremist elements within the Democratic establishment have lodged a successful secular-socialist coup. The alarming consequences of this progressive triumph became manifest throughout the pages of the DNC's 2012 platform. They were also on display during the subsequent Democratic convention.

Slippery was the slope into Democrats' anti-theist primordial bog. In 2004, there were seven mentions of God in the platform. In 2008, there was but one.[16,17] And by 2012 there were none. Zip, zero, nada. Godless.

That is, until some in leadership realized that political fallout was reaching, well, biblical proportions. In early September 2012 (just in time to make a late-bid pander), in a highly contentious and unprecedented move, the DNC held a special session where, to a volley of stadium-shaking boos, Democratic leaders narrowly passed a resolution to put "God" back in the platform.[18]

It was as transparent as anything political can be. It was done out of fear, not love; necessity, not respect; incredulity, not fidelity. Nonetheless, Democrats, like everyone, should be grateful that God is more faithful to them than they are to Him.

Still, what's equally revealing is what had replaced God. The term "government" was referenced repeatedly—55 times, in fact. Nearly each reference is premised on the dubious claim that big government can, and will, cure all of humanity's ills. The DNC even played a promotional video proclaiming: "The government is the only thing we all belong to."[19]

Yikes.

True, the 2012 Republican Party platform also mentioned government, but in the context of limiting its size and scope—of protecting individual liberty from the authoritarian monstrosity envisaged by Obama, Hillary Clinton, Bernie Sanders and the DNC. (Yes, I realize the Republican Party appears to have given up on that by 2016.) As Ronald Reagan observed, "Government is not the solution to our problem; government is the problem."

The Republican platform also acknowledged God. Twelve times, in fact. And each acknowledgement fell within the framework of "our country's Judeo-Christian heritage." This heritage is something the Democratic Party both stubbornly denies and viscerally abhors.[20] (And yes, again, I realize that by 2016 the GOP is moving dangerously close to the Democratic Party's denial of our godly heritage.)

Shortly after the DNC released its secularist platform in 2012, I tweeted, "Well, Democrats are officially 'godless'..."[21] Zack Ford, a progressive blogger with ThinkProgress.org, captured, I think, the general consensus among Democratic movers-and-shakers. He tartly replied, "Good!"[22]

Another of my Twitter followers, @redandright, answered, "In all fairness to the DNC, I think He [God] requested it."[23]

She may be on to something.

"How beautiful are your tents, O Jacob, and your dwelling places, O Israel! ... Blessed is the one who blesses you, and cursed is the one who curses you!" (Numbers 24:5, 9 – New English Translation)

No anti-God platform would be complete without taking Wite-Out™ to all things pro-Israel. Jews, take note: Democrats' 2012 platform also "yanked" all previous pro-Israel language, even refusing to acknowledge Jerusalem as her capital. Under President Obama and Hillary Clinton, this abject hostility toward Israel has only gotten worse and more pronounced since then.

This, too, should come as little surprise. Throughout his presidency, Barack

Obama has shown an overt hatred of Israel—something no other president in American history has done. Instead, Obama has unapologetically sided with the Palestinian Authority, the Muslim Brotherhood, terrorist Iran and other Islamo-fascist radicals, all of whom seek Israel's total annihilation.

Even so, after widespread Judeo-Christian outrage in 2012, language tepidly referencing Israel was once again restored to the Democratic platform. Another too-little-too-late act of desperation?

And then there's Democrats' sacred cow: abortion. Welcome to the modern Democratic Party, where the women are "sexually liberated" and their offspring gravely imperiled.

Indeed, it was genuinely sad to see such a parade of angry, hurting women take the DNC stage to command, with perverse pride, an invisible "constitutional right" to snuff out their very own young. (Bet she would've looked like you, Mom.)

The 2012 DNC party platform was no better. It "unequivocally" demanded un-fettered abortion on demand, at taxpayer expense, through the ninth month—"regardless of ability to pay."

By contrast, the Republican platform aligned with the actual Constitution, stating, "[T]he unborn child has a fundamental individual right to life which cannot be infringed."

To be sure, it would have been helpful if the DNC had included, in its Glossary of Terms: "Reproductive Freedom: noun 1) 'Sexual liberation' without consequence (i.e., hook-up, cover-up, pay-up and shut-up.)"

I know. I've declared "war on women." But we conservatives believe that sexual relativism comes at a cost—one we refuse to subsidize. I prefer to call it a "war for responsibility."

Speaking of the "War on Women," wasn't it rich? The DNC featured, as its heavy hitter in 2012, Bill Clinton—former Preezy of the Sleazy, serial sexual-harasser and, likely, so very much more. Although the time for praising him appears to be coming to an end as late 2015 and 2016 saw renewed focus on his history of sexually assaulting women.

The 2012 DNC also had an emotional tribute to late Senator Teddy "splash-'N-dash" Kennedy. I wonder if Mary Jo's folks got free admission. Hypocrisy, thy initials are D-N-C.

But at least the Democratic platform was "pro-education," right?

Well, for the record, being "pro-education" means teaching little Billy to read, not which eyeliner matches his skirt. (Yes, this godless manifesto went there too.)

Democrats signed off on every demand of radical "LGBT" pressure groups. They even put their official stamp of approval on same-sex "marriage," setting the stage for the Supreme Court, which is fully loyal to Democratic ideology, to illegally make it the "law" of the land in June of 2015, arrogantly rejecting the 32 states wherein "we the people" had spoken.

No, this ain't your father's Democratic Party. In fact, as the DNC goes godless, I suspect quite a few God-fearing Democrats contemplated breaking with tradition in 2012. I suspect even more do by now.

The 2012 Democratic Party official platform provided perfect insight into the raw hatred American progressives have for the foundations of America and for God. That hatred is so strong in them that they're not satisfied in merely removing any mention of God from the platform; they want to remove any mention or reference to Him, and His Son, from everything, everywhere in the United States—even in a memorial to Americans murdered by Islamic terrorists on September 11, 2001.

Chapter 4

Memorializing the World Trade Center Site with a Cross Becomes "Controversial"

> *"The god of this age has blinded the minds of unbelievers, so that they cannot see the light of the gospel that displays the glory of Christ, who is the image of God."*
>
> (2 Corinthians 4:4 – New International Version)

While America mourned the 11th anniversary of the September 11 Islamic attacks in 2012, atheist radicals were throwing fuel on the fire. While millions were praying for the friends and families of precious souls lost, self-styled progressives were preying upon the most significant symbol of hope to which many of the grieving clung: a cross at the World Trade Center Memorial site.

The 17-foot steel-beam cross, found amid the rubble of the once towering World Trade Center, was at the center of a lawsuit filed by the American Atheists Foundation.[24] While nearly the entire 9/11 memorial site remains purely secular in nature, these secular absolutists complained of unequal representation. Such a bizarre measure of inequality could arise solely in the blinded mind of a "free-thinking" relativist.

Fortunately, the Christ-hating heathens didn't have a legal leg upon which to be hopping mad. In cases like Abington v. Schempp, the U.S. Supreme Court has noted repeatedly that "religion has been closely identified with our history and government."

In fact, the High Court ruled explicitly in Lynch v. Donnelly that religious elements within a larger government display are perfectly constitutional where both a religious and a "secular purpose" are represented. There could be no better example than the case at hand.

The relic cross was dedicated to the World Trade Center Memorial. Workers, volunteers, indeed most of America, saw it as a profound symbol of hope after it was discovered amongst the debris. The cross, which many believe miraculous, brought tremendous comfort to those who lost loved ones in the cowardly, Islamic attacks.

American Atheists' complaint read like a bad joke. The group's president, David Silverman, insisted that he and his fellow God-deniers experienced debilitating physical reactions from simply witnessing the rubble cross. Such reactions allegedly included "inter alia, dyspepsia, symptoms of depression, headaches, anxiety, and mental pain and anguish."[25]

These materialist martyrs complained that the cross made them "feel officially excluded from the ranks of citizens who were directly injured by the 9/11 attack." (Well, cry me a river, princess. Suck it up and go see the school nurse.)

To be sure, our atheist flowers—like other living dead—were evidently so insecure in their lack of faith that the mere glimpse of a cross provoked a hiss, a dramatic cape-whirl-twirl and an abrupt retreat to the cold sanctuary of moonlit coffin (or Starbucks—whichever has Wi-Fi).

Am I trying to vilify David Silverman and his anti-Christian American Atheists? Not at all. I'd no sooner try to "milkify" milk. Actions define character. It's at once both refreshing and instructive to see the godless left cast off its Apollyon mask.

One of the organizations I've worked with is Liberty Counsel, a non-profit organization dedicated to defending and advancing life, liberty, natural marriage and the natural family. Mat Staver is its founder and chairman. He said of the case, "Atheist groups would like to see a total collapse of the free exercise of religion in America. The cross is a symbol of hope amidst the total destruction at Ground Zero. The lawsuit is further evidence of the War on Christianity in America. The 9/11 cross survived the terrorist attack by Muslim extremists, and it will survive the cultural attack by radical secularists."[26]

Indeed, radical secularists' War on Christianity has reached biblical proportions.

Benjamin Franklin once observed, "If Men are so wicked as we now see them with Religion what would they be if without it?"[27]

We know what we'd be. We're becoming it.

Yes, liberals' desperate attempts to secularize America and eradicate her rich, Judeo-Christian heritage must be vigorously combatted. The left's militant jihad to exorcise public recognition of God must not go unchallenged.

In this case it did not. And thanks, in part, to those who challenged the suit (through public statements, amicus briefs on behalf of the cross and other such actions) the atheists have to date failed in their efforts. As of July 2014, "A three-judge panel from the Second Circuit Court of Appeals ruled...that 'the cross at Ground Zero' at the museum does not violate the Establishment Clause of the U.S. Constitution."[28]

As Muslim radicals conduct murderous assaults on U.S. embassies around the world, secularist radicals are no less determined to kill freedom. There is, you see, a tie that binds. Both groups hate—with a visceral, all-consuming kind of hatred—the one true God. They hate all things Judeo-Christian. Many progressives so hate God that they fantasize about eliminating Him and Christianity from all aspects of American life. But they don't just limit themselves to fantasies and booing God. They are constantly and relentlessly working to make their fantasies reality. One way they're doing so is by attempting, through a back door approach, to effectively eliminate the First Amendment altogether.

Chapter 5

Gutting the First Amendment to Eliminate Protections for Christians

Freedom to follow God, worship Him and openly express and live out our sincerely-held religious beliefs are God-given, unalienable rights—not things any man can legislate in or out of existence. Part and parcel of this is the right to not be forced to violate one's conscience. But this fact doesn't stop secular leftists from attempting to override the constitutional guarantees that protect these rights. This is exactly what the anti-Christians want done with the First Amendment, primarily to suppress the freedoms of speech and religious expression it secures.

While reams have already been penned examining the implications of the 2014 Burwell, Secretary of Health and Human Services v. Hobby Lobby Stores, Inc. decision (that's the Hobby Lobby decision which reaffirmed that Obamacare cannot compel people to forfeit their First Amendment rights when running businesses, and thus are not forced to help others murder their unborn babies), most of what's been written, particularly in the liberal press, has missed the point entirely.

Though it was mildly pleasing that the Supreme Court wasn't quite ready to take gasoline to both the First Amendment and the Religious Freedom Restoration Act (RFRA), signed into law by Bill Clinton, a liberal, in 1993, it is alarming that only 56 percent of our sitting U.S. Supreme Court justices were still willing to give the U.S. Constitution a modicum of the respect, recognition and compliance it not only deserves, but requires. America was dragged before Emperor Obama's counter-constitutional, secular-progressive Obamacare firing squad and remarkably, miraculously, they missed.

But that win (having to call the preservation of the First Amendment a "win" tells you a lot about where we are today) gave us a false sense of security. As we Christians and conservatives celebrated with chest bumps and high fives, we remained bound, gagged and blindfolded while these progressive fascists reloaded. The next volley of cultural Marxist lead was just moments away. More on that in a bit.

I'm not trying to throw a wet blanket on that victory for Christians and conservatives. There was much to celebrate, and the ruling's broader implications were profound indeed. But the opinion simply didn't go far enough.

Yes, Hobby Lobby was, in part, about the non-negotiable fact that government cannot compel religious business owners of private, closely held corporations to be complicit in abortion homicide. It was also, tangentially, about the self-evident reality that women are not, never have been and never will be, entitled to expect Christian men, who are not their husbands, to pay for their birth control and abortion drugs so that they can have consequence-free sex or otherwise murder their pre-born babies. But Hobby Lobby was chiefly about one of our very first freedoms: religious liberty.

So how was it that this was a 5-4 decision? Even an elementary understanding of American history and a cursory analysis of both our U.S. Constitution and RFRA established that this opinion should have been roundly unanimous. The majority decision merely recognized, in the weakest of terms, Americans' God-given, inalienable, constitutionally guaranteed right to religious free exercise (yes, even for those pesky Christian business owners).

Still, while lovers of freedom rejoiced across the nation, the reality became more manifest than ever that there were—are—at least four domestic "enemies within" currently sitting on the highest bench in the land, not the least of whom is Ruth Bader Ginsburg.

Ginsburg revealed everything you need to know about Ginsburg a few years back: "I would not look to the U.S. Constitution, if I were drafting a Constitution in the year 2012," she disgracefully vomited in an interview about the fledgling Egyptian government. "I might look at the Constitution of South Africa. That was a deliberate attempt to have a fundamental instrument of government that embraced basic human rights. ... It really is, I think, a great piece of work that was done. Much more recent than the U.S. Constitution."[29]

Ginsburg hates the America of our founding. She hates our Constitution and, like all true progressives, endeavors to circumvent it at every turn.

And that's the prism through which we must interpret the parade of hyperbolic horribles in her scathing Hobby Lobby dissent. She excoriated the constitutionalist majority for its ruling, calling it a "radical" decision "of startling breadth." Still, when you cut through the alarmist tripe, she actually gets to the meat of the matter.

"In a decision of startling breadth," she wrote, "the Court holds that commercial enterprises, including corporations, along with partnerships and sole proprietorships, can opt out of any law (saving only tax laws) they judge incompatible with their sincerely held religious beliefs."

Uh, yeah, and?

Here's what Ginsburg actually meant: "I hate the First Amendment. It's broad, unalienable, and I want to alienate it. Oh, and dead babies. Lots of dead babies."

Ginsburg was right. The decision was "of startling breadth," but only if you happen to be a secular elitist hell-bent on marginalizing Christians and wielding unchecked power over your fellow Americans.

Indeed, the secularist left's utter meltdown over having had but a small measure of control over others wrested away is highly instructive. Still, why would we expect lefties to understand the First Amendment when the same Rhodes Scholars called a decision penned by Justice Alito "#ScaliaLaw" on Twitter?

In his concurring opinion, Justice Anthony Kennedy, who more often than not gets it wrong, got one right:

> *In our constitutional tradition, freedom means that all persons have the right to believe or strive to believe in a divine creator and a divine law. For those who choose this course, free exercise is essential in preserving their own dignity and in striving for a self-definition shaped by their religious precepts. Free exercise in this sense implicates more than just freedom of belief. ... It means, too, the right to express those beliefs and to establish one's religious (or non-religious) self-definition in the political, civic, and economic life of our larger community.*

Wow. And now for the pink elephant in the room: Although the Hobby Lobby decision did not directly address the raging cultural debate over counterfeit "gay marriage" and the irreconcilable friction this modern, sin-centric novelty has with the long-established and unalienable right to religious free exercise, it doesn't take a Phi Beta Kappa to read between the lines and discover, as Ginsburg and Kennedy evidently agreed, that the "startling breadth" of the decision most assuredly touches and concerns the debate head on. (And not in favor, I might add, of the homofascist "you-have-to-affirm-my-faux-marriage-or-go-to-jail" crowd.)

Or it should have anyway.

The 2014 ruling made it clear that, as both the First Amendment and RFRA already assure, the Christian baker, photographer, florist or any other business owner, is protected from being forced, under penalty of law, into indentured servitude—from having to give their God-given time and talent to create goods or services that require they violate sincerely held religious beliefs.

In other words, both the First Amendment and RFRA trumped any and all so-called "sexual orientation" laws. Or, as Ginsburg put it, private businesses "can opt out of any law (saving only tax laws) they judge incompatible with their sincerely held religious beliefs."

Yet that didn't happen as the June 2015 Obergefell v. Hodges decision—the one where the Supreme Court illegally legislated that same-sex "marriage" be instituted throughout the U.S.—showed.

And that's because, in part, the progressives ramped up their advocacy against freedom and Christianity after the Hobby Lobby decision. In the week or so that followed the decision, two new developments broke: 1) Democrats in Congress readied a legislative "Hobby Lobby fix" that stood exactly zero chance of passing and would be struck down as unconstitutional even if it did, and 2) The ACLU, AFL-CIO, National Gay and Lesbian Task Force, Lambda Legal and a hodgepodge of other left-wing extremist groups withdrew support for the ironically tagged "Employment Non-Discrimination Act" (not to mention the paradoxically named "Equality Act," which is even worse), the crown jewel of homofascism, because ENDA's paper-thin "religious exemption" did not adequately outlaw the practice of Christianity.

1 – The Hobby Lobby "Fix"

Addressing the High Court's Hobby Lobby decision from the floor of the U.S. Senate, then Senate Majority Leader Harry Reid, D-Nev., fumed, "We have so much to do this month, but the one thing we're going to do during this work period—sooner rather than later—is to ensure that women's lives are not determined by virtue of five white men."

"This Hobby Lobby decision is outrageous," continued Reid, "and we're going to do something about it."[30]

And, "do something about it" they tried. *TalkingPointsMemo.com* reported on legislation Democrats introduced soon after that would have done away with religious liberty protections altogether:

> *The legislation will be sponsored by Sens. Patty Murray, D-Wash., and Mark Udall, D-Colo. According to a summary reviewed by TPM, it prohibits employers from refusing to provide health services, including*

contraception, to their employees if required by federal law. It clarifies that the Religious Freedom Restoration Act, the basis for the Supreme Court's ruling against the mandate, and all other federal laws don't permit businesses to opt out of the Obamacare requirement.

The legislation also puts the kibosh on legal challenges by religious non-profits, like Wheaton College, instead declaring that the accommodation they're provided under the law is sufficient to respect their religious liberties.[31]

This reactionary response to the Hobby Lobby ruling was, of course, little more than an election-year fundraising scheme for the Democratic National Committee. The bill, as of the date of this writing, has never gone anywhere. But don't kid yourself. They'll never stop trying.

2 – Withdrawn Support for ENDA

The Washington Post reported in early July 2014 on the progressive establishment having a change of heart on one of its pet bills:

Several major gay rights groups withdrew support Tuesday for the Employment Non-Discrimination Act that would bolster gay and transgender rights in the workplace, saying they fear that broad religious exemptions included in the current bill might compel private companies to begin citing objections similar to those that prevailed in a U.S. Supreme Court case last week. ...

But the groups said they can no longer back ENDA as currently written in light of the Supreme Court's decision last week to strike down a key part of President Obama's health-care law. The court ruled that family-owned businesses do not have to offer their employees contraceptive coverage that conflicts with the owners' religious beliefs.[32]

Rep. Gary Glenn was a candidate for the Michigan State House and the president of the American Family Association (AFA) Michigan in 2014. (Glenn won his seat and serves as the representative for the 98th House district of Michigan. He also remains the president of AFA Michigan.) Glenn has been a national leader in defense of religious liberty for well upon two decades. Responding in an email at the time, he wrote:

The extremely limited religious exemptions typically included in discriminatory homosexual and cross-dressing "rights" laws have always been mere window-dressing with no real protection or effect, as witnessed by the ongoing persecution and discrimination under such laws against Christian business owners and community organizations such as the Boy Scouts, Catholic Charities, Salvation Army, and even the United Way.

But now that the U.S. Supreme Court's Hobby Lobby decision threatens to give real teeth to such exemptions, the AFL-CIO's in-house homosexual activist group has announced it will no longer support discriminatory "sexual orientation" legislation that includes even limited exemptions for religious institutions.

If this zero tolerance stance spreads to larger groups such as the Human Rights Campaign and National Gay and Lesbian Task Force [it now has], this could become the sticking point which hamstrings future attempts to pass federal, state, and local homosexual "rights" legislation. These supposed religious exemptions, which the AFL-CIO's homosexual lobby at least now says it will no longer support, have been a key propaganda point in blunting the opposition of churches and citizens concerned about the obvious threat such laws pose to religious freedom.[33]

According to their leftist proponents, ENDA and the Equality Act would merely insulate people who choose to engage in homosexual conduct (sexual orientation) or those who suffer from gender confusion (gender identity) against employment and housing intolerance. In truth, however, these two pieces of legislation effectively would codify the very things they purport to combat: workplace and housing discrimination.

Though in its current form ENDA contains an extremely weak religious exemption (the Equality Act has none) that might—and I mean might—partially protect some churches and religious organizations (until they're sued by "gay" activists), this so-called exemption would leave most others, such as Bible bookstores and many Christian schools and para-church organizations, entirely unprotected. Both bills would additionally crush individual business owners' guaranteed First Amendment rights.

Any "religious exemption" is meaningless. In 2013, Harry Reid promised homosexual pressure groups that Democrats would remove all protections for Christians and other people of faith on the flipside—after ENDA passed. The homosexual news site *Washington Blade* reported that homosexual activist Derek Washington of "GetEqual" confirmed Reid's promise. In a conference call with homosexual activists, Washington admitted that Reid vowed, as goes any religious exemption, "the main thing to do was get the vote taken care of, and then deal with it later. As oftentimes happens, you don't get something perfect the first time around, you go back and fix it later, so that was basically his take on it."

According to the *Blade*, "That account was corroborated by Faiz Shakir, a Reid spokesperson, who said the Democratic leader understands the concerns, but wants to get the bill passed first, then go back and address the exemptions."[34]

They stopped pretending in 2014 and it's only gotten worse since then. The Hobby Lobby decision exposed secular liberals for who they truly are. It blew back the propagandist curtain and exposed their truly sinister aims. They desire to neutralize the First Amendment so they can eliminate protections for Christians, so they can make it less difficult to wage progressive lawfare and silence all dissent.

And they're becoming more and more brazen in openly admitting their designs on fascism. On July 10, 2014 the editors of *Bloomberg View* published an article headlined, "Ban Gay Discrimination. No Exceptions."[35] It said:

> *A strange thing happened after the Supreme Court ruled on the Hobby Lobby birth-control case last week: Gay-rights organizations turned against legislation they once championed that would have outlawed workplace discrimination against gay people. They've also grown concerned about the executive order President Barack Obama has promised that would bar anti-gay employment practices by federal contractors.*
>
> *How could a decision allowing companies to opt out of the Affordable Care Act's contraception requirement make any difference to gay rights? By illuminating the power of religious exemptions. If a woman can be denied contraception by an employer for religious reasons, can the employer also fire the woman if she is a lesbian? Can it deny spousal benefits if she's married to another woman?*
>
> *Obama and, ultimately, Congress should take the Hobby Lobby warning seriously and make certain that gay people get the same workplace protections as the ones people are granted for their race, color, religion, sex or national origin—with no special exceptions for employers' religious beliefs."*

The Democratic-Media Complex has since put the wheels in motion. While actions speak louder than words, words often predict future actions. Secular progressives' words and actions rarely align. This is because the pseudo-utopian, wholly dystopian perch from which they view the world is so detached from reality that, from a cultural and public policy standpoint, they must disguise their intended actions in flowery and euphemistic language, or face near universal rejection.

When they don't like the terms, liberals redefine the terms to mean something they do not, never have and never can mean. Consider, for instance, the once meaningful words "marriage" and "equality." And this is how they are moving toward negating the First Amendment.

Other progressive doublespeak includes words like "invest" (meaning socialist redistribution of wealth), "tolerance" (meaning embrace immorality or face total ruin), "diversity" (meaning Christians and conservatives need not apply), "hate" (meaning truth) or "The Affordable Care Act" (meaning unaffordable, unsustainable and utterly inferior socialized medicine).

Even so, it's during those rare moments of candor that our cultural Marxist friends' rhetoric actually aligns with their intended actions. In other words, every so often, and usually by accident, they tell the truth.

Take this 2015 declaration by President Obama at Georgetown University. He was discussing his contempt for conservative new media in general and Fox News in particular: "[W]e're going to have to change how our body politic thinks, which means we're going to have to change how the media reports on these issues," he said.[36]

How Kim Jong-un of him. In sum: Goal 1) Control thought by, Goal 2) Controlling the media.

This is an idea older than—and as well-preserved as—Vladimir Lenin himself. How Dear Leader intended to reconcile his scheme to "change how the media reports on these issues" with the First Amendment's Free Press Clause, namely, "Congress shall make no law ... abridging the freedom ... of the press," is abundantly clear.

He didn't.

Our emperor-in-chief tried to force feed his once free subjects yet another unconstitutional executive decree—a Net Neutrality sandwich with a side of Fairness Doctrine.

Or take would-be President Hillary Clinton's comments in 2015 on the "rite" of abortion vs. the right of religious freedom.

Reported *LifeNews*:

> *The comment has Hillary Clinton essentially saying that Christians must be forced to change their religious views to accommodate abortions.*
>
> *"Far too many women are still denied critical access to reproductive health care and safe childbirth. All the laws we've passed don't count for much if they're not enforced," Clinton said, using the euphemism for abortion.*
>
> *"Rights have to exist in practice—not just on paper," Clinton argued. "Laws have to be backed up with resources and political will. And deep-seated cultural codes, religious beliefs and structural biases have to be changed."[37]*

That's a lot of "have tos." See the pattern here? Whether it's Obama saying government will "have to change how the media reports," or Hillary saying "deep-seated religious beliefs have to be changed," such despotic demands should spike the neck hair of every freedom-loving American.

And then there are those left-wing extremists whose designs on despotism require that Christians "must be made" to obey. Homosexual practitioner and *New York Times* columnist Frank Bruni is one such extremist. In an April 3, 2015 column titled, "Bigotry: The Bible and the Lessons of Indiana," Bruni quoted homosexual militant Mitchell Gold, a prominent anti-Christian activist: "Gold told me that church leaders must be made 'to take homosexuality off the sin list,'" he wrote. "His commandment is worthy—and warranted," he added.[38]

Of course, if homosexual behavior, something denounced as both "vile affections" and "an abomination" throughout both the Old and New Testaments, is no longer sexual sin, then there can be no sexual sin whatsoever. To coerce, through the power of the police state, faithful Christians to abandon the millennia-old biblical sexual ethic and embrace the sin of Sodom would likewise require that Christians sign off on fornication, adultery, incest and bestiality. Such is the unnatural nature of government mandated moral relativism.

"But this isn't free speech—it's hate speech!" come the mournful cries of the ill-informed and the ill-prepared, desperately afraid to debate the issues on the merits. "Hate speech is excluded from protection," opined CNN anchor Chris Cuomo in a tweet on the topic.[39] "But there is no hate speech exception to the First Amendment," replied UCLA law professor Eugene Volohk in a *Washington Post* op-ed. "Hateful ideas (whatever exactly that might mean) are just as protected under the First Amendment as other ideas."[40]

Of course this matters not to those to whom the First Amendment is meaningless. Indeed, one man's "hate speech" is another man's truth, and as I've often said, truth is hate to those who hate truth.

And boy do they hate it.

And so they mean to muzzle it.

The time of which many of us have long warned is no longer on the horizon. The left's full-on assault against freedom, most especially religious freedom, is at hand.

Which brings us to this modern age of American lawlessness. We're fast moving from a soft tyranny to hard tyranny, and progressive leaders like those mentioned above are, chillingly enough, emboldened to the degree that they will openly call for it.

Like our brothers and sisters around the world, American Christians must prepare for suffering.

So when I say the anti-Christians want to nullify the First Amendment, I'm not engaging in hyperbole. They are dedicated to achieving this so they can further their War on Christianity. And that war includes pushing faithful Christians to the far margins of society, eventually making it near impossible for Bible-believing, openly-professing Christians to hold down a job and advance a career.

Chapter 6

Christian? No Job for You!

The progressive thought police have long been dead serious about gutting religious liberty and free speech even before exposing their true intentions following the Hobby Lobby decision. In an April 2014 column titled, "Why Are They Called 'Homofascists'? Here's Why," I wrote that progressive, "Christian-hating fascists—but I repeat myself—are hell-bent on...pushing to the fringes anyone who publicly acknowledges natural human sexuality and the age-old, immutable institution of legitimate marriage as created by God."[41]

I was referring specifically to the left's well-organized and highly disturbing character assassination of former Mozilla CEO Brendan Eich for his private support of natural marriage. Mozilla constructively terminated Eich after progressive activists insisted it do so, all because he donated money (in 2008) to the Proposition 8 effort in California, an effort that was designed to protect marriage (and which succeeded at the time). I was also addressing the larger goal of the American left to completely shut down free speech and religious liberty, and to severely punish anyone who maintains both biblically and biologically correct views on human sexuality.

I closed my April 2014 column with this:

> They smell blood in the water. I've often said that these folks want those who speak biblical truth about human sexuality and legitimate marriage either 1) dead, 2) imprisoned or, if they can have neither of these, 3) marginalized to the point where they can't even support their families.
>
> Check No. 3 off the list. I guess they're working backwards.

The very next day, and as if right on cue, lefty rag *Slate* magazine vomited evidence of my claims. It could not have been better scripted if I'd written it myself.

In an article titled, "Purge the Bigots," *Slate* writer William Saletan penned these chilling words:

> *Some of my colleagues are celebrating. They call Eich a bigot who got what he deserved. I agree. But let's not stop here. If we're serious about enforcing the new standard, thousands of other employees who donated to the same anti-gay ballot measure must be punished.*

> *More than 35,000 people gave money to the campaign for Proposition 8, the 2008 ballot measure that declared, "Only marriage between a man and a woman is valid or recognized in California." Why do these bigots still have jobs? Let's go get them.*[42]

Now, to be fair, Saletan later claimed that his article was intended as satire to illustrate the hypocrisy of his own progressive movement. Many, if not most, of his readers seemed to miss the joke, and the article's comments section quickly filled with people agreeing that it was, indeed, time to "purge the bigots" (read: Christians).[43]

The Fox News Channel observed that the piece "may or may not be tongue-in-cheek."[44] Satire is traditionally somewhat clever, witty and fairly easy to recognize as such. Mr. Saletan's piece was none of these things. Nevertheless, I will give him the benefit of the doubt.

So we had Mr. Saletan playing the role of a modern Joseph Goebbels, Adolf Hitler's Nazi propaganda minister, in an effort, albeit a clumsy one, to underscore how utterly out of control his own progressive movement has become and, in the spirit of *argumentum ad absurdum*, gently coax his fellow bohemians from madness.

Slate was apparently in on the fun too, pretending, for a day, to be "National-sozialistischen Briefe," Goebbels' parallel publication, in an equally awkward attempt to use the power of metaphor as a scrub brush to wash away the stench of totalitarianism from an American left bathed in it.

But as you read the article a frightening reality quickly rose to the surface. It was neither funny nor untrue. None of it. The cultural Marxist American left is 100 percent serious about "purging" Christians from society.

They're as serious as Josef Stalin's heart attack.

Continued Saletan: "To organize the next stage of the purge, I've compiled the financial data into three tables" (he actually did this). He then listed details from, and linked to, the Proposition 8 hit list which was meticulously assembled and published by the *Los Angeles Times*.[45]

That was all by design. It was what led to Brendan Eich's career beheading. But Eich was just the opening act. The list provided the exact names, employers, places of residence and dollar amounts of every single person in America who donated even a dime to the Golden State's campaign to protect natural marriage. This was a level of voter intimidation and journalistic terrorism on the part of Eich, *Slate* and the *L.A. Times* that was unprecedented in American history.

Joking or not, Herr Saletan then gave the rainbow-shirts their jackbooted marching orders: "If we're serious about taking down corporate officers who supported Proposition 8, and boycotting employers who promote them, we'd better get cracking on the rest of the list," he said, concluding, "otherwise, perhaps we should put down the pitchforks."

You do understand this, right? The *L.A. Times* and America's larger progressive movement were dead serious about purging Christians and other traditionalists from both the workplace and society at large then, and they're dead serious now. It's going to get worse. Mozilla was just an opening salvo.

In the very same way Eich's forced resignation was deliberately calculated to terrorize any American who might resist the left's sexual anarchist agenda, and support some future, legally executed pro-family ballot initiative, the clear purpose behind releasing the Prop. 8 donor list was to instill fear in the hearts of Christians and other traditionalists who support natural marriage, family and human sexuality. It was a not-so-subtle shot over the bow to Americans: "Henceforth, you shall fear for your career and likely lose your job if you ever again openly, or even privately, via ballot measure, profess support for biblical Christianity."

An anonymous writer at *First Things* analyzed the hysteria and hostility that erupted after Mozilla named Eich, a Christian, CEO (and right before it subsequently fired him). This writer noted what the Eich affair means in the future for Christians—or anyone else—who dare oppose homosexuals and other progressive change agents:

> *Whether or not Eich keeps his position, this episode is instructive for those who hold out hope for a détente in the culture wars. The flawed analogy between the movement to end discrimination against African-Americans and the movement to allow gays and lesbians to marry is sincerely believed by many. But it is not merely a convenient piece of rhetoric or a skillful legal strategy. The moral force of the civil rights movement did not permit any sort of accommodation or compromise*

with bigots, and contemporary social conservatives who believe that they can negotiate more favorable terms of surrender have fallen prey to wishful thinking. What Thomas's statement and others reveal is that the same-sex marriage movement has inherited that same genuine moral outrage, that same crusading zeal. While supporters of traditional marriage would like to convince the world that they are correct, they may soon find it difficult enough just to establish that they are not monsters. What is certain is that this will not be the last time that a public example is made of a dissenter from the new moral order.[46]

The persecution isn't just coming. It has arrived. Christians are now very much in danger of losing our livelihoods simply for being Christian. But the anti-Christians are so emboldened—so crazed with raw power that even non-Christians in America cannot escape the War on Christianity. After all, anyone who eats delicious chicken sandwiches is now considered to have engaged in risky political activity.

Chapter 7

Eat at Your Own Risk

In July of 2012, Dan Cathy (then president and chief operating officer of fast food restaurant chain Chick-fil-A) appeared on *The Ken Coleman Show* and spoke with the radio host of the same name. *The Daily Caller* reported on this interview, noting how Cathy commented on the effort to destroy marriage: "I think we are inviting God's judgment on our nation when we shake our fist at him and say, 'We know better than you as to what constitutes a marriage,'" said Cathy.

"I pray God's mercy on our generation that has such a prideful, arrogant attitude to think that we would have the audacity to try to redefine what marriage is all about," he added.[47]

Christ-haters became apoplectic over these remarks. They tried to organize a boycott of the fast food chain but other Americans fought back, showing their support of Chick-fil-A (and opposition to the anti-Christians) by having a "Chick-fil-A Appreciation Day" on August 1, 2012. And it seemed to work… at first.

Those who wanted to silence speech that defended something good were initially shouted down through an unprecedented—dare I say miraculous—show of unity in the Body of Christ. Millions of God-fearing Americans took part in the "buy-cott" and Chick-fil-A saw its cup runneth over.

It was a beautiful thing to behold. It made you proud to be an American. Most of the characteristically cocky, progressive blogs and propaganda sites observed radio silence as left-wing elitists—media, activists, politicos and pundits—sat in stunned disbelief. Their wrongheaded Chick-fil-A boycott had backfired catastrophically.

Multiple elected officials, all Democrats, had previously disgraced both themselves and the offices they held by pledging to shut down Chick-fil-A in their cities, simply because they disagreed with its leadership's biblical viewpoint.

But the American people stood strong. And in response to the illegal threats of the mayors of Chicago, Boston, San Francisco and Washington, D.C. to ban Chick-fil-A from their respective jurisdictions, the residents of those great cities rebuked them with "freedom chicken" lines that wrapped around city blocks. "Mayor Emanuel," they declared, "your godless values are not 'Chicago Values!'"[48,49,50,51]

In fact, Pastor Rick Warren tweeted that Dan Cathy called him to say that sales for August 1, 2012 had smashed all records.[52]

Progressives were furious and they were determined to beat a dead chicken. As liberty-loving folks peacefully showed support for real marriage with nuggets and waffle fries, homosexual activists held a "kiss-in" at various Chick-fil-A locations two days later.

That effort failed—miserably. In fact, the effort failed so badly even Michelangelo Signorile, a radical, Christian-hating homosexual, admitted that it was a disaster:

How did we allow it to happen? Because there was no coordinated effort on our side. The controversy was largely driven by blogs, social media and very loosely organized grass-roots activists, with no coordinated leadership. The city mayors and politicians calling for banning Chick-fil-A gave an opportunity for the right to reframe the story. The mayors backed off quickly after many on the left decided it wasn't a good idea.[53]

Of course, Signorile wasn't entirely right in why their effort failed. The right didn't "reframe" the story and there wasn't a "controversy" in it. Instead, it was an attack that enemies of God launched which failed after Christians and other Americans fought back against it.

On top of this, we couldn't have asked for a starker contrast between the two efforts. Whereas marriage supporters peacefully patronized Chick-fil-A to demand tolerance for varying viewpoints, homosexual activists engaged in gross, sexually charged public displays deliberately designed to shock and offend children and families.

True colors are brightest. The vandalism, bomb threats and bullying of employees working at Chick-fil-A were nice touches too.[54,55,56]

Executives from corporations, large and small, should have sat up and taken notice of what happened. They should have learned to not be intimidated by insufferable homofascist organizations like the incongruously tagged "Human Rights Campaign" and "GLAAD," (formerly known as the Gay & Lesbian

Alliance Against Defamation). Their bark is much, much worse than their bite.

But they didn't learn that lesson and inexplicably continue allowing themselves to be intimidated. As previously mentioned, Americans' fighting back against the Christ-haters' attack on Chick-fil-A "seemed to work...at first." Regrettably, Dan Cathy later threw in the towel, unnecessarily, and completely undid this valuable pro-family victory, something Leon Stafford reported on in 2014 for the *Atlanta Journal-Constitution*:

> *"Every leader goes through different phases of maturity, growth and development and it helps by (recognizing) the mistakes that you make," Cathy said. "And you learn from those mistakes. If not, you're just a fool. I'm thankful that I lived through it and I learned a lot from it."*
>
> *Cathy talked about the events of the summer of 2012 in a wide-ranging interview that included his thoughts about the company's future and the path he wants to put it on as the newly named CEO. He got the title in November after his father, Chick-fil-A founder Truett Cathy, stepped aside at age 92.*
>
> *Still, as Cathy starts the job the company's link to the gay marriage debate lingers. And it still occupies a niche as the only major fast food chain that isn't open on Sunday, owing to the Christian, pro-family convictions of the elder Cathy—something Dan Cathy says he won't change...*
>
> *The company tried to extricate itself from the controversy by repeatedly asserting it does not discriminate against customers or employees on the basis of sexual orientation...*
>
> *For Cathy, who is in a cutthroat business where no player can afford alienating market segments, the lingering identity is troubling.*
>
> *"Consumers want to do business with brands that they can interface with, that they can relate with," Cathy said. "And it's probably very wise from our standpoint to make sure that we present our brand in a compelling way that the consumer can relate to."[57]*

Americans standing firm against the enemies of God and for Chick-fil-A in 2012 was a tremendous (and rare) victory in the escalating culture war. Christians and other pro-family Americans could have used that victory to rally the troops and bring about a much-needed boost in morale. Instead, Cathy essentially deflated the balloon in 2014, needlessly setting back the truth movement. Cathy's surrender emboldened the anti-Christians, and their attacks on Christianity have grown worse since—much worse. Such attacks include a near-deadly homosexual terrorist event that was inspired by progressives' demonization of Chick-fil-A and faithful Christians.

Chapter 8

Supporting Sexual Normalcy Threatens Your Life

The homosexual-led attack on Chick-fil-A following Dan Cathy's open expression of Christian faithfulness might have failed (at the time), but it helped stoke the American left's swelling hatred for Christ, His followers and His immutable sexual truths. Two weeks after the massive "Chick-fil-A Appreciation Day," a homosexual activist and supporter of the anti-Christian Southern Poverty Law Center (SPLC) attempted to mass murder American Christians.

On August 15, 2012, self-identified LGBT activist Floyd Lee Corkins entered the Washington-based Family Research Council (FRC), a mainstream Christian think-tank and pro-family organization, armed with a 9mm handgun and 15 Chick-fil-A sandwiches.

All that stood between Corkins and mass murder was FRC facilities manager and security specialist Leo Johnson. As Corkins shouted disapproval for FRC's Christian faith and cultural beliefs, Corkins fired at Johnson. The shot struck Johnson in the arm, severely wounding him. Yet despite this, he counterattacked, tackling Corkins and disarming him. (On a sidenote: Corkins somehow possessed the 9mm firearm despite it being illegal to carry a concealed weapon in Washington, D.C. "Gun control" strikes again.)

Cathy L. Lanier, the Chief of Police of the Washington, D.C. Metropolitan Police Department, later praised Johnson's actions: "The security guard here is a hero, as far as I'm concerned," she said.[58]

I agree. And upon hearing of Johnson's selfless act of heroism, I was reminded of John 15:13 (Berean Study Bible): "Greater love has no one than this, that he lay down his life for his friends."

But not everyone agrees that Johnson's heart was full of love. In fact, according to the aforementioned SPLC, Johnson's heart was, instead, full of hate. Indeed, the SPLC believes all of FRC is a seething cauldron of hatred. After all, the SPLC proudly "named the FRC an anti-gay [sic] hate group starting in 2010" because of its orthodox Christian positions on marriage and family.[59]

Tragically, Floyd Lee Corkins had fully absorbed the SPLC's propaganda. Almost as soon as the media began reporting on the terrorist attack there were signs that Corkins was an SPLC devotee. Tony Perkins, the president of FRC, spoke to the press in the aftermath of the shooting:

> *"And that does bring me to my final point," said Perkins. "Let me be clear, that Floyd Corkins was responsible for firing the shot yesterday that wounded one of our colleagues and our friend Leo Johnson. But Corkins was given a license to shoot an unarmed man by organizations like the Southern Poverty Law Center that have been reckless in labeling organizations hate groups because they disagree with them on public policy."*
>
> *"And I believe the Southern Poverty Law Center should be held account- able for their reckless use of terminology that is leading to the intimi- dation and what the FBI here has categorized as an act of domestic terrorism," he said. "There's no room for that in a society such as ours that works through differences that we have on issues in public policy through a peaceful means."[60]*

Perkins wasn't just angrily and baselessly venting following the violent attack. He wasn't just looking to blame the SPLC. As the evidence would later reveal, the SPLC was, in fact, and in large part, to blame. Corkins's trial revealed that he indeed did use SPLC resources in planning his attack. *The Washington Post* reported on this in February of 2013:

> *Corkins, who had volunteered at a gay community center in Northwest, told FBI agents that his goal was to target people opposed to same-sex marriage and "smother Chick-fil-A sandwiches in their faces," accord- ing to a plea agreement he signed in December. He had bought 15 Chick- fil-A sandwiches the day before, an apparent symbol of his antipathy for the head of the fast-food chain, who had recently spoken out against same-sex marriage.*
>
> *A detail sure to reignite the culture wars that erupted around the shoot- ing is the fact that Corkins told FBI agents that he identified the Family Research Council as anti-gay on the Web site of the Southern Poverty Law Center. The day after the shooting, Tony Perkins, the president of the Family Research Council, suggested that the center's labeling of the*

organization as a hate group had given Corkins a "license to perpetrate this act of violence." On Wednesday, Perkins said the revelation had validated his earlier comments.

A spokeswoman for the center said the group never listed the address for the Family Research Council on its Web site. The law center has said that Perkins's group deserves the label because of its claim, for instance, that pedophilia is a "homosexual problem."[61]

So, alongside violence-charged photos of actual hate groups like the Aryan Brotherhood and the KKK, the SPLC listed on its website the decidedly mainstream and always peaceful FRC.

The SPLC strategy was dishonest and reprehensible, yet at the same time it was clever. By comparing FRC and other Christian organizations with violent extremist groups, it groomed the public to believe that Christian organizations were equally violent and worthy of hatred by all.

Rather than debating—on the merits—the mainstream Christian groups with which it has ideological disagreement, SPLC chose, instead, the coward's way out: demonization and marginalization through false guilt by association.

It was a scheme that proved not only slimy but extremely dangerous. And it all was predictable.

If ever there were a time I'd have preferred not to have been right it was back in 2012 when Corkins attacked the FRC headquarters. But in November 2011 I essentially forecast both the FRC shooting and the SPLC's undeniable complicity therein.

In a column headlined, "Liberal violence rising," I wrote, "The SPLC's dangerous and irresponsible ('hate group') disinformation campaign can embolden and give license to like-minded, though less stable, left-wing extremists, creating a climate of true hate. Such a climate is ripe for violence."[62] (If anyone deserves to be taken out, rationalizes the unbalanced SPLC dupe, it's members of this or that evil "hate group" whom, as he's been repeatedly told, mean him great harm.)

Still, although there has always been a vast ideological divide between the SPLC and the tens of millions of Christian Americans represented by FRC, I at one time thought the SPLC might do some self-reflecting and ultimately decide to do the right thing and attempt to rehabilitate its badly damaged reputation. And I had thought this because I believed, wrongly, years ago that the SPLC had good intentions and that we could all find common and reasonable ground.

But I no longer do.

I no longer believe the SPLC has a sense of goodwill. In fact, based on what the FBI discovered and based on the group's own actions (and inactions), I and many others are left with no other inference but this: The SPLC—a left-wing extremist fundraising behemoth—may be intentionally inciting anti-Christian violence. As of January 2016, the SPLC still proudly lists the FRC as an "extremist" group on its website, even as it acknowledges how Corkins used its propaganda for terrorism:

> In August 2012, Floyd Corkins, 28, walked up to FRC's headquarters in Washington, D.C., and shot and wounded a security guard, who managed to subdue him, because he was opposed to the group's socially conservative policies. He pleaded guilty in February 2013 to three felonies: transporting a firearm over state lines, assault with intent to kill, and committing an act of terrorism while armed.
>
> Corkins, who was volunteering at an LGBT community center at the time of the shooting, told authorities that he had targeted groups that oppose same-sex marriage and that he was going to "smother Chick-Fil-A sandwiches in their faces," 15 of which he was carrying in his backpack at the time. Chick-Fil-A was then making national headlines because of its foundation's funding of some anti-gay groups and because of statements CEO Dan Cathy had made against marriage equality.
>
> Corkins told FBI agents that he used the SPLC website to determine that the Family Research Council was anti-gay, prompting Perkins to reiterate his earlier claim that SPLC had "given a license" to Corkins' attack because it had named the FRC an ant-gay hate group starting in 2010. "Only by ending its hate-labeling practices will the SPLC send a message that it no longer wishes to be a source for those who would commit acts of violence that are only designed to intimidate and silence Christians and others who support natural marriage and traditional morality," he said. In fact, the SPLC designation was based on FRC's distortion of known facts to demonize gay men as child molesters and similar false claims, and had nothing to do with FRC's support of "natural marriage" or its belief that homosexuality is a sin.[63]

The SPLC has no shame, particularly when considering how progressives attempt to blame conservatives for attacks with which they have no connection.

"When Congresswoman [Gabby] Giffords and several others were shot in Arizona by Jared Loughner, the left went into overdrive blaming Sarah Palin for a map that had a list of political targets on it. After the fact, we learned that Loughner was apolitical and he clearly had not used Sarah Palin's map of political targets. That did not stop the left from blaming the right," noted Erick

Erickson at *RedState*. "By the way, Palin took down her target map after the controversy. The Southern Poverty Law Center? Crickets ..."[64]

So what other explanation is there other than the SPLC is intentionally inciting anti-Christian violence? I understand that it's difficult to admit you're wrong, especially when the scheme seemed so delicious at the time. But once FBI evidence conclusively proves that you were, to a large degree, responsible for inciting an act of domestic terrorism, most reasonable people would take a deep breath, take a step back, admit fault and hobble forward in an effort to rehabilitate a reputation in ruin.

Is the SPLC a left-wing extremist group? Absolutely. Are they anti-Christian? Without a doubt. But few would have believed, until Corkins attacked the FRC in 2012, that it might intentionally, with malice aforethought, seek to incite anti-Christian bloodshed.

All of this involving the SPLC is bad enough. Yet it gets worse. The Obama administration has established deep, official ties with this radical, anti-Christian organization.

After Floyd Corkins pleaded guilty to attacking the FRC in 2013, Liberty Counsel released a statement on that plea and the SPLC. Part of that statement noted the Obama administration's ties to the anti-Christian group:

> *"The Southern Poverty Law Center has a long history of maliciously slandering pro-family groups with language and labels that incite hatred and undermine civil discourse," said Mat Staver, Founder and Chairman of Liberty Counsel. "In the issues of family and marriage, Christians are literally in the crosshairs of radical homosexual activists, and the SPLC is fueling the hatred and providing the targets. The SPLC should be held accountable for its reckless acts. Even more disturbing than the SPLC's irresponsible behavior is the fact that the Obama Administration is in bed with this group," said Staver. ...*
>
> *Weeks before Corkins pleaded guilty of terrorism and assault with intent to kill, a study from the* Combating Terrorism Center at West Point *entitled* Challengers from the Sidelines: Understanding America's Violent Far-Right *said the "violent far right" exhibits an intense fear or dislike of foreign people, "including people with alternative sexual preferences." The SPLC's warped view of reality has been adopted by the Obama Administration.* [65]

Staver wasn't exaggerating when he said the Obama administration is connected to the SPLC. In fact, that connection has grown stronger since 2013. It has ingrained this group within the U.S. government. And it has done so knowing full well that the SPLC labels mainstream Christians as "hate groups." The Obama administration is even pleased with how the SPLC smears faithful Christians, something it made clear to *CNSNews.com* in October of 2015 when the U.S. Department of Justice made a public and official appearance with the SPLC to promote their partnership:

> *"Homegrown violent extremists can be motivated by any viewpoint on the full spectrum of hate—anti-government views, racism, bigotry, anarchy and other despicable beliefs," Carlin told a gathering at George Washington University. The discussion was co-hosted by SPLC. "When it comes to hate and intolerance, no single ideology governs." ...*

> *SPLC's Intelligence Project Director Heidi Beirich participated with Carlin in Wednesday's discussion of domestic terrorism.*

> CNSNews.com *asked Beirich about their designation of the Family Research Council as a hate group.*

> *"I think there's a common misunderstanding about the way you get on our Hate List. We post groups on the basis of ideology, not whether they're violent or not," she replied.*

> *"Of course some of the groups are particularly violent, the Skinheads, Neo-Nazis, and what not," she continued. "Others are simply pushing propaganda that we consider hateful. For example, there's an organization called American Renaissance, it puts out reams and reams of information about why black people are inferior, it lies basically, so black people are dumber, they're psychopathic, they're more violent.*

> *"In the same way groups like the Family Research Council and the American Family Association do that but what they're putting out is anti-gay material so gay people are pedophiles, or molesters, or whatever the case may be, and that's why they're on the list and that's the direct analogy."*[66]

Jaw-dropping, no? The Obama administration has made it official U.S. policy to misrepresent faithful Christians and target them for marginalization and, potentially, even violence. It's open about doing so. And to understand just how significant it is for the U.S. government to openly partner with a group that labels Christians as "hateful" in its fight against what it deems right-wing "domestic terrorism"—one need only look to how President Obama and his Democratic Party are actively backing an actual domestic extremist group: the left-wing anarchist outfit known as "Black Lives Matter" (BLM).

Lee Stranahan, writing for *Breitbart* in October 2015, reported on how the Democratic Party has thrown all in with the extremist BLM:

The Democratic National Committee has formally invited the anti-po-lice Black Lives Matter to host a presidential town hall. It's the latest move by the Democrats to kowtow to a movement whose hero Assata Shakur is currently on the FBI's most wanted terrorist list. ...

While they did not support a full-fledged debate, the DNC response was rapid and enthusiastic, praising the "commitment to progressive values" of the group that screamed, "Burn everything down" at their Netroots Nation takeover. As posted by Black Lives Matter on their Facebook page, the DNC's Amy Dacey said in part that the group that chanted "Pigs in a blanket, fry 'em like bacon!" after the murders of police of-ficers would be "an ideal host for a presidential candidate forum" ... [67]

And for those who might suggest that President Obama is not associated with the Democratic National Committee's public support for Black Lives Matter (despite his being the de facto head of the Democrtic Party), Stranahan later reported on how this president has, himself, overtly lent support to the group (emphasis added in the original source):

As Breitbart News reported, President Obama defended Black Lives Matter at the Panel Discussion on Criminal Justice Reform at the White House Thursday, saying, "Sometimes, like any of these loose organizations, some people pop off and say dumb things."

However, the three self-described "queer women" who founded Black Lives Matter have made it abundantly clear that the group is not a ragtag, spontaneous movement, but rather the work of experienced community organizers working with unions and educators with the goal of reenergizing radical Black Liberation politics in the black community. ...

*"**We intended Black Lives Matter to be a hub for connection**, for Black Lives Matter to be a platform to tell our own stories in our own voices," Garza says. "**And for Black Lives Matter to be a platform also to reenergize radical politics in our community** [emphasis added]." ...*

Obama's whitewash of Black Lives Matter appears to be especially dis-honest since one of the group's other co-founders, Patrisse Cullors, has claimed to have met with the President—something that Breitbart News has reported, which seems to be confirmed by White House visitor re-cords. [68]

A homosexual activist who hates Christians attacks the mainstream FRC and attempts to slaughter the Christians therein. The Justice Department's inves-tigation reveals that the SPLC's propagandist materials both aid and motivate him to carry out this would-be bloodbath. Yet the administration of the President of the United States remains affiliated with the hard-left outfit responsible, the SPLC, even as this president directly expresses support for actual domestic extremists like the Black Lives Matter movement—a radical Marxist organization founded by "three self-described 'queer women'"—an organization whose members have actually called for, and even engaged in violence.

Simply astounding. While ours was a nation founded on Judeo-Christian principles, by vastly God-fearing Christian men, today's American government has officially aligned itself against Christians and with the anti-Christians, while sympathizing with and supporting criminals and worse.

And this hostility toward law-abiding Christians, this love of evil displayed by both private citizens and leftists in the U.S. government, regrettably extends into all aspects of American life—including the armed forces.

Chapter 9

Being a Faithful Christian in the U.S. Armed Forces Is Risky Business

While anti-Christian attacks on Christian troops in the U.S. armed forces have occurred to a small degree under other administrations, they have become systemic under the Obama regime.

In a statement released in May of 2013, President Obama's Pentagon threatened military personnel: "Religious proselytization is not permitted within the Department of Defense. … Court martials and non-judicial punishments are decided on a case-by-case basis. …"[69]

Merriam-Webster defines "proselytization" as an attempt "to recruit or convert especially to a new faith, institution, or cause." Sounds an awful lot like the Pentagon is threatening to court-martial any service member who obeys Christ's central command to "[g]o into all the world and preach the gospel to all creation." (Mark 16:15 – New International Version)

Hard to read it any other way.

Although the Pentagon later walked back its anti-Christian "proselytizing" policy within the realm of public relations (a policy that was drafted in concert with foul-mouthed atheist and anti-Christian bigot Mikey Weinstein), the DOD never offered much in the way of solid evidence that it has walked it back within the realm of application.[70]

I've got news for progressives. In America, serving God and serving country are not mutually exclusive. They never have been. In fact, until this president came along, the two went hand-in-hand.

In his farewell address, George Washington underscored the critical role religion and morality play to our nation's survival. He warned of people like Barack Obama and Mikey Weinstein: "Of all the dispositions and habits which lead to political prosperity, Religion and Morality are indispensable supports," he said.

"In vain would that man claim the tribute of Patriotism, who should labor to subvert these great pillars of human happiness, these firmest props of the duties of Men and Citizens. ... [R]eason and experience both forbid us to expect that national morality can prevail in exclusion of religious principle."[71]

It seems the central goal of this president and his Pentagon is to do that—to "subvert religion and morality" wherever they find it. George Washington called that unpatriotic. I agree.

Every brave serviceman or woman I've ever known loves serving this great nation. Every Christian I've ever known loves serving the one Holy and Sovereign Creator of the universe—King Jesus.

I served twelve years in the military. I'm proud of that. But it can't be easy now, laboring under an incompetent commander-in-chief who, over and again, has displayed overt hostility toward Washington's "indispensable" pillars of religion and morality. It can't be easy to serve under a president who constantly attacks your faith and freedom.

My friends at Liberty Counsel weren't about to let this attack on faith and liberty go unchallenged, and Mat Staver quickly condemned it: "It is beyond ironic that this administration chose to attack the religious liberties of the men and women who are charged with defending our nation's freedom across the country and around the world," he said.

"The military has a unique relationship with chaplains in order to meet the spiritual needs of our soldiers. To threaten court-martial to anyone who shares their faith is reprehensible and un-American. This absurd policy will undermine the military and destroy morale. It must be rescinded immediately, and those responsible for instituting it should be disciplined."[72]

As I've noted, there isn't much by way of credible evidence that the Obama administration ever walked back its anti-Christian policy within the realm of application. Those who instituted it certainly haven't been disciplined. And things have, of course, only gotten worse since then, with anti-Christian zealot Mikey Weinstein leading the attacks on Christian troops.

You can gain some understanding of just who Weinstein is, and just how frenzied he is in his secularist jihad to rid the armed forces of Christianity, by reading an op-ed he wrote in June 2015—an op-ed that he republished at his misnamed Military Religious Freedom Foundation (MRFF) website. Here is but one excerpt. It concerns the effect the Supreme Court's "gay marriage" ruling should have on Christian military chaplains:

> *Oh, but the ruling doesn't simply apply to civilians alone—the Supreme Court decision will permit same-sex marriage not only in all 50 states in the union, but on ALL United States Military bases as well. For the Military Religious Freedom Foundation, the only organization devoted solely to fighting the scourge of fundamentalist Christian extremism, the monumental importance of this occasion CANNOT be overstated enough. Indeed, our LGBTQ client base of over 900 servicemembers has been ecstatic, and I can scarcely write this opinion piece due to the fact that my phone is absolutely ringing off the hook with phone calls from exuberant servicemembers. Expect to hear wedding bells ring joyously across chapels as same-sex couples are joined in matrimony at military installations across the globe! ...*

> *These pernicious bigots must stop trying to claim "Christian Victimization" when, in point of fact, what they are seeing "Christian Equalization". ...*

> *Nobody is arguing that these losers don't have a right to their religious beliefs—that right is sacrosanct, and is backed by the highest law of the land—the U.S. Constitution. However, as long as these faux "victimized" chaplains insist on accepting a government paycheck from us, the taxpayers, while nurturing and maintaining the state of antagonism between their religion and the sexual/gender identities of servicemembers, then they don't belong in the military. At this stage, the only honorable thing that these losers can do is to fold up their uniforms, turn in their papers, and get the hell out of the American military chaplaincy. If they are unwilling or too cowardly to do so, then the Department of Defense must expeditiously cleanse itself of the intolerant filth that insists on lingering in the ranks of our armed forces.*[73]

And so, in just a few short years, America has gone from being a nation wherein disordered same-sex sodomy, which destroys unit cohesion and troop morale, is rightfully prohibited in the ranks of the armed forces, to a nation wherein a close ally of the U.S. Department of Defense (DOD) brazenly calls for the armed forces to purge Christians who won't bow to America's new Official Secularist Religion and its false god of Sodom.

Christian? Don't ask, don't tell.

Indeed, this bigoted anti-Christian rhetoric is par for the course for Weinstein and other progressives, and it's unconscionable that our executive branch would partner with him—with them. Unfortunately, it seems that the DOD *is* "them."

Nonetheless, a U.S. congressman called Weinstein on his demonstrable hatred of Christians and Christianity in 2014 when the U.S. House of Representatives Armed Services Committee held a hearing over concerns about the Obama DOD's established hostility toward religious freedom:

> *At a House Armed Services Committee's Subcommittee on Military Personnel on Wednesday, Rep. Randy Forbes (R-Va.) confronted one witness with derogatory remarks he made about Christians, which the lawmaker said exemplifies the threat to religious liberty in the U.S. Armed Forces.*
>
> *Forbes used his five minutes to ask Michael Weinstein, founder of the controversial Military Religious Freedom Foundation, about remarks he made about Christians.*
>
> *"In a Washington Post article on July 16, 2006 they attributed a quote to you that said: 'We've created this foundation to be a weapon. We're going to lie down a withering field of fire and leave sucking chest wounds,'" Forbes said. "Was that an accurate quote?"*
>
> *Weinstein did not answer the yes or no question but instead tried to defend his stance.*
>
> *"I want to make it very clear that we realize what we're facing is a tsunami of fundamental Christian..." Weinstein said.*
>
> *"Did you make that quote or not?" Forbes asked.*
>
> *Weinstein went on saying, "We are facing a tsunami of fundamental Christian exceptionalism and supremacy..."*
>
> *"Yes, of course I said those words. I'm proud of them," Weinstein added.*
>
> *Forbes then repeated another quote attributed to Weinstein.*
>
> *"A second one on June 16, 2013, you said, 'Today we face incredibly well-funded gangs of fundamentalist Christian monsters who terrorize their fellow Americans by forcing their weaponized and twisted version of Christianity upon their helpless subordinates in our nation's Armed Forces.' Did you make that quote?" Forbes asked.*
>
> *"I did," Weinstein said.* [74,75]

Yet the Obama DOD continued (and continues at the time of this book's publication) its ties with Weinstein, always ready to listen whenever this bona fide nut gives voice, whether from the floor of Congress or on MSNBC, to his latest conspiracy theories about Christians "terrorizing" the U.S. armed forces.

Even so, Weinstein's and the Obama administration's official policy against proselytization are far from the only examples of the rising attacks on Christianity in the U.S. armed forces.

The "Texas on the Potomac" blog of the *Houston Chronicle* reported in July 2013 that the persecution of Christians in the armed forces had gotten so bad that Republican Rep. Louie Gohmert (TX-01) spoke about "a section in the National Defense Authorization Act designed to expand religious freedom in the military."[76] The 2014 National Defense Authorization Act eventually became law in 2014 with that amendment attached.[77]

Things had gotten so bad that by April of 2014, the Strategic Studies Institute, part of the U.S. Army War College in Carlisle, PA, published a monograph on systematic anti-Christian hostility in the military. The SSI is an important organization within the Army and provides the following description of its purpose:[78]

> *The Strategic Studies Institute is the U.S. Army's institute for geostrategic and national security research and analysis. The Strategic Studies Institute conducts strategic research and analysis to support the U.S. Army War College curricula, provides direct analysis for Army and Department of Defense leadership, and serves as a bridge to the wider strategic community.*

In the monograph, titled, *A Soldier's Morality, Religion, and Our Professional Ethic: Does the Army's Culture Facilitate Integration, Character Development, and Trust in the Profession?*, authors Dr. Don M. Snider and Alexander P. Shine write about the increasing hostility towards faith in the armed forces under the Obama regime:

> *In October 2013, the Secretary of the Army directed a halt to all "briefings, command presentations, or training on the subject of extremist organizations until that program of instruction and training has been [re]created and disseminated." ...*
>
> *Of interest is the fact that during those briefings, Catholics, Evangelical Christians, and several apolitical religious advocacy groups in Washington, DC, had been labeled by Army instructors as "hate groups." News of this drew negative reaction from members of Congress who strongly addressed their concerns to the Secretary.*
>
> *How could such unprofessional conduct on the part of Army instructors happen "on several occasions over the past few months" without, apparently, corrective action being taken by uniformed leaders at each location, or even at some higher uniformed level? Why did they stand on the*

sidelines so long that it took the Secretary of the Army to act? Why did they not recognize what the Secretary did—that such representations are "inaccurate, objectionable, and otherwise inconsistent with Army policy," not to mention, common sense? ...

We contend that this example, one of several that we shall discuss, high-lights a much larger issue—that the Army's professional culture, as well as those of the other Services, has become increasingly hostile to almost any expression of personal moralities—and particularly those based on religion—so hostile that citizens can rightly wonder whether the conduct of the institutions continues to reflect the legal and moral foundations of the professions' own ethics."[79]

The American left's War on Christianity is real and undeniable. It has gotten so bad that in 2016 American troops who attempt to live out their Christian faith are under threat of persecution and prosecution by anti-Christian activists and government officials who want to ruin their careers and lives—all while the same Christian troops continue actively fighting and dying on behalf of anti-Christian/anti-Semitic/anti-American Muslims across the globe, including in Iran, Iraq, Afghanistan, Syria, Egypt, et al., where the U.S. government has aided and abetted the burgeoning caliphate in its establishment of official Islamic theocracies. It should come as no surprise, then, that we hear little to nothing from the American left as the U.S. government not only proselytizes on behalf of Islam (consider Obama's insistence that, "The future must not belong to those who slander the prophet of Islam."), but in conquering the world for "the prophet of Islam" by the sword.

In the meantime, the LGBT lobby's "gay" caliphate is trying to conquer the world one Christian bakery at a time.

Chapter 10

You Will Bake Phony Wedding Cakes or Else!

Anti-Christians have long abused the American judicial system through what's called "lawfare," in their ongoing multi-pronged, multi-theatre War on Christianity. Still, within just the past five to ten years, this leftist lawfare has escalated to unprecedented levels. In 2013, for instance, homosexual activists planned and orchestrated an attack on an Oregon Christian bakery because its Christian owners, Aaron and Melissa Klein, politely declined to desecrate God's natural design for marriage by participating in a so-called "same-sex wedding."

The Oregonian reported on the attack at the time:

> *A same-sex couple who requested a cake for their wedding in January but were refused service by a Gresham bakery have filed a complaint with the state, alleging Sweet Cakes by Melissa discriminated against them based on their sexual orientation.*

> *Oregon's Bureau of Labor and Industries' civil rights division will investigate to determine if the business violated the Oregon Equality Act of 2007, which protects the rights of gays, lesbians, bisexual and transgender people in employment, housing and public accommodations.*

> *...*

> *Rachel N. Cryer, 30, said she had gone to the Gresham bakery on Jan. 17 for a scheduled appointment to order a wedding cake. She met with the owner, Aaron Klein.*

> *Klein asked for the date of the wedding and names of the bride and groom, Cryer said.*

"I told him, 'There are two brides and our names are Rachel and Laurel,'" according to her complaint.

Klein responded that his business does not provide its services for same-sex weddings, she said.

"Respondent cited a religious belief for its refusal to make cakes for same-sex couples planning to marry," the complaint says. ..."

"We are committed to a fair and thorough investigation to determine whether there's substantial evidence of unlawful discrimination," said Labor Commissioner Brad Avakian. ...[80]

Mr. Avakian then revealed what he viewed as a "fair and thorough investigation":

"Everybody is entitled to their own beliefs, but that doesn't mean that folks have the right to discriminate," he said.

Here's the kicker. Read it closely:

"The goal is never to shut down a business. The goal is to rehabilitate," Avakian said. "For those who do violate the law, we want them to learn from that experience and have a good, successful business in Oregon."

George Orwell much?

Get the not-so-thinly-veiled threat? Christians have a right to own a "successful business" in Oregon, so long as they don't, well, act Christian—so long as they shelve their faith and submit to our ever-progressive government's anti-Christian demands. "The goal is never to shut down a business," but either you abandon the Judeo-Christian sexual ethic and dutifully observe postmodern sexual relativism, or government will shut you down in a Sodom and Gomorrah minute.

Left-wing bullies need to get this straight (so to speak): The godless have been trying to "rehabilitate" Christians for over 2,000 years. We haven't caved yet. What makes you think we will now? Those of us who wish to remain obedient to God will not—indeed, cannot—accommodate you and play along with your sin-centric "gay marriage" delusion.

Ain't gonna happen.

Ever.

Look, you have every right to dress up in two wedding gowns or two tuxedos, get pretend "married" and play house to your heart's content. You do not have the right, however, to force others to abandon their sincerely held religious beliefs, thousands of years of history and the immutable reality of human biology to engage your little fantasy. No amount of hand-wringing, gnashing of teeth, suing Christians or filing charges against those of us who live in marriage reality will make us recognize your silly so-called "marriage equality."

Rather than trying to compel these Christians to participate in their counter-Christian mock marriage, all Ms. Rachel and Ms. Laurel had to do was take their business down the street. There are, no doubt, many bakers who share their worldly sexual morals (or lack thereof).

Imagine if a Christian came into a "gay"-owned bakery and demanded a cake with these words: "Homosexual behavior is shameful: Romans 1:27." Think the left would be clamoring for charges against the baker if he refused? Me neither. In fact, I'd be the first to defend his right to "discriminate" against the Christian.

Or what if some anti-gun nut printing service refused to produce flyers for an NRA rally? Shouldn't they have that right?

Or if some hippy bed and breakfast owner refused to host a conference challenging global warming alarmism? Shouldn't he have the right to operate his business in accordance with his sincerely held beliefs?

Of course he should. And so should Christians.

But ... But ... discrimination! "Homophobia"!

I know. How dare I say that Christians should have rights just like everyone else?

Seriously, lefties, give it a rest. So-called "sexual orientation" laws are nothing like laws prohibiting racial, age, disability or sex discrimination. Those qualities are based on neutral, immutable characteristics. Even liberals admit that "sexual orientation" is based on "fluid" feelings and behaviors. It's about what you do, not who you are. It's about what you believe and whom you choose to have sex with, not the color of your skin.

Still, progressives will never give it a rest. And because Christians—true regenerated, Bible-believing Christians—will never compromise objective truth in favor of worshipping alongside progressives at the secularist altar of fleshly self-gratification, they become enraged. They've made it clear that they will never allow their fantastical moral relativist worldview and Christianity to coexist in harmony.

Thus, things have only gotten worse for the Kleins since 2013.

The Oregon Bureau of Labor and Industries found the Kleins "guilty" of refusing to violate their Christian faith and the state has ordered them to pay $135,000.

The Daily Signal reported on this unconstitutional injustice in October of 2015:

> *The agency that ordered Aaron and Melissa Klein to pay $135,000 in damages for refusing to bake a cake for a same-sex couple began the legal process last week to seize the money the Oregon bakers are refusing to pay.*
>
> *"Our agency has docketed the judgment and is exploring collection options," Charlie Burr, communications director for the Oregon Bureau of Labor and Industries, told The Daily Signal. "They are entitled to a full and fair review of the case, but do not have the right to disregard a legally binding order."*
>
> *Docketing the judgment is a preliminary step the agency must take in order to seize the Kleins' house, property, or other assets in lieu of payment.*
>
> *On July 2, Brad Avakian, commissioner of the Oregon Bureau of Labor and Industries, ordered the Kleins to pay $135,000 for the emotional, physical, and psychological damages they caused Rachel and Laurel Bowman-Cryer for refusing to make a wedding cake.*[81]

Just before Christmas 2015, Herr Avakian and the Oregon Bureau of Labor and Industries drained the Kleins' personal bank account of every last penny, including money set aside for tithing to their church, and putting food in the mouths of their five children.

What kind of America is this?

And this isn't an isolated instance of state persecution of Christians for refusing to participate in a phony, sin-centric, marriage mockery ritual.

"Gay pride" necessitates anti-Christian hate. It must. "Gay marriage" and other "sexual orientation"-based laws do violence to freedom and truth. They are the hammer with which the postmodern left is bludgeoning bloody religious liberty and the Judeo-Christian sexual ethic.

According to the unequivocal moral precepts of the Judeo-Christian tradition—explicit throughout both the Old and New Testaments—homosexual behavior is sin. Sin is evil. Homosexual behavior is the central, defining characteristic of so-called "gay marriage." Therefore, "gay marriage" is evil. Christians are obligated to avoid sin—to "do no evil."

I know—it's not popular to speak such simple truths in today's politically correct world. But I'm not out to win a popularity contest.

Neither is Ms. Barronelle Stutzman. Ms. Stutzman is the Christian owner-operator of Arlene's Flowers in Richland, Washington. She is, by all accounts, a lovely, sweet, elderly woman who both employs and regularly serves open practitioners of the homosexual lifestyle. Sadly, she has become yet another victim in this fast-growing string of secularist attacks against Christians and other morally minded people. And now that same-sex "marriage" is "the law of the land" (it's not—not really, anyway), I can assure you that we will see an explosion in the same kind of anti-Christian persecution Ms. Stutzman now suffers.

In 2013, one of Ms. Stutzman's frequent homosexual customers requested that she provide flower arrangements for his same-sex "wedding." She politely declined, saying that her Christian conscience and "relationship with Jesus Christ" prevented her from any involvement with counter-Christian same-sex "marriage." She was, quite simply, a Christian being Christian. The two hugged and parted ways.

Unfortunately, in our decaying culture, being Christian has fast become a most dangerous proposition. As each homofascist demand is checked from liberals' debauched wish list, it only gets worse.

As a result of her constitutionally guaranteed religious free exercise, Washington state Attorney General Bob Ferguson filed charges against Ms. Stutzman, seeking both a monetary judgment and an injunction to physically force her to violate her Christian conscience. He would compel her to either lend her artistic expression in support of counterfeit "gay marriage"—something Christianity steadfastly recognizes as mortal sin—or face further charges.[82,83]

Speaking of steadfast, to her credit, Ms. Stutzman has stood firm through it all. She has refused to cave under Ferguson's tyrannical torment. Ferguson, on the other hand, has revealed himself a creep and a coward—a progressive bully who apparently gets off on abusing elderly women. He's a disgrace to Washington state and should be thrown out of office and disbarred.[84]

Still, this type of government persecution must be expected. Ferguson is a liberal. The liberal viewpoint is that any viewpoint, save the liberal viewpoint, must be criminalized and prosecuted.

Like many of us, Joseph Backholm, with the Family Policy Institute of Washington, has long warned about the consequences of radically deconstructing the institution of natural marriage. "Now that the law says marriage is genderless," he wrote in 2013 of Ms. Stutzman's ongoing abuse, "those who think otherwise [must] ... conform or be punished. ... Now liberals believe they are legally entitled to someone else's labor."[85]

To homosexuals I say this: Yes, you are equal in God's eyes. You are loved. These things are true, not because of your homosexual lifestyle, but, rather, they are true in spite of it.

Most homosexuals know intuitively, I think, that their lifestyle is unnatural and immoral and that the oxymoronic notion of same-sex "marriage" is a silly farce. Thus, they must force others to affirm both their self-destructive lifestyle and their mock "marriages" under penalty of law. They must physically compel everyone to engage their "emperor's new clothes" delusion, so they can feel better about bad behavior.

Well, my friend, making everyone else "call evil good and good evil" won't fill that dark void in your soul. Only repentance and redemption through a personal relationship with Jesus Christ can do that.

When we give deviant sexual conduct preferred status in law, Christian morality becomes illegal. If you think government recognized "gay marriage" is harmless to society, you're playing the fool. It places the Christian sexual ethic and free exercise of religion in direct conflict with law. It's my sense that many liberty-minded people are finally coming awake to this disturbing reality.

Although we all sin, Christians are commanded to neither support nor engage in evil. Hence, Christians—true Christians—cannot engage in nor condone the unrepentant practice of homosexual behavior. Neither can we support sin-centric "gay marriage."

This rudimentary equation is built upon the natural laws of moral physics. Christianity is magnetically charged truth. Homosexual behavior is a magnetically charged lie—a spiritual and biological falsehood. Christianity and homosexual sin are as north to south. Polar opposites cannot occupy the same position in time and space. They repel one another. It's physically, spiritually and legally impossible for religious freedom and preferred legal status for sexual sin to coexist in harmony. Ms. Stutzman's persecution is just one of the increasing number of reminders of this timeless reality.

While there are dozens more, a third example of homosexuals and other anti-Christians using lawfare to attack someone who won't celebrate counterfeit "gay" weddings involves Jack Phillips, a Colorado cake artist who wouldn't bake a cake for two "Sin of Sodom" worshippers.

Mr. Phillips exercised his First Amendment religious rights in 2013 and politely declined to bake a "wedding" cake for a homosexual civil union. Colorado's "civil rights" Star Chamber ordered Mr. Phillips to deny his faith and bake these fake cakes, go out of business or even face prison.

He and his elderly mother (an employee) were additionally "sentenced" to attend "sensitivity training" (read: re-education camp).[86,87]

As Mr. Phillips has long indicated, he has no problem baking for homosexuals, but, as a Christian, he simply cannot and will not contribute his time and

God-given gifts to bake a "wedding" cake that mocks and defiles God's design for the immutable institution of legitimate marriage.

Nor would he bake for a white supremacist rally or any other similarly wicked event that likewise flouts biblical truth.

As a result, Phillips has said he will stop baking wedding cakes altogether.

That's how it works. Christian free exercise isn't outlawed all at once. Judges across our fruity plain simply order from the bench that millions of Christians, just like Aaron and Melissa Klein, Barronelle Stutzman, and Jack Phillips, must either deny recognition of God's natural order and Christ's admonition to "go and sin no more," or face prison for "contempt of court."

Welcome to America 2016, where evil is good, men are women, judges are tyrants, and Christians are persona non grata. There is no more in between. The anti-Christ left has thrown down the "gay marriage" gauntlet. It's either God or man.

But this doesn't mean that God-fearing folks like the Kleins, Ms. Stutzman and Mr. Phillips should give up. To the contrary, when it comes to sharing His truths, Christ taught His followers to never give up. And, as it has been since He first walked the earth, others Christians will be there, in support, to help them stand firm.

Consider, for instance, the non-profit legal group Alliance Defending Freedom (ADF). ADF has been instrumental in defending Ms. Stutzman, Mr. Phillips and many other Christians just like them. As late as October 2015, ADF and Mr. Phillips were still pressing fearlessly forward in fighting back against the progressive juggernaut in Colorado. *The Daily Signal* reported that ADF has taken his case to the Colorado Supreme Court:

> *Another layer has unfolded for cake artist Jack Phillips. He has asked the Colorado Supreme Court to rule that the government cannot force him to bake a cake in celebration of a same-sex wedding. ...*
>
> *Phillips, who says he doesn't think he committed an act of discrimination, has opted since March 2014 not to take any new orders for wedding cakes rather than be forced to create them for two men or two women.*
>
> *"In Colorado, bakers can refuse to make cakes with a message opposing same-sex unions but can be fined out of business if they decline to bake cakes celebrating same-sex unions," Roger Severino, director of The Heritage Foundation's DeVos Center for Religion and Civil Society, said. "There is something wrong when government respects the freedom of some to run their businesses according to their values while targeting others, especially people of faith, with lawsuits, penalties, and fines."*

In April, Alliance Defending Freedom pointed out that three Denver bakeries were not found guilty of discrimination when a Christian customer was declined a cake that reflected opposition to same-sex marriage, a view that violated the conscience of those cake artists. [88]

Let's hope and pray for the sake of religious liberty, freedom of conscience, our U.S. Constitution and the American way of life that Mr. Phillips prevails. Let's pray that Aaron and Melissa Klein and Barronelle Stutzman do as well. But even if they don't, we must all stand firm in our obedience to God—even if it means civil disobedience to man. No one said that being a Christ-follower is easy. "Easy" is not what we signed up for.

And so, American Christians now face a choice: "But if serving the LORD seems undesirable to you, then choose for yourselves this day whom you will serve. ... But as for me and my household, we will serve the LORD." (Joshua 24:15 – New International Version)

Whom will you serve?

But even if, and as, you choose to serve God, keep in mind that those who hate Him desire much more than simply forcing you to bake cakes and provide flowers for their marriage desecration ceremonies. They likewise intend to force Christians to join them in the denial of objective biological reality, and to stand silently by as they place your wives and daughters in harm's way.

Chapter 11

You Will Deny Reality or Face the Wrath of Municipal Government

Texas is thought to be one of the strongest conservative states in the Union. "Liberals will never take over Texas!" they say in the Lone Star State. And yet the former mayor of Houston, the largest city in Texas and one of the largest cities in the U.S., is among the most radical anti-Christians imaginable. Shamefully, she used her powerful position in this "conservative stronghold" to wage lawfare against Christians and, as a radical lesbian activist, to further the despotic "LGBTUVWXYZ" (or whatever alphabet soup of nonsense it is these days) agenda.

I was born in Waco, Texas, and lived in Houston, so I had a dog in this hunt. I still do. Really, we all do.

Annise Parker served as Houston mayor from January 2010 to January 2016 when her final term expired. Yet her anti-Christian extremism and tyrannical behavior should have disqualified her from the privilege of serving the people of south Texas long before that. Houston voters should have recalled her from office years ago, but they didn't and so she is now out of office solely due to term limitations.

You see, Parker, Houston's first openly homosexual, female mayor, was caught, cold, with her hand in the totalitarian cookie jar. She had, on multiple counts, betrayed her oath of office. She put her own radical self-interests above the best interests of her constituents and all but spit on the very U.S. Constitution she was sworn to uphold.

This woman revealed herself to be a single-issue-driven sexual extremist with zero regard for the rule of law when she decided to go after Houston citizens who fought back against an ordinance she helped pass that allowed men to go into women's bathrooms. Her dictatorial impulses saw her going so far as to target Houston churches and attempt to subpoena the sermons of pastors who helped lead the effort to put that ordinance up for a popular vote.

And while Parker backpedaled on her initial unconstitutional sermon subpoenas faster than a dyslexic cyclist in the Four de Trance, she, nonetheless, pushed ahead like Lance Armstrong on steroids with her unlawful subversion of Houston's citizen petition process (arbitrarily tossing out nearly three-quarters of validated petition signatures needed to put her utterly insane gender-neutral "bathroom bill" up for a vote by the very people whose privacy it sexually assaults). That single act of political corruption alone disenfranchised every single Houston resident.

Her gross abuses of power shocked and outraged millions of Americans across the country on every point of the political spectrum. Attorney, best-selling author and columnist David Limbaugh distilled nicely the controversy in an October 2014 *WND* column titled, "Fascist Leftists in Houston":

> *"There are at least three outrageous things about the Houston city government's recent actions pushing an ordinance to allow men and women to use each other's public restrooms," began Limbaugh. "The first is the substance of the ordinance itself, which allows men and women, irrespective of their biology, to use bathrooms designated for the opposite sex."*[89]

> *Indeed. As I noted in my own column the very next day, "[B]ecause it's now illegal to 'discriminate based on the basis of gender identity' in Houston, and since it's the only 'tolerant' thing to do, men who sign up for the ever-persecuted 'LGBT' class have secured the hard-fought 'civil right' to fully expose themselves to, and otherwise ogle, your daughters in the ladies' room."*[90]

Which brings us to Parker's second offense—another that, even after her withdrawing the unlawfully issued sermon subpoenas in a panicked frenzy, remained both unresolved and was never punished.

Continued Limbaugh:

> *The second outrage is that the city has greatly overreached in subpoenaing the pastors of the city for copies of their sermons and their communications to their congregations to determine whether they have violated this Godforsaken ordinance. Lest you think this was a mistake, the mayor tweeted, 'If the 5 pastors used pulpits for politics, their sermons are fair game.'*

Sermons are fair game? Uh, actually, no, Mrs. Stalin. In fact, hell no. Despite a bevy of progressive rationalizations to the contrary, this couldn't be further from the truth.

First, notwithstanding the decades of mythical "church-state separation" nonsense spread by the Communist-founded ACLU, there is no legal proscription that would, or even could, prevent pastors from "politicking from the pulpit." Doing so is their unalienable First Amendment-protected right. These are the issues that belong in the pulpit. This outrageous bathroom bill, and others like it, directly touch and concern matters of faith, morality and culture. Christians didn't politicize this debate; lefty nut burgers like Annise "I-am-lesbian-hear-me-roar" Parker did.

Furthermore, the 1954 Johnson Amendment, which itself is facially unconstitutional, only presumes to prevent pastors from endorsing or opposing, on behalf of their tax-exempt church, candidates from the pulpit. Nowhere does it even hint at prohibiting them from addressing, opposing or supporting legislation or ballot initiatives.

Moreover, none of the pastors whose sermons were subpoenaed were even party to the lawsuit a group of Christians filed against the city (and to which the city was supposedly responding with the subpoenas).[91] No reasonable judge or attorney would have dreamed of trying to make a case that anything they ever said or did could, in any way, be "reasonably calculated to lead to the discovery of admissible evidence," which, as any pre-law student with a pulse can tell you, is a fundamental must.

Finally, and as Limbaugh concluded:

> The third outrage is the city's lawless disqualification and rejection of valid petitions filed by voters to challenge the law. Voters submitted more than three times the legally required number of petition signatures to require city action (17,269 were required, and the voters submitted a whopping 55,000), and the city secretary initially certified them as sufficient in number. But the mayor and city attorney outright rejected the petition anyway, on the specious grounds that the petition signatures weren't valid.

This, my friends, was nothing short of fascism—lawlessness. It was unabashed political corruption, out front and in your face. Forget Parker's brazen attack on religious liberty and her twisted dudes-in-the-ladies'-shower ordinance. That disgusting abuse of power alone should've caused Houstonians to boot her out the door posthaste.

I don't care whether you're Republican or Democrat, conservative or progressive, this should shock and infuriate you. If Parker could get away with this kind of brazen political corruption while Democrats are in control, what's to stop Republicans from doing the same thing when they run the show?

Thankfully a number of Christians and other Houstonians fought back against Parker and her fellow Christ-haters. There was much at stake, and freedom, truth and women's right to privacy and protections against sexual harassment and potential sexual assault were ultimately victorious.

Houstonians succeeded in getting the right to challenge the nonsense that Parker and her allies created. They went to the ballot in November 2015 and voted on whether they wanted to subjugate their women to naked perverts in the shower; whether they wanted to reject a most fundamental aspect of natural law—the immutable biological fact that "God made them male and female," and that any other such "genders" as man may imagine are the delusional ravings of those in rebellion against God.

The ordinance that Parker and her fellow creeps rammed through to attack women and reality was known, of course, under the deceptively named, Houston Equal Rights Ordinance (HERO). The proposition that Houstonians wanted on the voting ballot (and which Parker and her allies tried to block) to allow them to repeal it was called Proposition 1. A "no" vote on Proposition 1 meant that Houstonians were voting against HERO. (In other words, the proposition was worded in such a way that voting "yes" meant that Houstonians wanted to keep HERO in place.)

The Christian Post explained in an October 2015 article how Houstonians succeeded in overturning Parker's initial rejection of valid petition signatures:

> *Opponents of the ordinance launched a petition that got more than 50,000 signatures; well above the 17,269 signatures needed to put the ordinance on the ballot.*

> *Although city officials attempted to throw out the petition, in July the Texas Supreme Court ruled that the ordinance must be put on the upcoming ballot.*

> *"The City Council is directed to comply with its duties, as specified in the City Charter, that arise when the City Secretary certifies that a referendum petition has a sufficient number of valid signatures. Any enforcement of the [Equal Rights] ordinance will be suspended," ruled the high court.*

> *"If the City Council does not repeal the ordinance by August 24, 2015, then by that date the City Council must order that the ordinance be put to popular vote during the November 2015 election."[92]*

This allowed Houstonians to determine in the November election what they wanted to do with HERO. And that determination was a matter of no small consequence. Again, a "yes" vote for Proposition 1 would have endorsed the HERO and would have effectively finalized Parker's effort to criminalize Christianity. Anyone who wouldn't defy their Christian faith thereafter—anyone who wouldn't join in the defiance of reality and assault on women—would be subject to punishment by the state, something the *Christian Post* reported on in a separate October 2015 article:

> *Family Research Council Action President Tony Perkins said that while the ad draws attention to the bathroom issue, voting against Proposition 1 is also about religious liberty.*
>
> *"This ad draws voters' attention to the fact that if parents—or anyone—dares to block a man from entering a woman's restroom, they are subject to fines up to $5,000 under Proposition 1," Perkins said in a statement.*
>
> *"Proposition 1 is about a lot more than even bathrooms. It's about criminalizing religious liberty. The ordinance also gives the government new grounds to impose punishing fines on bakers, florists, planners, musicians and others who refuse to yield their religious beliefs to this new morality.*[93]

You read that right. If Houstonians voted for Proposition 1 in November 2015, it would have forced Christians, under penalty of law, to stand by and allow their wives and daughters to be sexually harassed and, potentially, sexually assaulted in restrooms, locker rooms and public showers by men pretending to be women. The law would have treated the sexual harassers as the victims and those women who were sexually harassed as the criminals.

Fortunately, sanity prevailed and voters overwhelmingly rejected HERO by a margin of 62- to 38-percent.[94] It's simply remarkable what God can accomplish through His children when we choose to fight back against these sexual anarchists—those who seek to deconstruct and reinvent our once-great American culture into a perverted progressive dystopia that reflects their own secular, Christ-hating image.

And while it is indeed good news that Christians and other Americans soundly defeated this "progressive" regression in one city, the bad news is that the enemies of God are not about to throw in the towel. They continue working tirelessly to criminalize Christianity and codify sexual perversion in America's every nook and cranny, including within the bowels of federal government.

Chapter 12

You Will Lie about Marriage or the U.S. Government Will Send You to Prison

When the U.S. Supreme Court arbitrarily presumed to officially call God a liar on behalf of the American people in June 2015 (by way of the *Obergefell v. Hodges Supreme Court* "gay marriage" decision), the Christ-haters running the federal government began salivating—scheming myriad ways to use and abuse the U.S. government to target Christians. They soon enough found a flashpoint for their Alinskyite conniving—someone they could attack, demonize and make an example of at the national level.

In August of 2015, Liberty Counsel filed a request for a stay and an appeal of U.S. District Judge David Bunning's opinion ordering Rowan County Clerk Kim Davis to issue same-sex "marriage" licenses both in violation of her First Amendment right to religious free exercise and the biblical mandate that she must not participate in this explicitly sinful activity. Davis had been sued by the ACLU and two lesbian political activists. They sought licenses from Ms. Davis after learning of her religious objections to same-sex "marriage," and they refused to obtain a license elsewhere. Mat Staver and Liberty Counsel provided legal services for Ms. Davis. Staver said, "Just as Justice Alito predicted in his dissent in Obergefell, secularists are trying to 'stamp out every vestige of dissent' by targeting people of faith who do not agree with same-sex 'marriage.'"[95]

Judge Bunning wrote in his ruling:

> *Davis remains free to practice her Apostolic Christian beliefs. She may continue to attend church twice a week, participate in Bible study and minister to female inmates at the Rowan County Jail. She is even free*

to believe that marriage is a union between one man and one woman, as many Americans do. However, her religious convictions cannot excuse her from performing the duties that she took an oath to perform as Rowan County Clerk.[96]

Staver responded to Bunning's ruling:

"Judge Bunning's decision equated Kim's free exercise of religion to going to church," Mat Staver, one of her lawyers, said in a prepared statement. "This is absurd. Christianity is not a robe you take off when you leave a sanctuary." ...

"The First Amendment guarantees Kim and every American the free exercise of religion, even when they are working for the government."[97]

Staver also addressed how Kim's job fundamentally changed thanks to the lawless Supreme Court;

"Kim Davis did not sign up as a clerk to issue same-sex marriage licenses," he said. "Her job duty was changed by five lawyers without any constitutional authority. At a minimum, her religious convictions should be accommodated."[98]

Indeed, Davis's oath as county clerk was to defend and protect the U.S. Constitution and the constitution of Kentucky. As Chief Justice John Roberts rightly observed in his Obergefell dissent, the activist majority's opinion actually hijacks the democratic process and is in no way rooted in the Constitution: "[D]o not celebrate the Constitution," he said. "It had nothing to do with it."

The fact is that if Ms. Davis had issued counterfeit same-sex "marriage" licenses, she would have not only disobeyed God and directly participated in expressly sinful activity, she would have violated her constitutional oath.

To her credit, Ms. Davis stood her ground while the decision was appealed. Predictably, many leftists clamored for her imprisonment. They wanted her held in contempt of court and thrown in jail for refusing to at once affirm homosexual sin and violate God's commands.

Such is the new pagan orthodoxy. It's "here, it's queer, get used to it."

And jail her they did.

Mahatma Gandhi once said, "There is a higher court than courts of justice and that is the court of conscience. It supersedes all other courts."

He was partly right. Liberty of conscience is indeed sacred. There is, however, a higher court before which Mr. Gandhi—before which we all—will ultimately stand. It is Kim Davis's inevitable turn in the dock at this Supreme of all supreme courts that drove her steadfast refusal to mock God through mock "marriage."

Let's set aside for a moment all the legal and political wrangling over religious freedom.

What is it about Kentucky's Kim Davis that really had secularists, even some misguided and ill-informed church-goers, yanking their hair out in clumps? It seems many didn't—and still don't—merely dislike this accidental civil rights stalwart; they hate her with a white-hot hatred reminiscent of that levied against blacks during another civil rights struggle.

It was Rosa Parks then.

It's Kim Davis now.

Even so, while it may feel personal to them, it's not. The "throw-Kim-Davis-in-jail!" crowd doesn't hate this humble, unassuming Christian wife and mother of four so much for who she is (though many elitists insist upon sophomorically deriding her as some kind of intolerant, backwoods hick); they hate her more for what she represents—for Whom she represents—and, most especially, because, while making her stand, she was, and has remained, immovable.

After spending nearly a week in jail, Kim still wouldn't budge. Neither would she resign. Neither should she have resigned. If she had resigned, you see, the precedent would have been set. They wanted that precedent set.

And that's what's had them steaming.

If Kim Davis had stepped down from her elected position as Rowan County Clerk, it would've represented exile through attrition for her and her fellow believers. Christ-follower? Seeking elected office? Looking for a government job? Forget it. Christians need not apply. All the same, if you do apply, be sure to keep your mouth shut, your Bible closed and your First Amendment at home.

To Kim Davis and her supporters, her courageous stand represented unwavering faithfulness to the ultimate Lawgiver. To her detractors, it represented stubborn indifference to the laws of man. (The law, incidentally, remains unchanged and on the books as codified. Sections 402.005 and 402.020 of the Kentucky Revised Statutes have yet (as of this writing) to be amended by the legislature and, even now, restrict marriage to "the civil status, condition, or relation of one (1) man and one (1) woman").

Whatever your perspective, Kim's stand was bold. It was that boldness that has at once encouraged biblical Christians and terrified secular progressives. These things have a way of catching on, you see. This is how movements are born.

Before she was arrested, shackled and imprisoned by U.S. Marshals for her "crime" of conscience, Brian Beutler, senior editor of *The New Republic*, was among the torch-waving leftists demanding the government "throw Kentucky clerk Kim Davis in jail."

"Any attempt to force her hand risks making her a bigger martyr on the religious right than she already is," he wrote, "but that risk is small compared to the risk that allowing her to continue abusing her power without consequence will create a terrible precedent."[99]

And so she was thrown in jail.

It backfired magnificently. So much so, in fact, that Judge David Bunning suddenly and inexplicably walked back his contempt order and released her with no indication by Kim or her legal team that she intended to change her position one iota.

They aimed to make an example of her.

Instead, they made a martyr of her.

And she set the example for others to follow.

So, if jail wouldn't do it—if being thrown in jail wouldn't compel this brave woman to disobey God and violate her conscience—then what will?

They'll have to burn her at the stake.

To be sure, and based on the scores of death threats both Kim and her attorneys continue to receive, it seems many would love to see just that. In fact, it's exactly what *The Week* magazine senior correspondent Michael Brendan Dougherty suggested, if only satirically, in a column headlined, "Burn Kim Davis!" He wrote:

"Any normal punishment [i.e., jail] rewards her with the comfort of solidarity from right-wing Christians, or her own sense of moral self-approval," he wrote. "Therefore the only way to avoid granting her such 'martyrdom' is to actually martyr her. That's the really perverse thing about Christians who make a spectacle like this," he continued. "The only way the state can really punish them is to inform them that their suffering is meaningless and proving that God doesn't exist by sending them to the darkness of oblivion in torment. Justice Kennedy has issued his theological bull; let Kentucky officials in defiance of it be put on a pyre."[100]

Mr. Dougherty, a practicing Catholic, was being facetious, of course, and illustrating his point via reductio ad absurdum. Still, his point is well taken. Throughout the history of both Christendom and the United States, Christians have, with full knowledge and acceptance of the potential consequences, exercised a rich legacy of peaceful civil resistance to tyranny over conscience (e.g., Daniel, Mordecai, Christ's apostles, the signers of the Declaration of Independence, Martin Luther King Jr., et al.).

That's exactly what Kim Davis has done. I suspect, as she sees it, she would sooner be burned at the stake than face the flames of hell. For that, she is to be both admired and emulated. Imagine the possibilities if thousands of clerks, judges, pastors, photographers, bakers, inn keepers, florists, parents and other believers across this great nation came together, dug in their heels and said, "No! I will not violate my Christian conscience. Do as you may. Throw me in jail if you must, but I will not call evil good and good evil."

Indeed, throughout history Christianity has been shown to both blossom and flourish when Christ-followers are persecuted—when others attempt to quash their free exercise of faith.

In his "letter from the Birmingham jail," Martin Luther King Jr. famously declared, "One has not only a legal, but a moral responsibility to obey just laws. Conversely, one has a moral responsibility to disobey unjust laws."

"A just law is a man-made code that squares with the moral law or the law of God," he explained. "An unjust law is a code that is out of harmony with the moral law."

As it was with the national sin of systemic racism, there can be few things more "out of harmony with the moral law" than the inherently immoral notion of sodomy-based "marriage."

We are at an impasse.

Something has to give.

And something will.

Kim Davis is out of jail for the time being and that's a good thing. But she says it was well worth it. In fact, her courageous and principled stand for God's final word on marriage was responsible, in large part, for the November 2015 election of conservative Christian Governor Matt Bevin, as well as the Kentucky legislature's subsequent passing of a law that protects the rights of conscience and religious liberty of government officials like Kim Davis—a law that Bevin immediately signed.

It's also good that, more and more, Christians are saying loudly and proudly that they will never compromise their faith, no matter what the consequences. At the same time, we as Christians must continue to thirst for justice just as we are to celebrate persecution for Christ. Every God-fearing, freedom-loving Christian should be outraged at what happened to Kim Davis and what continues to happen to our other fellow Christian believers throughout the United States. We should be righteously enraged at how homosexual activists, like those who targeted Kim Davis for personal destruction, continue to lead this godless War against Christianity in an America that was founded on Judeo-Christian principles.

The anti-Christian nature of the homosexual activist lobby should be abundantly clear to every American Christian. Still, make no mistake about it—the war will not stop in the so-called secular world—at the government level. Homosexual activists and other secular progressives are hell-bent on conquering the American Church as well.

Chapter 13

Forcing Churches to Perform "Gay Weddings"

Churches in Denmark are now compelled, by law, to host same-sex "weddings."

America is next.

Tyranny's appetite is insatiable. The secular left's hunger for power and control over its detractors can never be satisfied. To outwardly succumb and affirmatively capitulate to their pagan demands will never be enough.

Thought control is the goal.

Denmark was the first nation to imagine same-sex "marriage" as a matter of law. It's now one of the first to compel, under penalty of law, churches to desecrate holy ground by hosting these sin-centric, pagan spectacles.

Columnist and AFR Talk radio host Bryan Fischer reported in 2014:

> Well, the day we prophesied has arrived. Churches in Denmark—and the U.S. will not be far behind—have been ORDERED to perform sodomy-based weddings whether they want to or not.
>
> According to the London Telegraph, a new law passed by the Danish parliament "make(s) it mandatory for all churches to conduct gay marriages." No options, no exceptions, no choice. Homosexuals are to be married wherever they want, regardless of whose conscience is trampled and whose sanctuary is defiled in the process. ...
>
> How long will it be before American churches will be ordered, as a condition of maintaining their tax-exempt status, to host same-sex ceremonies? How long will it be before American pastors are ordered to perform them?

Unless America's pastors rise up as one, now, that day will arrive like a thief in the night, a day when each pastor will be told that he must solemnize sodomy-based marriages in his church or his church's 501(c)(3) status will be revoked. At that point, he and his church will effectively be out of business.

Mr. Fischer was right. It's a foregone conclusion. We are no longer a constitutional republic. American pastors, like bakers, florists, photographers and every other citizen, will be confronted with a choice: Obey God or obey man. Pastors will be compelled, under threat of imprisonment, to participate in these unholy pagan rituals.

Pastors, priests, you will then face three choices: 1) Surrender, disobey God's law and obey man's, 2) Stand firm, disobey man's law and obey God's or 3) Use the opportunity to serve, speak truth in love and glorify Jesus.

I like No. 3.

When you men of the cloth are inevitably put to this test, I suggest you do the following. It will take great courage and the strength of the Holy Spirit.

"Preside" over the mock marriage and speak the following truths in love:

Let us begin with a reading from God's Holy Word, Matthew 19:4-5 (English Standard Version):

"He answered, 'Have you not read that he who created them from the beginning made them male and female, and said, "Therefore a man shall leave his father and his mother and hold fast to his wife, and the two shall become one flesh"?'"

Do we dare call the living Christ a liar?

I dare not!

As it is written: "Because of this, God gave them over to shameful lusts. Even their women exchanged natural sexual relations for unnatural ones. In the same way the men also abandoned natural relations with women and were inflamed with lust for one another. Men committed shameful acts with other men, and received in themselves the due penalty for their error." (Romans 1:26-27 – New International Version)

Dearly beloved, we are gathered here on this dark occasion because the government has threatened to imprison me otherwise. We are gathered here, presumably, to join "Party A" and "Party B" in "holy matrimony." I say "presumably" because this cannot be. God's infallible word calls this a farce and a lie. God's holy word calls this an abomination—a mortal sin.

He loves you enough, "Party A," "Party B"—all who are gathered here today—to tell you the truth. I love you enough to tell you the truth.

God warns, "Woe to those who call evil good and good evil." I will not call this evil good. You can persecute me, jail me or even kill me, but you cannot force me to deny Christ.

I am a sinner and can cast no stone. Neither can I condemn you. But, as did Jesus, I can tell you this: "Go and sin no more."

Repent, ask forgiveness and believe upon Jesus. Your eternity depends on it.

Then walk away and pray that these Holy Spirit-inspired words, these transcendent truths, pierce the hearts of those in attendance who labor under deception—who suffer under this "strong delusion."

That's what it means to "pick up your cross and follow Christ."

Still, my suggested prescription notwithstanding, the central point is that the day is rapidly approaching when the United States government will force American churches and pastors to defile marriage, under penalty of law.

But even this will not pacify the anti-Christians. As noted, tyranny can never be satiated. In fact, progressives are already in the process of suing an American Christian pastor in U.S. court on charges that he is guilty of "crimes against humanity" for following his Christian faith.

Chapter 14

Practicing Christianity Means Committing "Crimes against Humanity"

The ongoing lawfare persecution of attorney and pastor Scott Lively by anti-Christian activists presents one of the best case studies exposing the endgame goals of God-hating progressives. That is, to ultimately make the faithful practice of biblical Christianity a "crime against humanity."

Christians, pastors, take heed. In case you haven't noticed, times are a-changin'. Whether at home or abroad, if you follow God's command to speak biblical truth in all things, most especially, it seems, on matters of sex and sexuality, you will be persecuted.

"Remember what I told you: 'A servant is not greater than his master.' If they persecuted me, they will persecute you also. If they obeyed my teaching, they will obey yours also." (John 15:20 – New International Version)

I don't presume to compare my friend Scott Lively of Abiding Truth Ministries to Jesus Christ. None of us can compare, even remotely, to the one and only God-man—to the Lord of the universe and exclusive path to eternal salvation. That said, Pastor Lively is one of the most "Christ-like" people I've had the honor to know.

As did Christ, Scott Lively speaks absolute truth, in absolute love, with absolutely no fear of personal destruction or even death. He loves everyone, whether friend or foe, Christian or pagan, straight or "gay."

For example, Scott and his family took into their home and nursed, both physically and spiritually, the late Sonny Weaver, a former homosexual who died, as so many have, from AIDS—a natural consequence of unnatural behavior.

Sonny became homosexual after being raped at seven years old by a "gay" man in a local YMCA. He became a former homosexual after accepting Jesus as Lord of his life.

Lively loves those who seek to defend him just as he loves those who seek to destroy him—and, make no mistake about it, precisely because Pastor Scott Lively has chosen to both obey and emulate Jesus Christ, there are people, very powerful people, who seek to destroy him. These people, unless and until they come to know, accept and surrender to the Lord Jesus, are, and will remain, enemies of God.

And so Scott Lively prays for them.

Remember those pastors in Houston who were told to turn over their sermons to radical lesbian activist and (former) mayor Annise Parker? Remember that outrageous and blatantly unconstitutional act of governmental abuse? Remember Kim Davis?

These cases pale in comparison to what has been done—is being done—to Scott Lively.

Pastor Lively, you see, has, in the spirit of Saul Alinsky, been "Hitlerized" by a left-wing extremist group ironically calling itself the "Center for Constitutional Rights" (CCR). CCR is a George Soros-funded organization with, I kid you not, the beastly street address of 666 Broadway, New York, NY.

Because Lively exercised his God-given First Amendment rights, as well as his free speech rights afforded by the laws of Uganda, and spoke biblical truth about homosexual sin after having been invited there by a number of Ugandan pro-family groups, homosexual activists set out to make an example of him.

In March of 2012 CCR sued Lively in a Massachusetts federal court for "crimes against humanity"—the same charge filed against Nazis who stood trial in Nuremberg—on behalf of another moonbat organization called "Sexual Minorities Uganda," which, and again, you can't make this stuff up, prefers the moniker "SMUG."

And so Lively enlisted the pro bono legal services of Liberty Counsel.

We'll use Lively's own words to explain what is happening:

> *With full knowledge that these are bald-faced lies, SMUG asserts that 1) I masterminded the 2009 Anti-Homosexuality Bill in Uganda, which they call the 'Kill the Gays Bill' [in fact, Lively publicly opposed the bill, which has since been struck down by Ugandan courts], 2) inflamed passions against homosexuals in Uganda by characterizing all homosexuals as irredeemable genocidal child molesters, and 3) introduced to*

Uganda the heretofore unknown strategy of criminalizing public pro-motion of homosexuality as a means of opposing the rise of a homo-sexual movement in Uganda. The proof that these are lies is found in the very same documents they misuse against me.[101]

CCR and SMUG also tried to blame Lively for the murder of Ugandan ho-mosexual David Kato, a murder he also publicly condemned, making it the centerpiece of their lawsuit until, and as was noted in Liberty Counsel's Mo-tion to Dismiss, it was revealed that, as Lively predicted, Kato was actually murdered by his "gay" lover who confessed to the crime, was convicted and is now in prison.[102]

But all of this is incidental. It's a smokescreen. Keep in mind—we're talking about protected speech here. Lively is being tried for "crimes against human-ity" for merely uttering, publicly, millennia-old biblical orthodoxy relative to sexual morality.

So how could such an Orwellian lawsuit—clearly designed as a weapon to both harass and intimidate Lively and anyone else who might dare challenge the global homosexual activist political agenda—even make its way into a U. S. federal court?

Well, CCR and SMUG's angle was to circumvent that pesky ol' First Amend-ment, as well as Ugandan free speech laws, through a gross misapplication of the Alien Tort Statute. Normally, this would have been laughed out of court and, in fact, in 2013, even as this case was ongoing, the U.S. Supreme Court unequivocally ruled this very tactic to be unlawful.

But there's nothing normal about this case.

Meet federal Judge Michael Ponsor. Ponsor, who thumbed his nose at the Su-preme Court and denied Liberty Counsel's slam dunk Motion to Dismiss, is the textbook example of a judicial activist. He has admitted as much, once saying in another context that, "At some point I realized that judges are the unappointed legislators of mankind, and what we do is just as creative."[103]

But for this judicial activist, the case would seem personal. At his inaugura-tion to the federal bench he crowed, for instance, "We have a proud, vibrant gay and lesbian community."[104] Presumably he knows this because one of his ex-wives reportedly later "married" another woman. His daughter identifies as a lesbian as well.[105]

And so, to keep afloat the demonization of Scott Lively (of all Christians, re-ally) despite the Supreme Court's torpedo, and to keep alive this judicial abuse, harassment and intimidation—Ponsor, as promised, got "creative."

Still, the case will eventually be tossed. It's inevitable.

Yet, either way, for these anti-Christian extremists, the damage is done. The process is the punishment.

This was never about winning or losing.

It was always about intimidation.

And the intimidation doesn't just stop with threats to you as an adult. The American anti-Christians are already threatening to take away your children if you don't deny Christ.

Chapter 15

You're a Christian? We're Going to Take Your Children!

As has been repeatedly noted, it is those among the self-styled "LGBT" movement leading the War on Christianity. There is no other group of change agents as vicious and vindictive as those given over to this sexually deviant lifestyle. They are, even now, openly targeting our children through indoctrination by way of schools, entertainment and in every other arena wherein they can possibly gain access to young people.

But they are also using and abusing the fields of medicine and science, coupled with our judicial system, to get their hands on kids. They are, with increasing frequency, going so far as to threaten to take away children if parents oppose their attempts to indoctrinate them.

For example, in 2013, Republican New Jersey Governor Chris Christie signed A3371, a draconian piece of legislation that bars licensed therapists from helping children overcome unwanted same-sex attractions, behavior or identity.[106] This law bans help for minors even when—as is so often the case—those same-sex attractions arise from childhood sexual abuse by the likes of someone like Jerry Sandusky.

This law prohibits minors and their parents from receiving counseling they desire and forces counselors to violate ethical codes because they no longer are able to help clients reach their own counseling goals. This law enslaves children—whether abused or not—to a subjectively determined sexual identity that they reject.

The connection between homosexual abuse and "gay identity" is undeniable. Consider this: Researchers from the Centers for Disease Control and Prevention (CDC) have found that homosexual men are "at least three times more likely to report CSA (childhood sexual abuse)" than heterosexual men.[107]

For obvious reasons, this politically motivated law has been dubbed the "Jerry Sandusky Victimization Act." Liberty Counsel stepped in to protect New Jersey children, parents and licensed therapists. It filed suit to block the law, since it previously blocked a similar law in California.[108]

In his signing statement, Gov. Christie wrote, "Government should tread carefully into this area and I do so here reluctantly. I have scrutinized this piece of legislation with that concern in mind. However, I also believe that on issues of medical treatment for children we must look to experts in the field to determine the relative risks and rewards."[109]

Beyond the fact that Christie and the New Jersey Legislature have violated the First Amendment rights of New Jersey parents, children and counselors, there remains another problem with his assertion. It's not true. As with any form of therapy, the "experts" are all over the board on the issue of change therapy.

For instance, both New Jersey Democrats and Christie cited a 2009 American Psychological Association (APA) report as justification for this gross infringement on the right of self-determination.[110,111] Although, no doubt, the highly liberal APA supports this and similar Sandusky Laws for political reasons, the group's own task force on change therapy—led entirely by members who themselves are "gay"-identified or known political activists—admitted in 2009 that homosexuality itself refers to "feelings" and "self-concept."[112]

The taskforce confessed that such therapy has shown "varying degrees of satisfaction and varying perceptions of success."[113] It acknowledged within its own skewed, very limited "study" that some people had "altered their sexual orientation. ... [P]articipants had multiple endpoints, including LGB identity, ex-gay identity, no sexual orientation identity, and a unique self-identity.[114] ... Individuals report a range of effects from their efforts to change their sexual orientation, including both benefits and harm."[115]

Reports of "both benefits and harm"? Exactly what might be expected from any form of therapy.

But that's for adults. Here's what the APA report concludes about the effects of change therapy on children: "Further, the theories that such efforts are based on have not been corroborated by scientific evidence or evaluated for harm."[116]

In other words, there is no evidence that change therapy harms minors.

Get that? Gov. Christie signed into law a bill purporting to prevent harm to minors from change therapy, citing, as the reason, an APA report that admitted there is neither research nor empirical evidence to suggest that change therapy harms minors.

Is your head swimming? It should be.

The governor is one of three things. He is either: 1) ill-informed, 2) politically motivated or 3) stupid.

I don't know, I guess he could be 4) all of the above.

Meanwhile, many experts expressed outrage over this gross overreach by Christie and other New Jersey liberals. Dr. Nicholas Cummings, former president of the APA, wrote in *USA Today*: "Contending that all same-sex attraction is immutable is a distortion of reality. Attempting to characterize all sexual reorientation therapy as 'unethical' violates patient choice and gives an outside party a veto over patients' goals for their own treatment. A political agenda shouldn't prevent gays and lesbians who desire to change from making their own decisions."[117]

Dr. Cummings has testified to personally helping hundreds of formerly homosexual clients achieve the change they desired.

Things got more sinister yet. On August 22, 2013, mere days after Christie signed the bill into law, New Jersey Assemblyman Tim Eustace, who sponsored the bill and is openly homosexual, bombastically compared change therapy to "beating a child" and suggested that the government take children seeking change away from their parents. He told Talk Radio 1210 WPHT, "What this does is prevent things that are harmful to people. If a parent were beating their child on a regular basis we would step in and remove that child from the house. If you pay somebody to beat your child or abuse your child, what's the difference?"

Mat Staver responded on the same program: "It is shocking to hear the law's sponsor threaten parents that the state will remove their children from them if they provide the counsel they need and which helps them. This is the ultimate nanny state," he said.[118]

I'll take it a step further, and I think I speak for many Christian fathers. None of my three children suffer from unwanted same-sex attraction, but if any of them did and they decided to seek change therapy to reconcile their feelings with their faith, Mr. Eustace and the rest of his Gaystapo would be extremely ill-advised to crest my front porch with designs on taking my children.

Is this George Washington's America, or Joseph Stalin's Russia?"

And before anyone protests that Eustace's outrageous nonsense was just one homosexual saying something in a fit of anger that no one would take seriously, think again.

In late 2014 a boy named Josh Alcorn committed suicide. His suicide attracted national attention, with the horrific people in the liberal media regularly referring to him as "Leelah Alcorn," since he pretended to be a girl. His parents are professing Christians and they did what they could to help him. Their attempt to help him made the media and anti-Christians everywhere mad beyond words, and these filthmongers soon began to abuse his parents and even call for legal action against them.

The Inquisitr noted these mad attacks in January 2015 and collected some tweets from a particularly notable homosexual:

> *Leelah Alcorn, a 17-year-old transgender teenager from Ohio, took her own life last Sunday. She walked in front of an oncoming truck and was crushed to death. Leelah left behind a suicide note on her Tumblr blog, in which she said she had been forced by her devout Christian parents to undergo conversion therapy, which seeks to change sexual orientation through counseling. The practice has been banned in two states on grounds that it is medically unfounded and puts children in danger.*
>
> *As a result, Leelah's parents have been subjected to a torrent of abuse on social media. Today the Independent is reporting that gay rights activist Dan Savage has taken to Twitter, saying that Leelah's parents of [sic] should be prosecuted. ...*
>
> *Dan Savage ✓ @fakedansavage*
>
> *It risks incentivizing suicide—take revenge on hateful parents by killing yourself—but an example needs 2 be made of #LeelahAlcorn's parents 3:47 PM – 31 Dec 2014 Seattle, WA, United States . . .*
>
> *Dan Savage ✓ @fakedansavage*
>
> *We know that parental hostility & rejection doubles a queer kid's already quadrupled risk of suicide—rejecting your queer kid is abuse. 3:50 PM – 31 Dec 2014 Seattle, WA, United States*
>
> *Savage went on to say that "Leelah Alcorn's parents... should be ashamed—but first they need to be shamed. Charges should be brought."*
>
> *He also said the therapists who saw Leelah Alcorn should be charged, and suggested that her siblings should not remain with their parents. ...[119]*

The detestable cruelty of Savage is not unusual. He is a leader among the haters of Christ. Yet his cruelty in this case is particularly noteworthy because while he blames Josh Alcorn's parents for their son's suicide, he has openly bullied children and pined for the murders or deaths of people on a regular basis.[120,121]

And if you still aren't convinced that New Jersey Assemblyman Tim Eustace's threat to take children from Christian parents isn't an empty one, consider that homosexuals are pressuring the United Nations to deem conversion therapy (also known as reparative therapy) a form of torture. *Breitbart* reported on this effort in November of 2014:

> *A delegation of American LGBT activists is traveling to Geneva, Switzerland tomorrow to make the case to the UN Committee on Torture that "conversion therapy" is a form of torture and should be designated as such in international law.*

> *They intend to ask the Torture committee to declare "conversion therapy" a violation of international law under the UN Convention against Torture and Other Cruel Inhuman or Degrading Treatment or Punishment (CAT) that President Ronald Reagan signed in 1988 and was ratified under President Bill Clinton in 1994.*[122]

Indeed, the War on Christianity has ramped up to the level that the anti-Christians, led by LGBT activists, are working toward making it an international crime for Christians to direct the upbringing of their children with regard to sex and sexuality—the ultimate goal being that, should parents dare violate the anti-Christian's sexual anarchist orthodoxy, children will eventually be forcibly taken from the homes of Christian parents.

As mentioned at the end of Chapter 2, there are thousands of documented instances of the God-haters attacking Christians in America. So many, in fact, that it would be impossible to cover them all in a single volume. Still, consider, for one, the case of Beth Israel Deaconess Medical Center, "a teaching hospital affiliated with Harvard Medical School," "revok[ing] the appointment of [Dr.] Paul Church as a 28-year member of the medical staff" for not bowing at the altar of homosexuality. This just took place December 2015.[123] Or the fact that New York City has passed an ordinance that now makes it a punishable offense to refuse to call a man a woman and vice versa.[124]

Please stay alert, my friends, to what is happening from coast to coast. It is up to us, Christ's followers, His hands and feet, salt and light, to speak out boldly against all such evil and injustice, wherever it may occur.

PART 3

Chapter 16

Redefining Marriage = Attack on Christianity

The previous eight examples covered in Chapters 3-10, just a small sampling, were not the exception to the new normal rule. They are the rule. These very shocking examples of homosexualists, along with their anti-Christian progressive allies, are just the warm-up act. These attacks are intentional, and they are organized. The enemies of God are not only telling us that they hate us and want us either dead, silenced or marginalized into obscurity, they are now implementing their agenda in full force. In fact, the anti-Christians, under Barack Obama's presidential regime in particular, have institutionalized their War on Christianity as a matter of official government policy, and have made it clear that the destruction of marriage is the first step needed to ensure the eventual criminalization of Christianity altogether.

Many in the pro-family movement have long stressed that the cultural Marxist left's belligerent push for the judicial fiction that is "gay marriage" was never about gaining "equal access" to this biologically exclusive male-female institution, as they profess, but, rather, is, and has always been, about control.

While there are many layers to unfold, the almost instant explosion in government-sanctioned, anti-Christian extremism on display post Obergefell v. Hodges, confirms the poisonous three-fold agenda that underlies the "social justice" mob's flowery "marriage equality" propaganda. That is: 1) the ultimate destruction of marriage, 2) forced affirmation of sexual deviancy under penalty of law and 3) the eventual criminalization of Christianity.

1 – The Destruction of Marriage

Here's the bottom line: Homosexual activists don't want the white picket fence; they want to burn down the white picket fence. The endgame is not to achieve so-called "marriage equality" but, rather, to render marriage reality meaningless.

They are well on their way.

In a 2013 column headlined, "The Revolt of Intelligence Against 'Marriage Equality,'" worldview expert Rick Pearcey addressed one prominent "gay" activist's admission that the destruction of natural marriage signifies the left's ultimate cultural coup de grâce:

"Masha Gessen, a lesbian and a journalist, spoke frankly about this at a conference in Sydney, Australia, last summer. 'It's a no-brainer that we should have the right to marry,' she said. 'But I also think equally that it's a no-brainer that the institution of marriage should not exist.'"[125]

Austin Ruse at *Breitbart* reported on these comments and more in a 2014 post:

> She says, "I agree that we should have the right to marry, but I also think equally that it is a no-brainer that the institution of marriage should not exist. … Fighting for gay marriage generally involves lying about what we're going to do with marriage when we get there, because we lie that the institution of marriage is not going to change, and that is a lie. The institution of marriage is going to change, and it should change, and again, I don't think it should exist."[126]

Homosexual activist and pornographer Clinton Fein echoes Gessen's candid sentiments: "Demand the institution [of marriage] and then wreck it," he once wrote. "James Dobson was right about our evil intentions," he quipped. "We just plan to be quicker than he thought."[127]

(Fein claims his piece is satire and was used to bait "homophobes." The problem with this is that his "satire" is now reality. This is a technique anti-Christians often use: say what they really mean and when others note it, they say, "I was only kidding, you fool! Can't you recognize satire?")

The goal is to water down marriage until marriage is meaningless. And as evidenced by the burgeoning legal push for polygamous and incestuous "marriages"—even for the "right" to "marry" a robot—sexual anarchists are well on their way to achieving this goal.

Now that counterfeit same-sex "marriage" is the "law of the land," as the left inaccurately claims, a whole lot more of this marriage freak show must necessarily follow before marriage extinction inevitably occurs.

One of liberals' favorite Alinskyite defense mechanisms is to ridicule the opposition if confronted with some irrefutable argument against some hallowed left-wing delusion. Such is the tactic employed whenever a thinking person walks into the room and points out this big 'ol gay elephant: Now that the government pretends that some vague combination of "love" and "consent" are all that a "marriage" requires, then other "arbitrary" and "discriminatory" parameters beyond a binary male-female prerequisite must also go poof.

That is to say, since the Court magically divined some constitutional right to same-sex "marriage," then full "marriage equality" necessarily demands that polygamous, incestuous and any other equally aberrant nuptial cocktail be likewise permitted.

It's a "no-brainer," right?

The Supreme Court has a despicable history of radically redefining that which cannot be redefined. Though examples abound, I'm thinking specifically, as concerns the topic at hand, of the Court's 2003 holding in *Lawrence v. Texas*.

In *Lawrence*, the liberal majority, for the first time in history, arbitrarily mislabeled male-on-male sodomy—hitherto classified "a crime against nature"—as a "constitutional right."

In his characteristically brilliant dissent, the late Justice Antonin Scalia voiced my concerns better than I can: "State laws against bigamy, same-sex marriage, adult incest, prostitution, masturbation, adultery, fornication, bestiality and obscenity are likewise sustainable only in light of Bowers' validation of laws based on moral choices," he wrote. "Every single one of these laws is called into question by today's decision."

So, now that the High Court has removed one natural marriage parameter for one special interest group, "equal protection under the law" requires that it remove all natural marriage parameters for all special interest groups.

Liberty Counsel made these very points in a friend-of-the-court brief filed with the Supreme Court a few years ago: "Ultimately, there is no principled basis for recognizing a legality of same-sex marriage without simultaneously providing a basis for the legality of consensual polygamy or certain adult incestuous relationships," noted the brief. "In fact, every argument for same-sex marriage is an argument for them as well."[128]

Another brief filed by 18 state attorneys general voiced similar concerns: "Once the natural limits that inhere in the relationship between a man and a woman can no longer sustain the definition of marriage, the conclusion that follows is that any grouping of adults would have an equal claim to marriage," they wrote.

The brief further observed the self-evident "no-brainer" that legitimate marriage is "optimal for children and society at large."[129]

It's all very simple. If anything is marriage, then everything is marriage. And if everything is marriage, then nothing is marriage at all. "'Marriage equality' becomes 'marriage elasticity,' with the ultimate goal of 'marriage extinction.'"

I had sincerely hoped that the honorable and learned men and women who sit upon the highest bench in the land could recognize that all of these San Francisco-style social engineering games are a deceptive means to a destructive end. But my hope was clearly misplaced.

The desire of the enemies of God to destroy marriage has been achieved in the sense that they've destroyed the meaning of the word. And so for their next step, they are working to force everyone to affirm that it has been destroyed—to deny reality—or have or suffer the full weight of government sanction if they refuse.

2 – Forced Affirmation of Sexual Deviancy under Penalty of Law

The New York Times ran a revealing article in 2013 called, "The Gayest Place in America?". Can you guess where this "gayest" place is?

Well, it's not San Francisco, believe it or not.

If you guessed Washington, D.C., you'd be right.

> *When the District of Columbia is compared with the 50 states, it has the highest percentage of adults who identify as lesbian, gay, bisexual or transgender, according to Gallup. At 10 percent, that is double the percentage in the state that ranks No. 2, Hawaii, and nearly triple the overall national average of 3.5 percent. ...*
>
> *One answer seems to be that they have always been here. Gays and lesbians do seem to be drawn to politics in disproportionately high numbers. ...[130]*

Homosexualists, in large part, run Washington, D.C., and thus, are in the ideal strategic position to force Americans to affirm sexual deviancy under penalty of law. They have especially strengthened their influence and power under the Obama regime. It's little wonder, therefore, that this man, the most militantly pro-"gay" president in American history, was affectionately deemed, "The First Gay President™" (widespread rumors that he's *actually* homosexual notwithstanding.)

And just how "gay" is Obama?

I'm glad you asked.

The answer lies in the level of pro-LGBT deviance the federal government, under Obama's watch (and society at large), has embraced. If Hillary Clinton is elected president in 2016, she'll pick up where Obama left off, and, as many pundits, politicos and cultural commentators believe, will be even more radical in her tenure as POTUS.

Over many decades the anti-Christian left has put in place the official cultural, judicial, legislative and academic infrastructure needed to eventually silence all dissent and make unlawful the open recognition and adherence to biblical sexual morality by Christians.

But under Obama, it's gone gangbusters.

Newsweek declared Obama, "The First Gay President™," in 2012, putting that declaration on the cover of one of its issues along with his photo and a rainbow halo (the godlike imagery of homosexuality isn't creepy at all).[131] And the *Daily Caller* caught a homosexual talking head repeating this declaration in 2013: "MSNBC host Thomas Roberts said Monday that 'many people consider President Obama to be the first gay president.'"[132]

Furthermore, *National Journal* continued this line in 2014, proclaiming that, "On Gay Rights, Obama Has Built a Legacy."[133]

The Illinois Family Institute's Laurie Higgins wrote a column that my *Barb-Wire* website published in 2014. Her column looked at how "Obama Chooses Homosexuals over Veterans" and, so doing, indirectly exposed why anti-Christians have crowned, "The First Gay President™" with his inglorious rainbow halo:

> *Contrast Obama's miserable failure to address the needs of veterans with his vigorous efforts to satiate the desires of homosexuals. Here are just a few of his many efforts to revamp the moral structure of America and the world:*
>
> *On Saturday, May 31, 2013, in the midst of the VA hospital scandal, the Obama Administration announced that the National Park Service would begin installing "markers at significant locations that note the advancement of lesbian, gay, bisexual and transgender Americans."*
>
> *On Friday, May 30, 2013, in the midst of the VA hospital scandal, the U.S. Department of Health and Human Services decided that henceforth the overburdened Medicare system would pay for the absurdly named "sex reassignment surgery."*
>
> *He found time to be interviewed by lesbian journalist Robin Roberts*

about his evolutionary support for same-sex "marriage."

He found time to congratulate NBA player Jason Collins for announcing to America that he is homosexual.

He found time to congratulate football player Michael Sam on being the first openly homosexual NFL draft pick.

Obama repealed "Don't Ask Don't Tell," the policy that prohibited open homosexuals from serving in the military.

He appointed the controversial homosexual founder of the Gay, Lesbian and Straight Education Network (GLSEN), Kevin Jennings, to be his "safe school" czar.

He appointed openly homosexual John Berry to be the "Director of the United States Office of Personnel Management (OPM)" where he was "responsible for recruiting, hiring, and setting benefits policies for 1.9 million federal civilian employees." Berry was then appointed to serve as ambassador to Australia.

In a controversial recess appointment, he nominated lesbian Chai Feldblum to the Equal Employment Opportunity Commission where she sits as chair. Feldblum has long advocated the view that when in conflict, the sexual rights of homosexuals should trump the First Amendment religious rights of conservative people of faith.

In 2009, for the first time, an administration set aside a special block of tickets to the White House Easter Egg Roll for families headed by homosexuals and the gender-confused.

He hosted a purported "bullying prevention" conference at the White House to which he invited notorious, anti-Christian homosexual sex columnist Dan Savage.

In a 2011 formal address before the full General Assembly of the United Nations, Obama promoted the political goals of homosexuals.

Obama's Attorney General Eric Holder announced the Department of Justice would not defend the Defense of Marriage Act.[134]

And her list goes on.

I've personally dealt with the ramifications of the First Gay President™ and the homosexual assault on Christians in America.

Under President Obama, "justice" is anything but blind. Neither is it deaf. In fact, based on revelations throughout the years, it appears to be watching your every move and listening to your every word. Still, if you happen to be a federal employee, now it's even listening for your silence.

Whistleblowers within the U.S. Department of Justice contacted Liberty Counsel in 2013 to express grave concerns over one of this administration's attacks on freedom.

Our sources provided Liberty Counsel with an internal DOJ document titled, "LGBT Inclusion at Work: The 7 Habits of Highly Effective Managers." It was emailed to DOJ managers in advance of the left's so-called "Lesbian, Gay, Bisexual, and Transgender (LGBT) Pride Month."

The document was chilling. It was riddled with directives that grossly violated—prima facie—employees' First Amendment liberties.

Following are excerpts from the "DOJ Pride" decree. When it comes to "LGBT pride," employees were ordered:

"DON'T judge or remain silent. *Silence will be interpreted as disapproval.*" (Italics mine)

That was a threat. And not even a subtle one.

Got it? For Christians and other morals-minded federal employees, it's no longer enough to just shut up and "stay in the closet"—to live your life in silent recognition of biblical principles (which, by itself, is unlawful constraint). When it comes to mandatory celebration of homosexual and cross-dressing behaviors, "[s]ilence will be interpreted as disapproval."

The lawless Obama administration ordered federal employees—against their will—to affirm sexual behaviors that every major world religion, thousands of years of history and uncompromising human biology reject.

Somewhere George Orwell is smiling.

The directive included a quote from a "gay" federal employee to rationalize justification: "Ideally, I'd love to hear and see support from supervisors, so it's clear that there aren't just policies on paper. Silence seems like disapproval. There's still an atmosphere of LGBT issues not being appropriate for the workplace (particularly for transgender people), or that people who bring it up are trying to rock the boat."

Of course there's "still an atmosphere of LGBT issues not being appropriate for the workplace." When well over half of federal employees, half the country and most of the world still believe in objective sexual morality (and immorality), "the workplace," especially the federal workplace, should, at the very least, remain neutral on these highly controversial and behavior-centric issues.

Still, to borrow from self-styled "queer activist," anti-Christian bigot and Obama buddy Dan Savage, "it gets better":

"DO assume that LGBT employees and their allies are listening to what

you're saying (whether in a meeting or around the proverbial water cooler) and will read what you're writing (whether in a casual email or in a formal document), and make sure the language you use is inclusive and respectful."

Was that directive something issued by the DOJ or the KGB? "[A]ssume that LGBT employees are listening …"? And what are "LGBT allies"? If you disagree with the homosexual activist political agenda, does that make you the enemy?

Yes, in any workplace, language should remain professional, but who defines what's "inclusive"? Who decides what's "respectful"? If asked about "LGBT issues," for instance, can a Christian employee answer honestly: "I believe the Bible. I believe God designed sex to be shared between husband and wife within the bonds of marriage"? Or is that grounds for termination?

Here are some more DOs from the 2013 directive:

DO "Attend LGBT events sponsored by DOJ Pride and/or the Department, and invite (but don't require) others to join you."

DO "Display a symbol in your office (DOJ Pride sticker, copy of this brochure, etc.) indicating that it is a 'safe space.'"

Are you kidding? Did this administration really think it was legal to compel managers to "attend LGBT events," or to "display pride stickers" against their will? Does it still think that? That's compulsory expression. That's viewpoint discrimination. That's unconstitutional.

But there's more:

"DO use inclusive words like 'partner,' 'significant other' or 'spouse' rather than gender-specific terms like 'husband' and 'wife' (for example, in invitations to office parties or when asking a new employee about his/her home life)."

Oh, brother.

Sorry. Oh, gender-neutral sibling.

"DO use a transgender person's chosen name and the pronoun that is consistent with the person's self-identified gender."

In other words, lie. Engage in corporate delusion.

"DO deal with offensive jokes and comments forcefully and swiftly when presented with evidence that they have occurred in the workplace."

"DO communicate a zero-tolerance policy for inappropriate jokes and comments, including those pertaining to a person's sexual orientation and gender identity or expression."

So who gets to decide what's an "inappropriate joke [or] comment"? I thought we had a Constitution for that. It sure ain't Big Brother Barack. Sure, I get it, it's probably better not to start your work day with: "A lesbian, a tranny and two gays walk into a bath house…" but still, "no law … abridging the freedom of speech," means no law. No matter how much Obama wishes it so, we don't leave our constitutional rights at the federal workplace door.

The DOJ edict even addressed cross-dressing man woes:

> As a transgender woman [that's a man in a skirt], I want people to understand that I'm real. I want to be recognized as the gender I really am [again, you're a man in a skirt]. Yes, there was awkwardness with pronouns at first for folks who knew me before the transition. But it hurts when several years later people still use the wrong pronouns. And just imagine if people were constantly debating YOUR bathroom privileges. Imagine how humiliating that would be.

Tell you what, buddy, I won't "debate YOUR bathroom privileges" if you return to this planet. You'd better stay the heck out of the ladies' room while my wife or two daughters are in there; otherwise, we have a problem. Women have an absolute right not be sexually harassed in the workplace—a right to privacy when using the facilities. To constantly worry whether a gender-confused, cross-dressing man is going to invade her privacy creates a hostile work environment.

The "DOJ Pride" directive is a few years old now but it still serves as a perfect example of how Obama's love of homosexuality and hatred of Christianity has created a climate of fear and intimidation for Christians, conservatives and other values-oriented folks, both within and without the workplace.

Obama's enthusiasm for homosexuality and hatred of Christianity is so bad that it's essentially become religious to him. Media Research Center founder and President Brent Bozell wrote a column on this in July of 2014 with the title, "A New Evangelizing Foreign Policy":

> In this administration, there is no respect for opposing views on marriage or gender or homosexuality, especially those based on religion. They must be eliminated as "prejudice."

> In 2011, the State Department created a public-private Global Equality Fund to subsidize leftist LGBT advocacy groups around the world.

> They boast they've "provided over $7.5 million to civil society in over 50 countries worldwide" to build an "organizational capacity for human rights documentation, advocacy, legal reform, and organizational development" and "to combat negative social attitudes and societal discrimination." How's that for a good use of tax dollars?

And that's not all. In 2013, the U.S. Agency for International Development created an LGBT Global Development Partnership that will "contribute $11 million over the next four years to advocacy groups in Ecuador, Honduras, Guatemala and other developing countries."

In his new book "Making Gay Okay," Robert Reilly offers an entire chapter on the promotion of this libertine-left agenda as a major objective of U.S. foreign policy. In El Salvador, acting ambassador Mari Carmen Aponte wrote an op-ed in a Salvadoran newspaper in 2011 titled "For the Elimination of Prejudices Wherever They Exist."

Aponte wrote: "No one should be subjected to aggression because of who he is or who he loves. Homophobia and brutal hostility are often based on lack of understanding about what it truly means to be gay or transgender," an ignorance spread by "those who promote hatred."

Which includes nearly everyone who promotes the Bible.[135]

It's not just third parties analyzing Obama who make the assessment that hatred for Christianity and love of homosexuality has become a focus of religious zeal for him. He has basically said the same thing. *CNSNews.com* reported in September 2015 that he went to an "LGBT Fundraiser" and added his voice of support to those wishing to ban any attempts by children to quit engaging in homosexual behavior, or determine the root emotional cause of their unwanted same-sex attraction:

Speaking Sunday at the Democratic National Committee's "LGBT Gala," a fundraiser held in New York City, President Barack Obama called for legally prohibiting "conversion therapy" that aims to steer minors away from being transgender.

"We've come a long way in changing hearts and minds so that trans men and women can be who they are—not just on magazine covers, but in workplaces and schools and communities," Obama said at the fundraiser, according to a transcript posted by the White House.

"And to build on that progress, we should support efforts to ban so-called 'conversion therapy' for minors," Obama said. "So, we've got to keep striving every day to treat each other the way I believe God sees us, as equal in His eyes."[136]

If that heretical pronouncement wasn't religious enough, *Breitbart* reported that Obama said at that same event that homosexuality should take precedence over Christianity:

"We affirm that we cherish our religious freedom and are profoundly respectful of religious traditions," he insisted during a dramatic speech

at an LGBT fundraiser in New York City on Sunday night, praising the progress made on gay rights under his administration. "But we also have to say clearly that our religious freedom doesn't grant us the freedom to deny our fellow Americans their constitutional rights."[137]

So, it's of little surprise that, when a president, like Obama, along with five tyrannical liberal attorneys on the U.S. Supreme Court, arbitrarily make up newfangled "constitutional rights" out of thin air, that our actual constitutional rights (such as the unalienable right to religious freedom) end up taking a beating.

Other news from the past two years or so—between 2014 and 2015—further confirms just how "gay" Obama is. He has become the world's chief evangelist for this new homosexual-based cult in the U.S., going so far as to make the radical LGBT agenda America's chief export throughout the world. It's become one Obama's top priorities (if not his top priority).

This president has especially misused and abused the U.S. Department of State to evangelize homosexuality and gender confusion in every corner of the world.

CNSNews.com reported in June of 2014 that Secretary of State John Kerry insisted that foreign governments had to accept the homosexual "spouses" of homosexuals the U.S. sent to their nations on official U.S. business:

> *He said the federal government recognizes same-sex marriages of foreign diplomats stationed in the U.S., and it expects all other countries to do the same in their treatment of U.S. personnel deployed abroad.*

> *"Let me be clear: We oppose any effort by any country to deny visas for spouses of American staff," he said. "It's discriminatory, it's unacceptable, it has no place in the 21st century."*

> *Kerry told a "Pride" event at the State Department that the U.S. also is considering "all visa applications made by same-sex spouses in the same manner as those made by opposite-sex spouses."[138]*

Secretary of State John Kerry also issued a direct insult to Christians in June of 2014, honoring Masha Gessen—the same Masha Gessen mentioned last chapter, who boasted of the homosexuals' / anti-Christians' ultimate goal of redefining marriage in order to ultimately destroy it.

Reported *Breitbart*:

> *One of the speakers was journalist and LGBT activist Masha Gessen, who has been an outspoken critic of the Russian government on LGBT issues. She has written a book about Vladimir Putin, for a time headed the Moscow office of the US Radio Liberty, and has been a prolific contributor to New York Times blogs.*

Secretary of State John Kerry introduced her: "The government in Moscow may look at Masha as a troublemaker to contend with, but here in the United States, we know that she is a wonderful person—a mother, a journalist, an extraordinary human rights defender—and we are honored by her presence here."[139]

It's not difficult to find other news reports wherein the Obama regime has used the State Department to evangelize for homosexuality and cross-dressing in other countries. *The Associated Press* reported in June 2014 that the president was pushing full speed ahead despite multiple nations' vociferous objections and deep-seated traditional values relative to sex and sexuality:

President Barack Obama has taken the U.S. gay rights revolution global, using American embassies across the world to promote a cause that still divides his own country.

Sometimes U.S. advice and encouragement is condemned as unacceptable meddling. And sometimes it can seem to backfire, increasing the pressure on those it is meant to help.[140]

Meanwhile, *Reuters* published an article in June of 2014 stating that the "U.S. cuts aid to Uganda, cancels military exercise over anti-gay law."[141] And *Reuters* reported in October of 2014 that the, "U.S. raps Kyrgyzstan for proposed 'gay propaganda' law."[142]

Aleteia reported in February 2015 that a Nigerian bishop warned that Obama's evangelization for homosexuality would come at any price, writing that, "It's so bad, he says, that the United States has made clear it will not help Nigeria fight the Boko Haram terror group unless the country modify its laws regarding homosexuality, family planning and birth-control."[143]

The Associated Press reported in August 2015 that the U.S. and Chile were working together to talk about how badly the Islamic State treats homosexuals.[144] (Seriously, this is what the Obama regime thinks is important to address regarding Islamic terrorism.)

And *CNSNews.com* reported in October 2015 on the Obama regime's "planning to spend $49,083 in taxpayer funds for a one-time grant to establish a network to support the LGBT community in India."[145] Who cares about the massive U.S. deficit and debt? Obama has homosexual evangelism to push.

It's the "gospel" of "gay"!

The State Department website is another place to visit if you'd like to get a handle on just how much of a priority evangelizing homosexuality throughout the entire world is to this president and his acolytes.

Remarks by John Kerry in November of 2014, archived on the Department of State website, are particularly instructive, because, not only do they expose the importance of spreading homosexuality throughout the world to the Obama regime, but, because they show just how much the regime is willing to lie in order to advance this ungodly endeavor:

> On this year's Transgender Day of Remembrance, we honor the memory of the innocent souls who died because of who they are and who they love.

> Today and every day, the United States stands with the LGBTI community and its allies to stop all acts of hate and violence against gender non-conforming people.

> I will never forget standing on the steps of the U.S. Capitol in 1998 to honor Matthew Shepard, a young man killed just because he was gay. His mother, Judy, had a profound lesson for all of us: Loving one another doesn't require us to compromise our beliefs. Love only demands that we choose compassion over intolerance.[146]

Not only are people *not* systemically targeting for murder those who pretend to be of the opposite sex, but Kerry repeated the lie that Matthew Shepard was murdered because he liked having sex with men. Shepard was murdered by a man with whom he had sex, likely over a dispute involving drugs.[147]

But who cares about the truth, I guess, when progressives have a War on Christianity to wage?

Still, while the Obama regime places no value on truth, and suffers little concern for who it offends, most nations of the world do value truth and are offended. They are not happy with what the U.S. government is doing in its insatiable thirst to globally further this cancerous sexual anarchist agenda.

Al-Monitor reported in June 2015 that a "US ambassador's visit to LGBT event sparks outrage in Jordan."[148] Meanwhile, *CNSNews.com* had several stories in July of 2015 of how irate leaders of other nations have become at Obama with his evangelizing for homosexuality.

First, *CNSNews.com* reported that Kenyan politicians bluntly told Obama not to proselytize for homosexuality before he arrived in country for a visit:

> Irungu Kangata, a lawmaker in President Uhuru Kenyatta's The National Alliance (TNA) party, was blunter: "We are telling Mr. Obama when he comes to Kenya this month and he tries to bring the abortion agenda, the gay agenda, we shall tell him to shut up and go home." ...

> Kenya's The Daily Nation quoted several other lawmakers' views on the matter.

"Anybody who tries to come and preach to this country that they should allow homosexuality, I think he's totally lost," said TNA lawmaker Jamleck Kamau.

"And I would also like to add, our son from the U.S., Barack Obama, when he comes here, to simply avoid that topic completely," added Kamau, "because Kenyans will not be happy with him if he comes to bring the issue of homosexuality in this country."

"Liberal thoughts are being entertained in some countries under the guise of human rights," the speaker of the National Assembly, Justin Muturi, told an Anglican Church congregation. "We must be vigilant and guard against it. We must lead an upright society and not allow obnoxious behavior as we have a responsibility to protect our children."

Rose Mitaru, one of 47 female lawmakers representing counties across the country, said that allowing same-sex marriage in Kenya would open "floodgates of evil synonymous with the biblical Sodom and Gomorrah."[149]

Not that Obama or his regime cared what the Kenyans thought. The same CNSNews.com story reported that the White House essentially flipped the Kenyan people the bird:

White House press secretary Josh Earnest indicated Monday that Obama would not avoid the topic during his visit.

"We have been clear that when the president travels around the world, he does not hesitate to raise concerns about human rights," he told a press briefing, in response to a question on the Kenyan criticism.

"I'm confident the president will not hesitate to make clear that the protection of basic universal human rights in Kenya is also a priority and consistent with the values that we hold dear here in the United States of America," Earnest said.

But Kenya likewise refused to back down. The Kenyan president, speaking for untold billions worldwide, told Obama exactly what he thought of the American president's disgraceful, pro-debauchery evangelism efforts as the two held a joint press conference in Kenya. CNSNews.com reported on July 27, 2015:

Kenyan President Uhuru Kenyatta pushed back gently against President Obama's promotion of homosexual and lesbian rights on Saturday, saying Kenyans had more pressing concerns to deal with, including health, education and "ensuring inclusivity of women."

While Kenya and the U.S. shared many values, Kenyatta said during a joint press conference in Nairobi, "there are some things that we must admit we don't share—our culture, our societies don't accept. It is very difficult for us to be able to impose on people that which they themselves do not accept."

"This is why I repeatedly say that, for Kenyans today, the issue of gay rights is really a non-issue," he added. "We want to focus on other areas that are day-to-day living for our people."[150]

CNSNews.com also reported in July 2015 on a similar situation in 2014, which involved the President of Uganda. He bluntly insisted that America's sexual-anarchist-in-chief not spread his own demonic love for sin in the Christ-centered nation of Uganda:

Like the way President Barack Obama was told by the president of Kenya this week that "gay rights is really a non-issue" and not accepted by Kenyans, Uganda's president told Obama last year that, unlike in America, homosexual behavior is a "no-go" subject, "never supported by Ugandans," and Obama should "respect African societies and their values."

Ugandan President Yoweri Museveni also explained that Ugandans—a country that is 84% Christian—reject the notion that unnatural behavior is a "human right," and added that the behavior homosexuals engage in is "terrible."[151]

Obama's attempt at evangelizing homosexuality on the African continent became so pervasive, in fact, that on at least one occasion a number of Africans interpreted his efforts as a punitive attempt to force compliance...or else. *The Pulse* reported in July 2015 that Obama was attempting to push Nigeria, against the will of its people, into legalizing same-sex "marriage."

The United States of America has said that it would continue to mount pressure on Nigeria until the country legalizes same-sex unions.

The US is expected to begin making its case against Nigeria's anti-homosexuality law during President Muhammadu Buhari's visit to Washington on July 20.

This was revealed on Monday, July 13, 2015, by the US Assistant Secretary of State for African Affairs, Linda Thomas-Greenfield during a live-web chat with journalists. ...

Thomas-Greenfield also said that pressuring Nigeria to reverse the anti-gay law did not amount to interference with the country's sovereignty.

She said:

"This is very much a work in progress, but I think you will agree with me that the law in Nigeria really went far in discriminating against this

community but also people who associate with them. So, we will continue to press the government, to press the legislature to change these laws and provide human rights for all Nigerian people regardless of their sexual orientation."[152]

Once again, the pushback was viewed by America's arrogant chief executive as irrelevant.

So paramount was (and is) the LGBT propagandist agenda to Barack Obama, that he ordered his State Department to both undermine America's Judeo-Christian heritage and spread the homosexualists' political demands across the globe with a State Department position called the "Special Envoy for the Human Rights of LGBTI Persons." *Reuters* reported on the creation of this bizarre, sex-centric position in February of 2015:

The United States Department of State on Monday named its first-ever special envoy to advocate globally for the human rights of lesbian, gay, bisexual and transgender (LGBT) people.

Randy Berry, an openly gay senior diplomat, has served as U.S. Consul General in Amsterdam since 2012. His earlier foreign service postings included Nepal, Bangladesh, Egypt, Uganda, South Africa and New Zealand.

"Defending and promoting the human rights of LGBT persons is at the core of our commitment to advancing human rights globally—the heart and conscience of our diplomacy," said U.S. Secretary of State John Kerry in announcing the groundbreaking appointment.

In his new role, Berry is charged with advancing government initiatives to reduce violence and discrimination against LGBT people around the world, including in the more than 75 countries where consensual same-sex relationships are criminalized.

He also will be able to utilize the State Department's Global Equality Fund, created in 2011 to provide critical emergency, short-term, and long-term assistance to protect and advance the human rights of LGBT communities in over 50 countries.[153]

And Berry has been perversely busy about the task of encouraging sodomy in this new position ever since.

By June of 2015 he was leading a coalition of homosexual State Department personnel in trying to inject homosexuality—anti-Christian advocacy—into every aspect of U.S. dealings with other nations. Reports *CNSNews.com*:

International free-trade agreements like those being negotiated with countries in the Pacific and Europe should help to export American values such as human rights, including for lesbian, gay, bisexual, transgender and intersex (LGBTI) people, according to seven openly homosexual U.S. ambassadors.

The seven, joined by the State Department's first "special envoy for LGB-TI persons," Randy Berry, signed a joint letter published Tuesday in the national gay and lesbian news magazine The Advocate, *and re-posted by the White House.*

"Through the President's trade agenda, we will not only support more American jobs, but we can also promote greater justice beyond our borders," they wrote.

"We are committed to working closely with the White House to ensure that any trade arrangement approved by Congress is a force for progress on human rights for everyone, including for LGBTI persons."[154]

Berry also attended a "Gay" Pride Parade in Brazil in June of 2015, "and hoisted the homosexual rainbow flag just by the US flag in the US Consulate General in Rio de Janeiro," as we reported at *BarbWire.com* at the time.[155] He additionally promoted in *Voice of America* (a U.S. propaganda publication and organization) that same month.[156]

Striking as all this official sodomy-based evangelization may seem, the God-haters, not surprisingly, remain unsatisfied. They demand more affirmation of their sin-centered lifestyle choices. When, in their hearts, people know that they are violating God's laws, no amount of worldly affirmation of those violations will remove that nagging self-reproach.

Breitbart reported in June 2014 that Democratic Senator Edward Markey of Massachusetts introduced the International Human Rights Defense Act of 2014 in an attempt to legislate the Special Envoy position that Obama eventually executively created in 2015.[157,158] Markey's bill specified that he wanted legislation and a Special Envoy who would do even more than what Randy Berry has done (so far):

One area where the US under Obama has not retreated, indeed has ramped up American pressure, is in the promotion of LGBT rights. He issued a 2011 Presidential Memorandum that did just that.

Senator Edward Markey of Massachusetts and 24 Democratic senators want to make this policy a part of U.S. law.

In legislation introduced last Friday, LGBT rights would become an official foreign policy priority of the United States and would include US training of "professional foreign military."

The legislation would require the participation of all federal contractors, put US pressure on international institutions, and work in all global "sectors" including "economic, education, health, nutrition, legal and judicial..." The legislation calls for US pressure on individuals and also the family.

The legislation would also mandate that non-gay LGBT campaigners be given special refugee status in the United States.

The bill would establish a Special Envoy within the State Department, appointed by the President, to carry out the bill's mandate. The Special Envoy would "direct all activities, policies, programs and funding relating to the human rights of LGBT people... for all bureaus and offices of the Department of State and in the international programs for all other Federal agencies. ..."

Under the law there would be a "global strategy requirement" such that within 180 days after enactment the Special Envoy must create a five-year global plan that will first "fully implement" President Obama's 2011 Presidential Memorandum that first made LGBT the president's foreign policy priority.[159]

This is madness—official U.S. government madness. It's evil, and it's placing America in the path of God's well-deserved wrath. Notice how the bill (which has not passed into law as of the date of this writing) would mandate that the full U.S. government evangelize homosexuality—and, as a natural corollary, attack the Christian sexual ethic—as "an official foreign policy priority of the United States, and would include US training of 'professional foreign military.'"

The enemies of God want the U.S. armed forces to spread homosexuality throughout the world, against the will of those nations with whom it deals. What's it called when a national government uses its military power to advance its policies? It's called war. It's called imperialism. It's called conquest. Anti-Christians demand that the U.S. wage war against natural human sexuality (and marriage) and for homosexuality (and counterfeit "gay marriage"). And while the legislation has yet to pass, Obama (again) did create his homosexualist Special Envoy position to get the ball rolling. He has likewise been highly successful in "fundamentally transforming" (fully homosexualizing) the U.S. armed forces into a military force that would be much more willing to spread the homosexualist agenda across the globe...by whatever means necessary.

In addition to having been a driving force behind the effort to repeal the ban on homosexuals in the armed forces, Obama now works to make the U.S. Department of Defense even more sexually deviant.

His fellow anti-Christians in the U.S. Congress, as of 2015, began pushing to repeal the ban on so-called transgender people in the armed forces.[160] Yet even as it is still illegal (as of this writing) for these sexually confused souls to serve as the wrong sex in the U.S. armed forces, Obama has openly ignored the law (as is his way)—and mocked those who call him out on his lawlessness.

Buzzfeed reported in June of 2015 that Obama hosted multiple currently serving troops at the White House even as their sexual deviancy put them in violation of the standards of the U.S. armed forces. And he didn't just host them—he celebrated their deviancy and lawlessness:

> *The White House took a new position in February on transgender military service: Being transgender should not be a reason to bar people from serving. President Obama seemed to inch closer to making that a reality on Wednesday, when an out transgender airman in the U.S. Air Force attended an LGBT pride reception at the White House—at the president's invitation—even though official policy still states transgender people must be discharged.*
>
> *"I know that I am allowed to serve openly, and I know that the policy will be changed very soon," Senior Airman Logan Ireland told* BuzzFeed News *in an interview after the event.*
>
> *"People at the Pentagon want this changed," he added. "They are losing valuable people and prohibiting people from enlisting."*
>
> *Senior military officials are so supportive of Ireland, he said, they put him on official orders to attend and granted him an exception to appear in a man's uniform. Yet he is one of a select few who can serve in a uniform that corresponds with his gender identity. Ireland's fiancé, Army Cpl. Laila Villanueva, a transgender woman, attended in civilian clothes.*
>
> *"We are trying to make a statement to say, if you are letting me go by male dress and appearance standards," Ireland said, "then why not let my fiancée" wear the uniform that corresponds with her gender identity? "She is also active duty in the Army. And there are other people from other branches of the military who are transgender who are not able to go by the same standards I am." ...*
>
> *But, Ireland was the only active duty trans service member who was specifically invited to the White House after coming out. Asked if Ireland should be discharged in accordance with current military policy, a White House spokesman cited comments from the president's press secretary, Josh Earnest, earlier in the week.*

"I will reiterate the President's view—and it's one that is shared by his Secretary of Defense—and it's that Americans who are qualified to serve should be able to do so, and deserve to be treated with dignity and respect," Earnest had said.[161]

The insanity that naturally comes from progressives waging a War on Christianity extends further into the world of United States national security than just the U.S. armed forces. Both the Central Intelligence Agency and Defense Intelligence Agency now celebrate "LGBT Pride Month."[162,163] And the United States of America has even codified its evangelization of homosexuality through its national security structure by way of the official 2015 National Security Strategy (NSS), a strategy developed directly by the White House and issued with the president's signature. The NSS Fact Sheet states what the intended purpose of the NSS is:

National Security Strategy provides a vision and strategy for advancing the nation's interests, universal values, and a rules-based international order through strong and sustainable American leadership. The strategy sets out the principles and priorities that describe how America will lead the world toward greater peace and a new prosperity.[164]

And just how does the Obama White House think it will accomplish that? Under the "Advance Equality" subsection of the "Values" section of the NSS it states the following:

We will be a champion for communities that are too frequently vulnerable to violence, abuse, and neglect—such as ethnic and religious minorities; people with disabilities; Lesbian, Gay, Bisexual, and Transgender (LGBT) individuals; displaced persons; and migrant workers.[165]

And under the "Empower Civil Society and Young Leaders" subsection of the "Values" section of the NSS it states the following:

Restrictions are often seen through new laws and regulations that deny groups the foreign funding they depend on to operate, that criminalize groups of people like the LGBT community, or deny political opposition groups the freedom to assemble in peaceful protest. The United States is countering this trend by providing direct support for civil society and by advocating rollback of laws and regulations that undermine citizens' rights.[166]

The progressives' War on Christianity is so furtively embedded into official American government now that it has officially become part of the U.S. National Security Strategy by way of "protecting" (read: advancing the sexual anarchist political cause) homosexuals throughout the world.

Still, to truly comprehend how dedicated the anti-Christians are to their war, and, consequently, how utterly dangerous and out of touch with reality they are, one need only read what Rosa Brooks wrote in *Foreign Policy* in June 2015. Brooks's bio line in the column included describing her as having "served as a counselor to the U.S. defense undersecretary for policy from 2009 to 2011," meaning she was serving at a senior level in the DOD. Her column was titled, "Can Gay Marriage Defeat the Islamic State?". And even as it's subtitled with, "A few—admittedly sappy—thoughts on the power of #LoveWins," it is as devoid of any intelligent thought as its primary title suggests:

> *The first set of images, from early June, shows masked gunmen surrounding a crowd of people, mostly men. Some of the faces in the crowd show fear or hatred; others are studiously blank. But all eyes are fixed on the rooftop of a nearby building, where a blindfolded man is dangling upside down, his ankle held tightly by another masked man. Next image: The blindfolded man's body plummets headfirst toward the pavement below. Final image: a crumpled, bloody heap on the ground, surrounded by a sea of faces. Headline and caption, from Fox News: "ISIS conducts more executions of men for being gay. ... On June 3, 2015, Islamic State (ISIS) operatives in Iraq's Ninveh [sic] province published photos of a public execution in Mosul of three men convicted of acts of homosexuality. The three men were blindfolded and dropped head first from the roof of a tall building in front of a large crowd of spectators, including children."*

> *The second set of images shows another crowd, thousands of miles away from the first. This crowd is full of men and women, all ages and all races, and they're waving American flags and rainbow-colored flags. This crowd isn't flanked by gunmen; no one looks frightened or enraged. This crowd is laughing and embracing; a few people are weeping, their faces lit with relief and joy. Caption from the Washington Post: "Gay rights supporters celebrate outside the Supreme Court in Washington after justices ruled that same-sex couples have the right to marry, no matter where they live."*

> *I know which crowd I'd rather be in.*

> *Do you want to fight the Islamic State and the forces of Islamic extremist terrorism? I'll tell you the best way to send a message to those masked gunmen in Iraq and Syria and to everyone else who gains power by sowing violence and fear. Just keep posting that second set of images. Post them on Facebook and Twitter and Reddit and in comments all over the Internet. Send them to your friends and your family. Send them to*

your pen pal in France and your old roommate in Tunisia. Send them to strangers.[167]

Obviously, any true Christian will agree wholeheartedly with Brooks that it's evil beyond words that Muslims across the globe, like the Islamic State, are publicly executing people for engaging in sodomy—just as they execute many times more for merely following Jesus Christ.

Even so, her suggested approach is utterly insane (and wicked). You don't fight evil with evil. Don't believe for a moment that you will ever reason with LGBT activists like Brooks, or find much common ground beyond agreeing that people should not be tortured, even if they engage in sinful sexual behaviors. Obama and the rest of the anti-Christians do evil, while believing, I think, that they are doing good. They're deceived. There is no evidence that we can sway them from that deception—from doing the evil under which they suffer.

Only the Holy Spirit can do that.

Understand that it is no exaggeration to say that the enemies of God demand that the U.S. wage war to advance the homosexual socio-political agenda. Many are beginning to recognize that we are indeed at war—a war for the global culture. It's good versus evil and the homosexualists are demonstrably on the side of evil—even as likewise evil Islamists persecute a handful of them in Muslim nations.

Writing for Reuters in, "The coming clash of civilizations over gay rights," in 2013, John Lloyd spun it this way:

Not so long ago how a country's administration handled its 'homosexual problem' would be thought of as its business. Many still think that way. But most Western democracies don't. They haven't just adopted legislation that enjoins equality of treatment for all, irrespective of sexuality. They have taken seriously, for the most part, the claims made by gay organizations for many years: that discrimination against gay men and women is an affront to civil liberties, and that when some states pursue discriminatory policies, those who do not should make their disapproval clear. Gay rights are now part of the world's clash of cultures.[168]

So, again, if you think that we Christians will be able to get far in the U.S., or appeal to liberal officials in the federal government to protect our First Amendment rights as we resist unjust laws that now force us to violate Christianity (even as these same liberals help illegal aliens break the law, the head of the IRS break the law, or Hillary Clinton break the law), then you are sorely mistaken.

Again, only a national spiritual revival—an act of the Holy Spirit—will change the heart of a fallen nation.

The God-haters are positioned everywhere, throughout every major institution (government, academia, entertainment, media, et al.) and are looking for every opportunity to persecute Christians—up to and including throwing us in jail—if we refuse to deny Christ and publicly affirm homosexual sin and same-sex "marriage." The Obama administration is fully on board and is doing all it can to see that they're successful. Once they've forced many Christians, as a matter of law, to affirm sexual deviancy (Step 2 of their above-mentioned plan), they will then move seamlessly to their third and final step: The outright criminalization of Christianity (true Christianity, anyway).

3 – The Criminalization of Christianity

As we've now seen in the U.S. since the Supreme Court opined that same-sex "marriage is the law of the land," progressives can now force Christian individuals and business owners—such as bakers, photographers, innkeepers and florists—to lend their talents to sin-centered "gay weddings" through the power of the police state. This amounts to a systemic, immoral and profoundly unconstitutional trampling of the First Amendment.

What is now happening is that progressives are creating a deviant-sexual-behavior-based "LGBT" suspect minority class with all the associated trimmings. In the eyes of government, Bible-believing Christians are now treated as modern-day racists. Any outward expression of the Judeo-Christian sexual ethic is trumped by newfangled "gay rights" and deemed verboten. For all intents and purposes, Christianity is on its way to being criminalized. This is not mere speculation. It's been the plan all along.

Case in point: Chai Feldblum, President Obama's EEOC commissioner—a lesbian activist who supports "plural marriage"—has promised as much. She admits that progressives "want to revolutionize social norms" and believes that "gay sex is morally good."[169] She calls the clash between religious liberty and so-called sexual liberty a "zero-sum game,"[170] meaning someone wins and someone loses. Guess who loses? Feldblum has "a hard time coming up with any case in which religious liberty should win."[171]

Even so, back in 2013 I was reminded by a close friend and fellow Christian attorney that, "God is in control, and that has to be more than a slogan at times like this."[172]

Since, no doubt, the Obama NSA has already read our entire email exchange from back, I thought I'd go ahead and share excerpts with you as well. My colleague's insights are profound. I found them encouraging. I hope you do, too.

"Amen," I replied. "At the risk of sounding a bit apocalyptic, I'm fully convinced that this is part of His divine plan—perhaps to begin separating the wheat from the chaff. We have arrived: 'As it was in the days of Noah, so it will be at the coming of the Son of Man.'" Matthew 24:37 (New International Version).

"I agree with you," he responded, "and that conviction makes all this much easier. What depresses me is the astonishing disconnect and irrationality that sin so easily produces, and how quickly it spreads; we are truly sheep and fully as stupid without a Good Shepherd.

"In my 35 years as a Christian, I never seriously believed we might end up in prison for our faith—except, perhaps, for something like a pro-life demonstration. This is the first time it seriously occurs to me that the trajectory of the nation is such that it is possible in five to 10 years. Oddly, this thought does not discourage or scare me; in fact, it's almost a joyful thought that we might have the privilege to suffer for our faith. Rejoice greatly when men revile and persecute you for my name's sake, for your reward is great in Heaven (a rough paraphrase of Matthew 5:12).

"It may be that the truly toughest tests we had were earlier in our lives," he continued, "before we got fully engaged and in the movement. ... Now we're part of networks with support from like-minded people, and we're largely insulated from what the opposition can do to us. The real heroes are our clients who speak up at the risk of losing their livelihood, getting thrown out of school, or getting death threats from the tolerance crowd. I feel now like my faith costs me less than when I was in private practice before hostile judges and antagonistic media hit-men."

"You nailed it," I replied. "What an honor that our Creator chose us before time began to be part of a Gideon's army of truth-tellers and defenders of the faithful. It's an amazing time to be alive. But, as you mentioned, although we're on the front lines, we also have tremendous support. It's quite liberating to be written off by the world and, consequently, free to speak and behave in a way that reflects the reality that we couldn't give a rat's behind what the world thinks of us. Those we represent rarely have that luxury.

"Whether it's one day or hundreds of years," I continued, "I really believe we are living in the last days (in the total scheme of time and space). I just hope that when and if the time comes, the Holy Spirit gives me the strength of character to not only refuse to deny His truth, but to be like our martyred brothers and sisters who walked up and kissed the stake before being burned alive on it.

"Anyway, that's enough trying to cheer each other up for now," I joked. "Keep on keepin' on, my friend."

Do I really believe American Christians will be burned at the stake over counterfeit "gay marriage"? No. Or probably not, anyway. Do I believe Christians will face real persecution, such as loss of livelihood, civil penalties, physical abuse or even jail? Absolutely.

Still, come what may, we Christ-followers must always remember this admonition from Romans 12:12 (New International Version): "Be joyful in hope, patient in affliction, [and] faithful in prayer."

In other words, mock "marriage" or not: Keep on keepin' on, my friend.

And you'll need to keep a positive attitude for the coming persecution, because the progressives really are passionate about criminalizing true Christianity.

The secular-left's goal of fully destroying Christianity in America obviously has its dire consequences (many of which have been detailed above), but there will be additional consequences beyond these—chief among which is that anti-Christians will (and already are) endeavor to fill the Christianity vacuum with a secularist religion of their own—one that sets them up as their own little gods to be self-worshipped.

Chapter 17

Establishing the New Religion

The anti-Christians regularly present themselves as rational, "science-minded" people who don't believe in supposedly superstitious things such as God and religion. The reality, of course, is that they are the most religious people of all. Yet, instead of believing that the one true God, Creator of heaven and earth, is God, they believe themselves to be little gods and their own little subjective worlds, deceptive words and relative "truths" to somehow represent reality.

Regardless of what you believe now, did you actually think the debate over gay "marriage" was about marriage? Have you really come to believe that this cultural kerfuffle has anything to do with "civil rights" or "equality"? Have you bought into the popular premise that this is a legitimate discussion on federalism—that it's a reasonable disagreement over whether the U.S. Constitution's equal protection clause requires that newfangled gay "marriage," something rooted in same-sex sodomy, a deviant and disease-prone behavior our Constitution's framers officially declared "the infamous crime against nature," be made law of the land?

A lot of people have, so don't feel bad if you are among them. A lot of reasonable, well-meaning and even, at times, intelligent people have taken the bait.

But that was all window dressing. It was superficial. It was collateral. It was chaff, a diversion, a squirrel.

At its core, this increasingly heated fight over gay "marriage" is about two diametrically opposed and profoundly incompatible views of reality (or lack thereof). It's the modern manifestation of a millennia-old clash between worldviews. This ugly cultural conflict is, in reality, neither legal nor political in nature, but, rather, is fundamentally a philosophical debate. Ultimately, it derives from, and is illustrative of, deep-seated spiritual warfare. Quite simply, the clash over gay "marriage" is emblematic of the larger, and much older, clash between good and evil.

And it has reached critical mass.

On the one hand, on the natural marriage side, we have a worldview that recognizes absolute truth—that acknowledges the fixed moral and natural law, authored and enforced from time immemorial by the sovereign and loving Creator of the universe. This same Creator, incidentally, just happened to design and define the very institution over which we quarrel. Those with this worldview concede that every man, woman and child is accountable to this sovereign Creator and will, one day, stand before Him to face final judgment for what they did or did not do during their infinitesimally short-lived stint here on earth.

This, though not a comprehensive representation, is the biblical worldview.

On the other hand, on the unnatural marriage side (or the "marriage equality" side as these self-styled progressives euphemistically prefer), we have a worldview that denies absolute truth. It imagines there are no fixed lines of demarcation between right and wrong—that morality, that reality, is entirely relative and, therefore, the very notion of good and evil, right and wrong, sin and repentance are but false and limiting constructs concocted in the narrow minds of a dull bevy of sheepherders some thousands of years ago.

Since those with this worldview either deny God's very existence altogether or, alternatively, believe that some version of god, like marriage, can be defined, or redefined, in the mind of the beholder, they claim accountability to no one (except godless political correctness) and, thus, declare reality to be that which they, the secular progressive intelligentsia, proclaim it to be (e.g., that man-made, credulity-straining, reality-warping and oxymoronic counterfeit called same-sex "marriage").

Supreme Court Justice Anthony Kennedy, who happens to be both a big fan of unnatural marriage and one of the aforementioned intelligentsia, summarized this worldview neatly when he wrote the following in Planned Parenthood v. Casey. He did so while attempting to rationalize government-sanctioned child sacrifice, the evil twin to gay "marriage": "At the heart of liberty is the right to define one's own concept of existence, of meaning, of the universe, and of the mystery of human life," he pontificated.

In other words, man is the measure of all things. Man is god, and there is no god but man. According to Kennedy, and as was first suggested by a garden snake a very long time ago, truth is defined by man's "individual concept of existence."

This, of course, is empirically stupid.

And so both of these worldviews cannot be right. It's impossible. The law of non-contradiction precludes it.

Blogger Matt Walsh also recognizes that the anti-Christians are religious zealots, determined to force everyone to convert or die. He wrote about these secularist fanatics in a 2014 blog post on his website:

> The Cult of Leftism has many tenets, and it demands full compliance with all of them, but nothing in its creed compares to the sanctity of their two great sacraments: child murder and sodomy. You must not question these, but tolerance alone will not be good enough. You must celebrate them, too. You must worship at their altar. You must sing hallelujah at the mention of their names. You must fight for a society where infanticide and gay sex are awarded a protected and privileged position. When a man decides to kill babies for a living, you must call him a "health care provider" and a "healer." When a man decides to announce to the world that he enjoys sex with other men, you must call him a "hero" and a "pioneer." You must quite literally give him awards for his courage.
>
> Nothing less will be allowed.
>
> I hope that all of my fellow Christians and conservatives soon catch on to this reality. It seems that many in our camp have been too afraid of confrontation and too addicted to approval and affirmation, so we sent up the white flag and surrendered the culture entirely. "Hey, you do you, it's none of my business," we said, and moved on to arguing over safer things, like the economy or foreign policy. We rejected political candidates who dared to venture onto the forbidden soil of "social issues" and instead nominated milquetoast moderates who run around regurgitating platitudes about how we should "just talk about jobs." But the progressives have concentrated almost exclusively on winning the culture and reshaping our society in their image. While conservatives set up shop way off in the outskirts, liberals have burrowed right into the heart of America and gone to work subverting and perverting our civilization at its most foundational level.
>
> It's because they've claimed so many victories that they have earned the luxury to demand more than a cowering tolerance from their ideological opponents. Conservatives and Christians who tried to keep their hands clean by merely putting up with the slaughter of children and the destruction of the nuclear family are now faced with a dilemma. They

can't just tacitly endorse evil anymore—they are going to be required to give their enthusiastic and active approval. Silence will be viewed as dissent, and dissent is the highest crime.

So I suppose my point here is simple: if you aren't willing to become a liberal, you might as well finally stand up and condemn it. There is no middle ground anymore. There never was to begin with, but even the illusion is fading. Either fight for life, family, and Truth, or else join the ranks of the nihilists and hedonists. The distinction between the two sides is not a murky no-man's land colored in hues of gray; it is a stark and sudden line in the concrete. You are either for truth or you are not.

Either/or, black or white, right or wrong. Sorry, there are only two options, and you have to choose one. Progressivism says that you are either with it or against it, and on that point I agree.[173]

Indeed, the secular left represents today's Baal worshippers. "What has been will be again, what has been done will be done again; there is nothing new under the sun." (Ecclesiastes 1:9 – New International Version)

Modern-day progressives labor under an awkward misconception; namely, that there is anything remotely "progressive" about the fundamental canons of their blind, secular humanist faith. In fact, today's liberalism is largely a sanitized retread of an antiquated mythology—one that significantly predates the only truly progressive movement: biblical Christianity.

While visiting the Rivermont Evangelical Presbyterian Church in Lynchburg, VA a few years back I heard a troubling, albeit thought-provoking, sermon. Pastor John Mabray addressed the ancient Canaanite practice of Baal worship and, though he didn't reveal it by name, connected the dots to its present-day progeny: liberalism. Baal, the half-bull, half-man god of fertility, was the focal point of pagan idolatry in Semitic Israel until God revealed His monotheistic nature to Judaism's forebears.

In his sermon, Pastor Mabray illustrated that, although they've now assumed a more contemporary flair, the fundamentals of Baal worship remain alive and well today. The principal pillars of Baalism were child sacrifice, sexual immorality (both heterosexual and homosexual) and pantheism (reverence of creation over the Creator).

Ritualistic Baal worship, in sum, looked a little like this: Adults would gather around the altar of Baal. Infants would then be burned alive as a sacrificial offering to the deity. Amid horrific screams and the stench of charred human flesh, congregants—men and women alike—would engage in bisexual orgies. The ritual of convenience was intended to produce economic prosperity by prompting Baal to bring rain for the fertility of "mother earth."

The natural consequences of such behavior—pregnancy and childbirth—and the associated financial burdens of "unplanned parenthood" were easily off-set. One could either choose to engage in homosexual conduct or—with child sacrifice available on demand—could simply take part in another fertility ceremony to "terminate" the unwanted child.

Modern liberalism deviates little from its ancient predecessor. While its macabre rituals have been sanitized with flowery and euphemistic terms of art, its core tenets and practices remain eerily similar. The worship of "fertility" has been replaced with worship of "reproductive freedom" or "choice." Child sacrifice via burnt offering has been updated, ever so slightly, to become child sacrifice by way of abortion. The ritualistic promotion, practice and celebration of both heterosexual and homosexual immorality and promiscuity have been carefully whitewashed—yet wholeheartedly embraced—by the cults of radical feminism, militant "gay rights" and "comprehensive sex education." And, the pantheistic worship of "mother earth" has been substituted—in name only—for radical environmentalism.

But it's not just self-styled "progressives" or secular humanists who have adopted the fundamental pillars of Baalism. In these postmodern times, we've also been graced, regrettably, by the advent of counter-biblical "emergent Christianity" or "quasi-Christianity," as I prefer to call it.

This is merely liberalism all dolled up and gratuitously stamped "Christian." It's a way for left-wing ideologues to have their "religion" cake and eat it too. Under the guise of "social justice," its adherents often support—or at least rationalize—the same pro-homosexual, pro-abortion and radical environmental policies pushed by the modern-day Baal worshipper.

Though the "Christian left" represent what is arguably a negligible minority within larger Christianity, the liberal media have, nonetheless, embraced their cause and seized upon their popularity among elites as evidence that the so-called "Christian right" (read: biblical Christianity) is losing influence—that Christianity is, somehow, "catching up with the times."

Because emergent Christianity fails the authenticity test whenever subjected to even the most perfunctory biblical scrutiny, I suspect it will eventually go—for the most part—the way of the pet rock or the Macarena. But this does not absolve leaders within the evangelical community from a duty to call leaders of this counter-biblical revolution on their heresy. It's not a matter of right versus left; it's a matter of right versus wrong—of biblical versus non-biblical.

Nonetheless, the aforementioned pillars of postmodern Baalism—abortion, sexual relativism and radical environmentalism—will almost certainly make rapid headway over the next four to eight years, with or without help from the

Christian left. The gods of liberalism have a new high priest in Barack Obama, and enjoy many devout followers in the Democratic-controlled Congress, liberal media and halls of academia. Both Obama's social agenda and that of the 111th Congress are rife with unfettered pro-abortion, freedom-killing, pro-homosexual and power-grabbing environmentalist objectives. The same kind of "hope, action and change," I suppose, that was swallowed up by the Baalist Canaanites of old.

So, today's liberalism is really just a very old book with a shiny new cover. A philosophy rooted in ancient pagan traditions, of which there is naught to be proud.

There's "nothing new under the sun," indeed.

And modern-day Baal worship is all the rage.

This is why progressives are both warring to destroy Christianity, and why they intend to replace it with their own religion—worship of man, sex and the gods of secularism—once their goals are achieved. This is what they've been leading up to for decades, and relates directly to why Kennedy believes, like so many progressives do, that man has "the right to define one's own concept of existence, of meaning, of the universe, and of the mystery of human life."

This is idolatry. And idolatry leads to God's judgment.

Chapter 18

God's Judgment Is Coming

The aforementioned verse, Ecclesiastes 1:9 again states, "What has been will be again, what has been done will be done again; there is nothing new under the sun."

The Apostle Paul likely wrote his letter to the Romans about 25 years after Christ's death and resurrection (sometime between A.D. 55-57). Throughout the book of Romans, Paul warned of God's unfolding wrath against the Roman Empire—indeed, all of humanity—for mankind's embrace and practice of pagan morality.

Approach Paul's words with a modicum of objectivity and the reader is left with this dreadful realization: The words of Christ's hand-picked messenger likewise paint an eerily accurate portrait of America, A.D. 2016. The negligible difference is that ancient pagan morality has been sanitized with a new euphemism: postmodern "progressivism."

It is unbridled hubris that presumes America—lest she depart the wide path to ancient Rome—will not suffer that empire's same fate.

"The wrath of God is being revealed from heaven against all the godlessness and wickedness of people, who suppress the truth by their wickedness, since what may be known about God is plain to them, because God has made it plain to them," Paul wrote. "For since the creation of the world God's invisible qualities—his eternal power and divine nature—have been clearly seen, being understood from what has been made, so that people are without excuse." (Romans 1:18-20 – New International Version)

Of course, an entire book could be written on this passage alone, but, essentially, Paul is noting that knowledge of God's existence, eternal power, divine nature and moral law are self-evident. His truths are written on the hearts of every man, woman and child—Jew, Christian and pagan alike. Those who deny this reality are "without excuse."

Yet, excuses we make.

Pull your eyes from your smartphone, America. Look around you. God's wrath is "being revealed from heaven" once more. Paul's words in the Bible to the Romans sound as if they could be spoken to Americans of today.

> *For although they knew God, they neither glorified him as God nor gave thanks to him, but their thinking became futile and their foolish hearts were darkened. Although they claimed to be wise, they became fools and exchanged the glory of the immortal God for images made to look like a mortal human being and birds and animals and reptiles. Therefore God gave them over in the sinful desires of their hearts to sexual impurity for the degrading of their bodies with one another. They exchanged the truth about God for a lie, and worshiped and served created things rather than the Creator—who is forever praised. Amen. (Romans 1:21-25 – New International Version)*

Again, there is nothing new under the sun. Sexual impurity in all its ugly forms—fornication, adultery, homosexuality, pornography, et al.—is celebrated by these progressive "fools." American culture revels in the degrading of our bodies while purity is mocked. God has given us over to sinful desires.

Furthermore, and as mentioned in the last chapter, while good earthly stewardship is a sound biblical principle, the pantheism and idolatry of which Paul warned (worship of creation and/or false idols over the Creator) prospers yet today in its contemporary, totalitarian forms: radical environmentalism and new ageism.

> *Because of this, God gave them over to shameful lusts. Even their women exchanged natural sexual relations for unnatural ones (lesbianism). In the same way the men also abandoned natural relations with women and were inflamed with lust for one another. Men committed shameful acts with other men, and received in themselves the due penalty for their error. (Romans 1:26-27 – New International Version)*

Was Paul rebuking progressives on the U.S. Supreme Court, President Obama, liberals in Congress and other cheerleaders for these "shameful lusts" and "unnatural relations"—or was he just describing the disproportionately powerful and "inflamed-with-lust" homosexual lobby they represent?

Probably both.

Either way, God's "due penalty" is non-discriminating. America's official endorsement of "gay marriage," "gay pride," homosexualist indoctrination in our schools, "transgender" bathroom bills and bans on counseling to help with unwanted same-sex attraction will not end well.

Ask the Romans.

> Furthermore, just as they did not think it worthwhile to retain the knowledge of God, so God gave them over to a depraved mind, so that they do what ought not to be done. They have become filled with every kind of wickedness, evil, greed and depravity. They are full of envy, murder, strife, deceit and malice. They are gossips, slanderers, God-haters, insolent, arrogant and boastful; they invent ways of doing evil; they disobey their parents; they have no understanding, no fidelity, no love, no mercy. Although they know God's righteous decree that those who do such things deserve death, they not only continue to do these very things but also approve of those who practice them. (Romans 1:28-32 – New International Version)

Where to begin.

We have arrived. Shame on you, America. Our children—our adults—are depraved. They are "occupied" by envy. They attack innocent people, beating and killing them for sport. They murder one another in the streets without love or mercy. They disobey, gossip, slander and hate God. They are insolent, arrogant, boastful "little monsters." They invent ways of doing evil. Hannah Montana is what America once was. MTV Miley is America today. She "evolved" because we "evolved." You saw it on display. It's ugly. It's Satanic.

It's progressive.

Still, though we have become a Romans 1 nation and, absent widespread spiritual revival, will fall as did Rome, those who embrace and follow truth—who is Jesus the Christ—are a Romans 8 people:

> Therefore, there is now no condemnation for those who are in Christ Jesus, because through Christ Jesus the law of the Spirit who gives life has set you free from the law of sin and death. For what the law was powerless to do because it was weakened by the flesh, God did by sending his own Son in the likeness of sinful flesh to be a sin offering. And so he condemned sin in the flesh, in order that the righteous requirement of the law might be fully met in us, who do not live according to the flesh but according to the Spirit. (Romans 8:1-4 – New International Version)

That's the good news. But that's a book for another day.

Right now the bottom line is: if progressives successfully conclude their War on Christianity in America, America is doomed.

So America, to our own detriment, is just begging for God's just and righteous judgment—up to and including destruction—unless something drastically changes. And this finally brings us to the question: How did we ever get to this point? As mentioned earlier, something changed in the 1990s that enabled the anti-Christians to escalate their War on Christianity to the point where they are, today, fast approaching ultimate success.

PART 4

Chapter 19

LGBTQI and the 1990s

This rapid escalation of the War on Christianity has been occurring in part because of a major shift in the American socio-political landscape, beginning back in the 1990s. This shift ultimately led us to where we are today. Many folks, even now, recognize that something big took place; they just can't put their finger on exactly what.

Rush Limbaugh talked about the most recent consequences of this massive, decades-old cultural paradigm shift on the July 2, 2015 edition of his top-rated radio talk show, specifically referring to the June 2015 U.S. Supreme Court ruling designed to undo the institution of natural marriage:

> *Here's the next question: Are any of you surprised by the utter lack of any public protest, anger, uprising, against the assault on our traditional culture that was affirmed last week by decisions of the US Supreme Court? If you put it another way: What is your reaction to the apparent public acceptance of all of these seemingly overnight shifts in our culture and society? Why is there no objection, anger—uprising, if you will? Why does there seem to be practically blanket acceptance for all of this that ten years ago would be unthinkable?*[174]

There are most certainly multiple layers beneath why this rapid transformation has taken place, and so quickly, but for the sake of brevity let's focus on two of the big ones.

First, the enemies of God carefully organized and meticulously developed a specific and detailed strategy which led to victory after victory in the courts, the legislatures, academia, the media and through all corridors of elitism from the 1990s through today.

Limbaugh talking about the Supreme Court ruling on marriage is highly relevant to the overall War on Christianity. The victories of the anti-Christians came about in large part because of a well-defined strategy by some of their most active participants: the radical "LGBT" political lobby. They crafted this strategy in the late 1980s in an article and a book.

MassResistance is a nongovernmental organization tracking and fighting back against the war homosexuals are leading against American Christians. One of the things MassResistance does best is identify the ways in which the homosexual movement has used propaganda to manipulate the American public into accepting as good and wholesome that which even twenty years ago was largely recognized as evil and twisted.

MassResistance has a webpage called, "Strategies of the Homosexual Movement: 'The Overhauling of Straight America.'" This page reprints a 1987 article written by Marshall K. Kirk and Erastes Pill and published in *Guide Magazine* (which MassResistance describes as "a homosexual publication"). MassResistance makes an important note in its introduction to the article: homosexuals settled on appealing to people's emotions, rather than to their intellect, or to the facts.

> *This landmark article has become a "bible" of the homosexual movement, and has since been widely re-published on the Internet and elsewhere. It outlines strategies and techniques for a successful widespread propaganda campaign to confuse and deceive the American people and demonize opponents. Like all propaganda, their methods are based not on solid intellectual arguments, but instead upon emotional manipulation of the public in an attempt to gain widespread sympathy and approval for homosexual behavior.[175]*

Appealing to emotions over reason is critical to the success of all goals of progressivism. The anti-Christians emotionalize everything, while Christians (and Republicans and conservatives) attempt to appeal to people's reason and intellect. That's why, in large part, we're getting our butts handed to us on a platter.

Beyond this, Kirk and Pill explained up front that their plan would concentrate on desensitizing Americans to homosexuality and cross-dressing behaviors. From there everything else would follow:

> *The first order of business is desensitization of the American public concerning gays and gay rights. To desensitize the public is to help it view homosexuality with indifference instead of with keen emotion. Ideally, we would have straights register differences in sexual preference the way they register different tastes for ice cream or sports games: she likes*

strawberry and I like vanilla; he follows baseball and I follow football. No big deal.

At least in the beginning, we are seeking public desensitization and nothing more. We do not need and cannot expect a full "appreciation" or "understanding" of homosexuality from the average American. You can forget about trying to persuade the masses that homosexuality is a good thing. But if only you can get them to think that it is just another thing, with a shrug of their shoulders, then your battle for legal and social rights is virtually won. And to get to shoulder-shrug stage, gays as a class must cease to appear mysterious, alien, loathsome and contrary. A large-scale media campaign will be required in order to change the image of gays in America.

Those two short paragraphs neatly summarize what homosexuals did and achieved over the next two decades. Indeed, American society today looks at sexual preference the way it looks at flavors of ice cream—you like this flavor and I like that one (and both are okay). And from this desensitization campaign Kirk and Pill achieved the bulk of their agenda—they were entirely right that the battle for legal and social power would eventually be won. Those legal and social powers have now served to disabuse Christians of their most fundamental human and constitutional rights.

Kirk and Pill expanded on their desensitization campaign by specifying six steps necessary to achieve total victory. Those steps are highly detailed, but a summary glance at a few of them reveals things that have now become very familiar—things that those of us who have paid close attention to the culture wars will easily recognize as items that have already been realized in the left's "fundamental transformation" of the American cultural and political landscape. An excerpt from Step 1 alone provides a fascinating, and eerie, example:

Step 1: Talk about Gays and Gayness as Loudly and as Often as Possible.

The principle behind this advice is simple: almost any behavior begins to look normal if you are exposed to enough of it at close quarters and among your acquaintances. The acceptability of the new behavior will ultimately hinge on the number of one's fellows doing it or accepting it. One may be offended by its novelty at first—many, in times past, were momentarily scandalized by "streaking," eating goldfish, and premarital sex. But as long as Joe Six-pack feels little pressure to perform likewise, and as long as the behavior in question presents little threat to his physical and financial security, he soon gets used to it and life goes on. The skeptic may still shake his head and think "people are crazy these

143

days," but over time his objections are likely to become more reflective, more philosophical, less emotional.

The way to benumb raw sensitivities about homosexuality is to have a lot of people talk a great deal about the subject in a neutral or support-ive way. Open and frank talk makes the subject seem less furtive, alien, and sinful, more above-board. Constant talk builds the impression that public opinion is at least divided on the subject, and that a sizable seg-ment accepts or even practices homosexuality. Even rancorous debates between opponents and defenders serve the purpose of desensitization so long as "respectable" gays are front and center to make their own pitch. The main thing is to talk about gayness until the issue becomes thoroughly tiresome.

And when we say talk about homosexuality, we mean just that. In the early stages of any campaign to reach straight America, the masses should not be shocked and repelled by premature exposure to homo-sexual behavior itself. Instead, the imagery of sex should be downplayed and gay rights should be reduced to an abstract social question as much as possible. First let the camel get his nose inside the tent—only later his unsightly derriere!

Where we talk is important. The visual media, film and television, are plainly the most powerful image-makers in Western civilization. The average American household watches over seven hours of TV dai-ly. Those hours open up a gateway into the private world of straights, through which a Trojan horse might be passed. As far as desensitization is concerned, the medium is the message—of normalcy. So far, gay Hol-lywood has provided our best covert weapon in the battle to desensitize the mainstream. Bit by bit over the past ten years, gay characters and gay themes have been introduced into TV programs and films (though often this has been done to achieve comedic and ridiculous affects [sic]). On the whole the impact has been encouraging. The prime-time presen-tation of Consenting Adults on a major network in 1985 is but one high-water mark in favorable media exposure of gay issues. But this should be just the beginning of a major publicity blitz by gay America.

The reference to using Hollywood to transform Americans' beliefs about ho-mosexuality is particularly noteworthy, because throughout the 1990s and into the 2000s both the anti-Christians in general, and the anti-Christians in the entertainment industry, have constantly maintained that entertainment does not affect how people think and behave. In other words, as the anti-Christians used Hollywood to subvert America and change the minds and hearts of the American people, they at once boldly lied about doing so throughout.

Movie critic, radio talk show host and columnist Michael Medved identified how Hollywood denied any responsibility for influencing culture in his seminal 1990s book, *Hollywood vs. America*. Here is an excerpt from the opening of Chapter 15 ("Denial Behavior") dedicated to documenting how Hollywood lied:

> *First, the industry apologists insist that popular entertainment is by its very nature inconsequential, and that no one is seriously damaged by the fleeting images or subtle themes in a movie, TV show, or popular song. As the Hollywood establishment never tires of pointing out, several decades of research by social scientists have failed to produce conclusive, irrefutable proof that brutality and promiscuity in a product of the mass media can* **cause** *destructive behavior in the real world. (Emphasis in the original)*[176]

Kirk followed his article with Pill by writing a book, *After the Ball: How America Will Conquer Its Fear and Hatred of Gays in the '90s*, with Hunter Madsen and which was published in 1989.[177] The book further expanded on the Kirk-Pill article and made it perfectly clear that the effort to mainstream homosexuality was also an explicit attack on Christianity.

Kirk and Madsen devised an insidious three-pronged approach the homosexual lobby has masterfully implemented in subsequent years: Desensitization, Jamming and Conversion.

"Desensitization," wrote Kirk and Madsen, means subjecting the public to a "continuous flood of gay-related advertising, presented in the least offensive fashion possible. If 'straights' can't shut off the shower, they may at least eventually get used to being wet."

"Jamming" refers to the public smearing of Christians, traditionalists or anyone else who opposes the "gay" agenda. "Jam homo-hatred (i.e., recognition of objective sexual morality) by linking it to Nazi horror," wrote Kirk and Madsen. "Associate all who oppose homosexuality with images of 'Klansmen demanding that gays be slaughtered,' 'hysterical backwoods preachers,' 'menacing punks,' and a 'tour of Nazi concentration camps.'"

"In any campaign to win over the public, gays must be portrayed as victims in need of protection so that straights will be inclined by reflex to adopt the role of protector. ... The purpose of victim imagery is to make straights feel very uncomfortable," they suggested.

Still, perhaps Kirk and Madsen's most revealing admission came when they wrote, "[O]ur effect is achieved without reference to facts, logic, or proof."

And so, words like "homophobia" and "heterosexism" were manufactured from thin air, not because they have substance, but, rather, because they were effective jamming tools. Anyone who holds traditional values relative to human sexuality suddenly became a "homophobe," a "hatemonger" and a "bigot."

Not even churches are safe:

> Gays can undermine the moral authority of homo-hating churches over less fervent adherents by portraying [them] as antiquated backwaters, badly out of step...with the latest findings of psychology. Against the atavistic tug of "Old Time Religion" one must set the mightier pull of science and public opinion. ... Such an "unholy" alliance has already worked well in America against the churches, on such topics as divorce and abortion. ... [T]hat alliance can work for gays.

Oh and how it has.

"Conversion" means, in the words of Kirk and Madsen, "conversion of the average American's emotions, mind, and will, through a planned psychological attack, in the form of propaganda fed to the nation via the media."

An even longer excerpt of the book, provided by MassResistance, shows just how well-planned this attack was:

> It isn't enough that antigay bigots should become confused about us, or even indifferent to us—we are safest, in the long run, if we can actually make them like us. Conversion aims at just this.

> Please don't confuse Conversion with political Subversion. The word 'subversion' has a nasty ring, of which the American people are inordinately afraid—and on their guard against. Yet, ironically, by Conversion we actually mean something far more profoundly threatening to the American Way of Life, without which no truly sweeping social change can occur. We mean conversion of the average American's emotions, mind, and will, through a planned psychological attack, in the form of propaganda fed to the nation via the media. We mean 'subverting' the mechanism of prejudice to our own ends—using the very processes that made America hate us to turn their hatred into warm regard—whether they like it or not. ...

> The objection will be raised—and raised, and raised—that we would 'Uncle Tommify' the gay community; that we are exchanging one false stereotype for another equally false; that our ads are lies; that that is not how all gays actually look; that gays know it, and bigots know it. Yes, of course—we know it, too. But it makes no difference that the ads are lies; not to us, because we're using them to ethically good effect, to counter negative stereotypes that are every bit as much lies, and far more

wicked ones; not to bigots, because the ads will have their effect on them whether they believe them or not.[178]

Those brief selections are astonishing to read in the present day, not just because they are so bold in their hatred of foundational American principles and Christianity (and so brazen in terms of admitting to lying about it), but because it is clear that the homosexual movement succeeded in its effort to brainwash a large percentage of the American populace—**whether they liked it or not**—into rejecting good and embracing evil.

Anyway, as Kirk and Madsen both astutely understood and surprisingly admitted, homosexual activism was and is really a big game of hide the ball. In order to achieve widespread acceptance of "gayness," they had to remove the focus from what homosexuality actually is (deviant and disordered sexual conduct) and, instead, shift it to the cleverly manufactured specter of "gay rights."

To cut through much of their propagandist sugarcoating, one need only consider what two men must actually do in order to "consummate" a so-called "gay marriage." Kirk and Madsen understood this. Most people are naturally repulsed by the mechanics of homosexual conduct, but everyone is for "civil rights."

So, America, here's a refresher. Homosexuality 101: The central, defining feature of homosexuality is same-sex sodomy, a filthy practice—both from a moral and biological standpoint—that spreads disease, ruins lives and mocks both God and nature.

With the aid of a willing media and a like-minded Hollywood, societal desensitization has been largely achieved. The film, television and mainstream news industries have been effectively utilized to foster a modern-day fairy tale that creates a dishonest and sympathetic portrayal of a lifestyle that, in truth, is emotionally, spiritually and physically sterile.

Reality is replaced with fantasy. Gone are references to, or images of, the millions of homosexual men wasting away in hospice due to behaviorally related diseases such as HIV/AIDS, hepatitis and syphilis. (Unnatural behaviors beget natural consequences.)

The homosexual pressure group GLAAD even offers awards to the television networks that most effectively carry the homosexual lobby's water. The more distorted and positive the portrayal of homosexual conduct, and the more frequently the networks show such portrayals, the more likely networks are to win GLAAD's coveted prize.

As Kirk and Madsen put it, homosexuals should be portrayed as the "Everyman." "In no time," they said, "a skillful and clever media campaign could have the gay community looking like the veritable fairy godmother to Western Civilization."

Prophetic words from two very smart men.

What's even more interesting of late is how the anti-Christians have largely dropped the lies about Hollywood's intentional propagandist influence on our culture. LGBT activists like those at GLAAD now boast openly of how the entertainment industry has transformed Americans' thoughts and hearts on homosexual sin—how Hollywood has influenced Americans into embracing all forms of sexual deviancy...just as the authors of "The Overhauling of Straight America" and *After the Ball* both predicted and planned.

For instance, after the U.S. Supreme Court mocked God by presuming to change His definition of marriage last year, about half of America cheered this miscarriage of justice. Hollywood liberals (but I repeat myself) were among the loudest cheerleaders for this newfangled "right" to sodomy-based marriage.

The Hollywood Reporter published a lengthy article on its website that included many tweets from celebrities and politicians who sang the praises of these five rouge lawyers on the High Court.[179] Meanwhile, the *Atlantic* published, "The Modern Family Effect: Pop Culture's Role in the Gay-Marriage Revolution" (with a subheading of, "TV has convinced America that same-sex couples can be just like straight ones. What's next?").[180] And the *Los Angeles Times* cheered the heresy with, "Years before court ruling, pop culture shaped same-sex marriage debate."[181]

The pretense slipped well prior to 2015, with the *Hollywood Reporter* publishing a 2012 piece headlined, "THR Poll: 'Glee' and 'Modern Family' Drive Voters to Favor Gay Marriage— Even Many Romney Voters," while *USA Today* announced in 2013 that, "Hollywood: Gay marriage's best man—Films and TV helped clear a path for acceptance in pop culture."[182,183]

So when people wonder to themselves, "What happened that brought about this desecration of marriage, the celebration of homosexual sin and the growing hatred for Christianity and Christians?"—they need look no further than to the homosexual movement's organized and well-planned strategy to brainwash the American people through news and entertainment. This caused many to "ally" themselves with the homosexualist radicals and against Christians and foundational America principles.

Another, and, perhaps even more distressing reason for the sin lobby's success, is that American Christians chose to play "nicer than Jesus" and ultimately raised the white flag.

Chapter 20

Lukewarm Christians Choose the Surrender Strategy

As previously noted, The Moral Majority significantly helped the Republican Party and the conservative movement in the 1980s. Christians within this massive grassroots network buoyed the GOP to multiple victories throughout the decade of big hair and parachute pants, as well as through the ensuing 1990s, even as many Republican leaders secretly reviled the very system of values that made these Bible-believing Christians who they were, favoring, instead, the increasingly immoral values of the secularist cultural elites within both the RNC, the DNC and the larger progressive movement. The late 90s saw the beginning of both Republicans and conservatives moving away from committed Christians and their values like lepers. The excuse? "We need a big tent!"

Republicans' and conservatives' unilateral surrender to leftist ideology, particularly on the "social issues," was damaging enough to the GOP and conservativism (not to mention society at large), but to make matters far worse, many Christian leaders began to emulate this mass capitulation by adopting a surrender strategy of their own. The judgment to hoist the tattered white flag, apologize for inconvenient and unpopular biblical truths, coupled with many Christian leaders being "ashamed of the gospel," has now become thoroughly ingrained in American Christianity—particularly in Mainline Christianity, and, at a fast-growing rate, in evangelical circles—in much the same way that surrendering and apologizing for being conservative has become part and parcel of what it means to be establishment GOP.

The idea that, in order to remain culturally relevant, surrender is a must has become so prevalent in American Christianity, that there are quite literally professing Christians who have now resorted, pathetically so, I might add, to begging for "mercy" from those whom they perceive as our secularist conquerors. *The New York Times*, for example, published in March 2014, "The Terms of Our Surrender," by Ross Douthat. His fearful groveling was both thick and embarrassing:

> *I am being descriptive here, rather than self-pitying. Christians had plenty of opportunities—thousands of years' worth—to treat gay people with real charity, and far too often chose intolerance. (And still do, in many instances and places.) So being marginalized, being sued, losing tax-exempt status—this will be uncomfortable, but we should keep perspective and remember our sins, and nobody should call it persecution.*

> *But it's still important for the winning side to recognize its power. We are not really having an argument about same-sex marriage anymore, and on the evidence of Arizona, we're not having a negotiation. Instead, all that's left is the timing of the final victory—and for the defeated to find out what settlement the victors will impose.*[184]

Disgusting, no? Can you imagine the Apostle Paul, Peter or John making a similar argument? "Well, the Romans have thrown several of us to the lions now. It was a good run, but time to throw in the towel. Let's deny Christ as they command and 'find out what settlement the victors will impose.'"

Douthat, and the many gutless Christian wonders just like him, should be ashamed of themselves. I can't know for sure, but I imagine Christ Jesus isn't exactly busting buttons off His robe with pride.

I'm not the only one who thinks so. Many of my fellow believers are revolted by this widespread "Douthatian" groveling as well. Linda Harvey, a good friend and *BarbWire* contributor, wrote a column in October 2015 taking our fellow believers to task for their lukewarm Christianity:

> *Has the Christian church sinned against homosexuals or those who claim they were born in the wrong sex body?*

> *For that matter, are some people unchangeably "lesbian, gay, bisexual or transgendered"? Christians who follow Scripture will quickly refute claims that excuse these sins. These identities are not natural to the human condition nor to God's created order.*

> *So why are Christian leaders like Rev. R. Albert Mohler, Jr. implying otherwise as they confess the alleged "sins" of the Christian church against these sexual rebels?*

> *Rev. Al Mohler stated last week in response to a homosexual activist demonstration at the Southern Baptist Theological Seminary, where he is president, that, "The Christian church has sinned against the LGBT community by responding to this challenge in a superficial way." He*

went on to talk about redemption in Christ but seemed to be dodging the central issue of immoral conduct. He conceded a ton with this apology statement, which surely was greeted with cheers by the protesters.

First, what "LGBT community" is this Christian theologian talking about? Why use homosexual lobbying terms? There is a wicked homosexual political movement, but in God's eyes, none would be known as "lesbian, gay, bisexual and transgendered." Scripture resoundingly condemns these grave offenses. It is extremely disheartening for believers to hear our leaders cave in and use such ungodly, sin-affirming, misleading terms—as if some people are different humans and indeed victims of institutional Christian "bigotry." ....

We deserve an apology for the sin of homosexual pride parades. We deserve an apology for demanding the framework of marriage be re-made in your image, instead of the structure designed by God.

Our children deserve an apology for the millstone-worthy offense of being led into sin, being taught the lie that people are born to engage in sodomy or to amputate healthy body parts. The resulting corruption of untold numbers of children can only be surmised.

An apology needs to come from the Human Rights Campaign, Fairness Louisville, GLAAD, NGLTF, and many other groups. Their leaders are in serious spiritual danger unless they repent.[185]

Another *BarbWire* contributor and popular Christian novelist Lee Duigon, likewise recognized, and wrote about, the growing problem of Christian wussification:

Who do these church leaders think they are—Senate Republicans? They're crying "uncle" when the people of God have not yet begun to fight.

Why do "young believers"—if indeed this is true, and not just a projection from the minds of exalted high surrender monkeys—think the world is right to embrace sin, and the church wrong to reject it? If they do believe that, it's only because the churches and Christian parents have refused to obey God's command to teach their own children, and entrusted Christian children's education to anti-Christian schools controlled by anti-Christian teachers' unions.

You don't have to have the military genius of Hannibal or Patton to figure out that allowing the enemy to train your troops is a very bad idea.

Gasp! Did I say "enemy"? That's not very winsome, is it? Sorry, but I don't do winsome. The teachers' unions, the homosexual activists, the

151

atheist militants, the abortion fans who chant "Hail, Satan," and the statist schmucks who staff "human rights" agencies really are the enemy.

They must be defeated. Not charmed, not appeased, but put out of business. And the way to do that is by depriving them of their food and fuel—our children's souls and minds.

We won't convert them by any amount of winsome groveling. Their minds are closed; they are implacable. Unlike church leaders, they understand perfectly that a house divided will not stand. They are convinced that Christianity is wrong, stupid, out of date, contemptible, and an obstacle to their utopian humanist schemes. They want to get rid of Christianity, and they won't stop until they do it.

They mean to do it, and are doing it, by using the schools and the media to fill young people's minds with absurd but powerful visions of sexual freedom, economic equality, and cumbaya-loosey-goosey-party-time-forever gibberish. It works!

Of course it works. Look what they're doing to our culture.[186]

I wrote about the same thing in 2014.

"For the time is coming when people will not endure sound teaching, but having itching ears they will accumulate for themselves teachers to suit their own passions." (2 Timothy 4:3 English Standard Version)

Dear false prophets, false teachers and Christian apostates of every stripe:

We've all heard this phrase: "You know who you are!" It's an expression typically levied in the context of some corrective admonition, intended for some person or persons, busy about some misbehavior. While sent via certified mail, this is one of those rare open letters to whom the preponderance of intended recipients have, somehow, managed to convince themselves, and one another, that they're not even home. Most of you decidedly do not know who you are. You're living on Deception Lane.

Indeed, this letter, for many who read it, will be marked "return to sender." Such is the nature of deception. Those who labor beneath it have become so accustomed to its crushing weight that they've lost all sense of it. It is my humble hope and simple prayer that, if this is you, upon reading this letter the Holy Spirit might, instead, plant a seed of revelation in your soul and water it with His Word of life and truth, so that, for you, it might blossom to repentance and right-standing with God the Father.

To be sure, the guidepost for that which makes up the false church is not rooted in my opinion. I'm a fallen sinner, saved by grace and worthy, by my own merit, of nothing more than the lake of fire. The guidepost for that which constitutes the false church is the Word of God:

> But false prophets also arose among the people, just as there will be false teachers among you, who will secretly bring in destructive heresies, even denying the Master who bought them, bringing upon themselves swift destruction. And many will follow their sensuality, and because of them the way of truth will be blasphemed. And in their greed they will exploit you with false words. Their condemnation from long ago is not idle, and their destruction is not asleep. ... (2 Peter 2:1-3 – English Standard Version)

More from 2 Peter 2:

> For they mouth empty, boastful words and, by appealing to the lustful desires of the flesh, they entice people who are just escaping from those who live in error. They promise them freedom, while they themselves are slaves of depravity—for "people are slaves to whatever has mastered them." If they have escaped the corruption of the world by knowing our Lord and Savior Jesus Christ and are again entangled in it and are overcome, they are worse off at the end than they were at the beginning. It would have been better for them not to have known the way of righteousness, than to have known it and then to turn their backs on the sacred command that was passed on to them. Of them the proverbs are true: "A dog returns to its vomit," and, "A sow that is washed returns to her wallowing in the mud." (2 Peter 2:18-22 – New International Version)

Let's define the terms:

The Church: The Body of Christ—those regenerate, sanctified Christ-followers who have sincerely called upon the name of the Lord Jesus Christ, King of the universe, Creator, Soul-saver and sole Savior of mankind, and have been forgiven, redeemed and saved by grace. The Church recognizes God's holy word as infallible, unchanging and eternal. The terms "orthodox," "conservative," "fundamentalist" or "Religious Right" are sometimes used pejoratively by those outside the Church (and at times from within) in an effort to undermine the Church and water down the Word of God. The Church is hated by the world because the world first hated Christ and, as such, must suffer persecution.

The false church: The body of self-identified Christians who may, or may not, have begun the process of sanctification through belief upon and acceptance of Christ. The false church either rejects the infallibility of Scripture outright, or seeks to rationalize and radically "reform," revise or reinterpret Scripture to justify sin. False-church apostates are Olympic caliber mental and exegetical gymnasts who systemically call good that which the Word of God calls evil. They imagine many paths to God and hold that the Holy Spirit-inspired men used of God to record the Holy Scriptures were, truth be told, rather uninspired after all. Thus, our apostate friends attempt to satisfy their spiritual hunger with Christianity à la carte, taking that which is palatable and leaving behind those bitter morsels given to curb the carnal appetites. The false church is loved by the world and can be summed by its central doctrine, coined long ago by its founding father, which is this: "Did God really say?"

With my apologies to Jeff Foxworthy, if you believe that "many paths lead to God" and that Jesus was joking when he said, in no uncertain terms, "I am the way and the truth and the life. No one comes to the Father except through me," then you might be an apostate (see John 14:6 – Berean Study Bible).

If you have marched with, frequented or otherwise support Planned Parenthood—if you believe that there is any biblical justification whatsoever for one person to dismember alive another person in her mother's womb, a most murderous, tortuous and excruciating end—then you might be an apostate.

If you demand a "free Palestine," actually believe that Israel is intentionally targeting innocent Arab citizens in Gaza and elsewhere and, therefore, is guilty of genocidal "war crimes," then you have aligned yourself with the Islamic terrorist group Hamas, a group indistinguishable from ISIS, a group that admits using its own women and children as human shields and actually does target innocent Israeli citizens with thousands of rockets and suicide bombs on a regular basis. If this is you then, as with Islam and the rest of the pagan world, you are an enemy to Israel and, as Scripture warns, just might be an accursed apostate.

If you, as my good friend Dr. Michael Brown puts it, are among the growing numbers of those who engage "the fundamental error of 'gay Christianity,' namely, people interpreting the Bible through the lens of their sexuality rather than interpreting their sexuality through the lens of the Bible," then you might, you just might, be an apostate.[187]

C.S. Lewis wrote, "There are only two kinds of people in the end: those who say to God, 'Thy will be done,' and those to whom God says, in the end, 'Thy will be done.' All that are in Hell, choose it. Without that self-choice there could be no Hell."[188]

These are matters of eternal weightiness and consequence. For as it is written:

> Not everyone who says to me, "Lord, Lord," will enter the kingdom of heaven, but only the one who does the will of my Father who is in heaven. Many will say to me on that day, "Lord, Lord, did we not prophesy in your name and in your name drive out demons and in your name perform many miracles?" Then I will tell them plainly, "I never knew

you. Away from me, you evildoers!" (Matthew 7:21-23 – New International Version)

For those who hear God speak to them, "Away from me" will be the most pure, righteous, just and all at once terrifying words ever breathed.

I pray you don't hear them.

You can find many more examples of this burgeoning Christian surrender and embrace of heresy by doing a simple web query with the search phrase, "Christian culture war surrender."

Far too many Christian leaders have succumbed to the Devil's agents on earth and have believed the world's false charges of "bigot," "hater" and "homophobe" as legitimate criticisms (they are not), arrogantly parroting such accusations against those believers who remain steadfastly grounded upon the rock of biblical truth. "We've been too mean. We haven't been 'Christ-like,'" they claim. "Our rigid closed-mindedness and self-righteousness is driving people away from the Church and alienating younger folks—millennials and other."

Nonsense.

Do the secularist enemies of Christ worry about driving people away from the idolatry of self-worship by pushing too hard? Does their nastiness and refusal to compromise their faith in earthly evil alienate young people and push them to the societal margins? Does their love for wickedness draw those on the path to perdition even closer to destruction? No! The world loves them for it. This self-righteous rebellion against God vaults them to the highest levels of sociopolitical power and grants them control over nearly every aspect of civilization. They now run the United States from their temple of Baal.

The effectiveness of this LGBT-led indoctrination campaign has been so fruitful that America's Christian leaders are falling away at record numbers. Not only have they capitulated, but many now find themselves blindly serving as anti-Christian propagandists in their own right, doing the work of their enemies by spreading the same false gospel that Kirk, Madsen and others forecast in their propagandist scribblings.

While claiming to be agents of Christ, many Christian leaders today have become, instead, His enemies.

The Old Testament of the Bible is filled with examples of godly men being "closed-minded," "bigoted," "too mean" and "driving people away" from God's saving grace. They were "mean" to His enemies and they drove people away whose primary purpose, as tools of Satan, was to corrupt and destroy the Israelites.

Moreover, the New Testament is likewise filled with manifold examples of godly men being "too mean" and "driving people away from church" by preaching God's unchanging truths. Christ Himself, were He present in His earthly form today, would be declared by our own sappy modern-day Pharisees as a "rightwing fundamentalist evangelical."

Contrary to modern American Christianity's pathetic caricature of the Lord, Jesus was not some passive, emasculated wussy who constantly took abuse and surrendered truth for the lie. Jesus loved all and, even now, desires that "none should perish," but His definition of "love" looks nothing like today's sin-affirming and perverted counterfeit "love."

Love, without truth, is hate.

Reflect on how Christ actually "did unto others." American Christians and their out-of-context-scripture-quoting secular progressive bedfellows would crucify Him all over again today. If an unbeliever were to read the Bible for the first time he would likely be shocked (and they are) at all the supposedly "un-Christ-like" words and deeds of our God incarnate:

> *"Do not think that I have come to bring peace to the earth. I have not come to bring peace, but a sword. For I have come to set a man against his father, and a daughter against her mother, and a daughter-in-law against her mother-in-law. And a person's enemies will be those of his own household. Whoever loves father or mother more than me is not worthy of me, and whoever loves son or daughter more than me is not worthy of me. And whoever does not take his cross and follow me is not worthy of me. Whoever finds his life will lose it, and whoever loses his life for my sake will find it." (Matthew 10:34-39 – English Standard Version)*

This is not the Jesus of the modern megachurch supposition.

Christ instructed His followers not to cast pearls before swine. That is to say, He told His followers not to waste time trying to share the Gospel with stubborn hearts that remained in overt and implacable rebellion against God even after hearing the truth repeatedly. Not only that, but he referred to such unbelievers as swine—as pigs! Can you imagine the outcry from modern American Christians if Jesus used such words to describe today's apostate Christians and secular progressives? They'd boycott any company, university, public forum or media outlet that gave Him a platform to "spread his hate."

And if there were ever any doubt that Jesus did not want His followers perpetually wasting their precious temporal time on men and women so ensconced in wickedness that they refused to repent, He made this directive clear once more when He instructed His followers to wipe the dust off their feet of the home or town of those who refused to accept the Gospel. Again, modern American Christian leaders would have been scandalized with Christ telling people not to endlessly share the Gospel with hard-hearted unbelievers.

Christ repeatedly talked to His followers about hiding the truth from those who wanted nothing to do with it. He directly praised God the Father for hiding the truth from the "wise and learned" while revealing truth to children. And when He relayed the parable of the seeds being sown on a variety of soil types (a story meant to impart that many people would reject the Gospel), He told His disciples—after they asked Him why He spoke in parables—that it was to hide the truth (the secrets of heaven) from certain people.

Modern American Christians simply would not stand for such "hate" and "self-righteousness" had they been on earth with Jesus in bodily form. They would, and do, denounce and crucify Him today (which they do figuratively) just as they did in reality over 2,000 years ago. They would smear Christ Himself as "un-Christ-like."

Intentionally hiding the Gospel from wicked men? Calling them pigs? Saying that some people are unworthy of the Gospel? Talk about "driving people away from the Church."

Remember the man who came to Jesus and wanted to follow Him after he buried his father, only to have Jesus tell him to let the dead bury the dead, and that he should instead go and witness for the kingdom of God. Many of today's American Christians would've lost their noodle had they heard this admonition live and in person. "Couldn't Jesus have shown a little human compassion here? How does He expect to win people to God if He doesn't even have enough humanity to let a man whose father just died grieve and properly bury him? What an insult—an outright assault on basic decency!"

And who can forget the way Jesus treated a Canaanite woman when she came to Him and begged Him to heal her demon-possessed daughter. Instead of instantly crying and sympathizing with her, as today's American Christian leaders would insist on fellow Christians doing, Jesus ignored her and even told His disciples He was only there to help fellow Jews. Think about the hysteria that would come from American Christian leaders were any Christian to say that today? He'd be called everything from a "racist," "bigot," "xenophobe" and worse. And yet Jesus didn't stop there.

When the woman wouldn't leave and kept imploring Him, He actually had the gall to tell her that it wasn't right to throw food for children to dogs.

Think about that. It'd be the cover story of every newspaper. Life would momentarily come to a halt in modern America if any prominent Christian were to say something so blunt today. The internet would explode with outrage.

Christian leaders would stop whatever it was they might be doing to immediately issue apologies and statements of disgust and denunciation, repudiating said Christian leader as hostile to the cause of Christ. Christianity's "War on Women" refrain would pollute the airwaves. They would call Jesus disgusting and misogynistic—they'd say He referred to women as "dogs."

Meditating on how many modern American Christians might react to another Christ-follower saying exactly what Christ said 2,000 years ago isn't merely an exercise in empty theorizing. It happens all the time. Writers at the "Unholy Bible" blog, for instance, essentially made the same point laid out above, criticizing what Jesus did and showing how, if He said the same things today, there would be a massive public outcry, first from the enemies of God, and then, from a parade of American Christian leaders "ashamed of the Gospel."[189]

There is nothing new under the sun. Perhaps the best parallel of how Jesus might today be condemned by many American Christian leaders is to reflect upon how, in just a few short days, He went, two millennia ago, from being a beloved hero of the people to the victim of torture and crucifixion. Jesus rode into Jerusalem with fawning fans placing their clothes on the ground in front of Him, shouting for joy and singing songs of exaltation, to, just a week later, clamoring, at the behest of the Jewish leaders, for His execution at the hands of the Roman government over that of a convicted murderer. Imagine all the op-eds, opinion pieces, columns, tweets and comments on news programs and talk shows if a modern American Christian likewise enjoyed, and then lost, that level of support over the span of a week. He'd be considered a complete and utter failure who simply didn't know how to lead or to connect with people. Such a fall from grace, it would be said, should be a warning for other non-politically correct leaders to heed. There would be calls to purge anyone who attempted to emulate Him and calls to overhaul the entire movement.

This is exactly how, regrettably, many modern American Christians think and behave today—particularly Christian leaders. In an effort to be liked, we begin to think as our enemies want us to think—behave as they want us to behave. And we openly ignore, deny, and obfuscate what the Bible clearly says and teaches. We twist how Jesus actually lived and what He actually said. We've given up—thrown in the towel. We have no fight left, it seems. We have perfected, however, the art of surrender.

Still, there does yet remain a remnant. There are believers who actually maintain the courage of their convictions. There are a handful who still speak the hard truths, whatever the cost may be—and, in so doing, are winning lost souls to the true Christ of the Bible.

And these lost souls—particularly those living the LGBT lifestyle, desperately need the Christ of the Bible. Their temporal—and eternal—lives depend on

Him.

"Projections have shown, for instance, that if current trends continue, half of all gay and bisexual men will be HIV-positive by age 50." – *The Wall Street Journal*, Sept. 25, 2014[190]

This jaw-dropping revelation is based on an article in *AIDS and Behavior* about the homosexual lifestyle.[191] *The WSJ* report further warns: "Gay and bisexual men represent an estimated 2 percent of the U.S. population but more than half of all people living with HIV and 66 percent of new HIV infections. They are the only population group in the United States for which HIV infections are rising."

What do you say of an adult or adults who, for selfish political reasons, encourage sexually confused children to adopt a sex-centric identity and lifestyle laced with a 50-50 chance of HIV infection? I'd say they're guilty of child abuse. Adults are supposed to protect children from touching the red-hot stove, not push their face down on it.

This is true hate.

Scripture admonishes, "The wages of sin is death" (Romans 6:23). Unnatural behaviors beget natural consequences. It is hateful to promote a sin-centered lifestyle to children, to anyone for that matter, which leads to disease, death and, unless repented of, eternal separation from God.

It bears repeating: "[H]alf of all gay and bisexual men will be HIV-positive by age 50."

The wages of sin is death.

Yet in today's upside down world it is we who are disingenuously accused of "hate"—those of us who remain compassionate and bold enough to warn our fellow fallen human beings of the spiritual, emotional and, yes, even the physical death that comes as a natural consequence of unnatural behaviors. A toxic cloud of political correctness distorts reality, choking off any honest appraisal of these self-destructive sexual behaviors. We truly live in a dark age that calls evil good and good evil.

Homosexual conduct is always sin. It always has been. It always will be. It is never good, healthy, normal or natural.

The wages of sin is death.

I'm honored to say that I'm one of those "haters" called by God to sound the alarm. While folks do send me positive and encouraging notes on a regular basis, I likewise receive a steady stream of hate mail—chiefly when I write (or speak) on the issues of marriage, God's moral law and His natural order for human sexuality.

While the positive correspondence is always heartening, it is, believe it or not, the nasty stuff—the uglier the better—that especially lifts my spirits. Christ's promises are true: "Blessed are ye, when men shall revile you, and persecute you, and shall say all manner of evil against you falsely, for my sake." (Matthew 5:11 – King James Version)

When God calls you to be an instrument of His truth, the biblical harmonies you play will often strike sour with those in rebellion against Him, sending them into blind rage and deep denial. This is a spiritual battle old as time itself. It is between good and evil. It is sublimely humbling to be used of God in this way. All we, all you, as faithful Christians can do is to speak truth in love and pray that those truths plant a seed that bears fruit in the hardened hearts of lost souls.

I have seen this happen many times.

One example occurred in October of 2009. I was keynoting a fundraiser for the pro-family group "Americans for Truth About Homosexuality" (AFTAH) in suburban Chicago.

Outside the event, and watched closely by police, was a mob of angry "LGBT" protesters. A young woman who claimed to be with the press was present at the banquet. It was quickly discovered that she was actually with the mob outside and had somehow managed to sneak in. Rather than kick her out, Peter LaBarbera, founder of Americans for Truth, asked her to stay and join us for the banquet. He requested only that she put away her video camera, which she did.

This young woman, who identified as a lesbian, sat at a table with some of the most loving and godly women I know. They showed her the love of Christ. Among them was Sandy Rios, my dear friend.

After I gave my remarks, this young lady—we'll call her Marie to protect her from being hanged for high treason by the "equality" crowd—rushed over to me with tears in her eyes. "They lied!" she exclaimed of the protest organizers outside. "You don't hate us. You don't hate me. You really do care. And you're funny!" she added of some of the humor I typically, though not always successfully, weave into my writing and speaking.

"I'll admit it," she continued, "What you said was hard to hear. But they lied to me. You don't hate anyone."

A number of us then prayed for this priceless daughter of God the Father. She stayed around and visited with us until well after the event ended. Sandy Rios and I then walked her out, where we were greeted with scowls and profanity-laden taunts by the activists outside.

"What are you doing with them!" demanded one of the protesters of our new friend. To even my surprise, she ignored them, reached over and gave me a big hug.

She saw that we loved her. She saw that Christ, in us, loved her. He died for our sins, her sins, and for the sins of each of her fellow protesters.

We learned that her friends, her ride home, had abandoned her and, as I recall, Sandy drove her home that night, continuing to minister to her along the way and for some time thereafter.

Yes, they lied. We don't hate you.

This is the true face of the vast majority of so-called "anti-gay" Christians. This story is but a microcosm for the larger movement.

It is truth.

And it is love.

But sadly, truth is hate to those who hate truth.

To you homosexual activists, I say this: We will not be daunted. We will not be intimidated. We will never quit.

We do this in obedience to the Holy Spirit.

Like He did before us, we are going to love you.

But, as did He, we are also going to tell you the truth.

And we're going to do it whether you—or the professing Christians on our own side who oppose fighting evil—like it or not.

Yet those of us advancing the Kingdom of God are few and far between. Many professing American Christian leaders, again, have chosen to surrender to the enemy.

And because Christian leaders have chosen surrender as a strategy, we continually become further and further undermined and defeated, falling deeper into our culture of losing and leading other people astray.

This is why we now have many American Christian leaders "dialoguing" with the enemies of God, while the enemies of God have made it abundantly clear that they want nothing to do with open and honest dialogue in the first place. They're simply looking for new ways to subvert truth and twist their adversaries into knots so that we become more and more like them—so we will, like them, increasingly advocate against truth and that which lies in the best interest of all mankind.

A willingness to "dialogue" with progressives became popular in the late 1990s and early 2000s, with homosexual activist groups leading this manipulative charge in deceiving American Christians into believing that they actually desire common ground—that they hope to engage in open and honest debate. Mel White, for instance, a former ghostwriter for Jerry Falwell, Christian pastor and founder of Liberty University (where I currently serve as an associate dean), declared himself a homosexual and later founded an activist group called SoulForce. This antichrist organization was specifically designed to target churches and Christian colleges to undermine, under the guise of seeking "common ground with fundamentalist Christians," these hitherto Bible-believing institutions.[192,193] White and SoulForce certainly weren't the first group of deceived souls attempting to subvert Christianity in America, but neither were they the last. Many similar such organizations have, like a cold sore on the face of the earth, sprung up since, engaging in the same type of subversive, anti-Christian propaganda perfected by SoulForce.

Still, no matter how many of these progressive organizations come and go, many Christians still fail to get it—we still believe, somehow, that these people are sincerely interested in legitimate debate and that we can win them over to the truth if we're only nice enough. This is false. They don't want compromise or understanding—they never did. They want surrender and outright defeat.

My dear friend and Christian radio talk show host Janet Mefferd often notes the absurdity of mealy-mouthed Christians "dialoguing" with these folks. She says that such "compromise" often leads to apostasy on our part, if not outright heresy:

> "Evangelicals Open Door to Debate on Gay Rights." *Just the kind of headline I never enjoy, but it ran June 8 in* The New York Times *over a story about "influential evangelicals" meeting with homosexual activist Matthew Vines at Biola University last month, complete with a* Times *reporter and photographer on hand. …*
>
> *And might I ask: What exactly is in any of this "dialogue" for Bible-believing Christians? The story states that this group ultimately disagrees with Vines on homosexuality, but look at the headline! "Evangelicals Open Door to Debate on Gay Rights." That, my friends, is how the world interprets this so-called "dialogue." The New York Times knows, and Vines knows, exactly what's going on here. Why don't we? …*
>
> *Vines and those like him have a clear agenda: They reject the teachings of Scripture on homosexuality, and you will be made to feel like a bigoted homophobe until you do, too. For his part, Vines isn't "dialoguing" with you so you can convince him he needs to repent. He's "dialoguing" in order to bring you over to his side of the aisle. And with more than 30 such meetings under his belt so far, he's probably going to have a lot of success in the end. …*

... We are surrounded by what many of us refer to as Big Gay, Inc. And within this movement are a certain number of individual, church-focused "LGBT prophets" whose goal is to undermine the inerrant and infallible Word of God by getting conservative evangelicals to buy into the "gay Christian" and "homosexuality isn't really a sin" lies. And with the inch-deep understanding of the Bible that most Christians have today, this movement has already deceived and will continue to deceive many.

That's why this useless and ultimately subversive "dialoguing" nonsense has to stop. We must not allow ourselves to be their useful idiots.

*We are to have **no fellowship** with darkness. We can't "dialogue" with any professing Christian who's in open rebellion against the Word of God. We can't "dialogue" with anybody who is deceiving and misleading the Body of Christ on any sin while claiming to be a Christian! (also see I Corinthians 5)[194]*

Mefferd is exactly right. The subversion she identifies, along with the illicit fellowship with progressives whose only purpose is to defeat Christians and lead others astray, should be clear to all Christians. But American Christianity has already surrendered so much truth, that in increasing numbers and with increasing frequency, we are losing the ability, the discernment, to even recognize that we've been duped.

But, in case I'm somehow cheering you up, it's actually much worse than all that. Many professing American Christians aren't just satisfied with surrendering to anti-Christian attacks and joining in fellowship with homosexual activists and other heretics. As mentioned, it's become en vogue for an increasing number of these apostates to join in with progressives in attacking actual Christians who won't surrender—those of us who choose to fight back.

Cal Thomas is a syndicated columnist and professional pundit. He is also a professing Christian. After Kim Davis, the aforementioned Rowen County, Kentucky civil servant, went to jail rather than defy her faith by issuing marriage licenses to homosexuals pretending to be married, Thomas wrote a column attacking, not the closed-minded homosexual bigots attacking Davis, but his fellow Christian instead:

And what, you might ask, pleases God the most? It is the sharing of His salvation message with members of that other kingdom, which has the additional benefit for those who accept it of changing their outlook on some of those very things most Christians believe. In other words, changed hearts are usually followed by changed minds.

Kim Davis chose the wrong issue for her "martyrdom." Amazingbible. org lists more than 600 sins mentioned in the Bible, including adultery,

> *fornication, divorce and lying. If Davis wants to be consistent, she would refuse a marriage license for anyone who has sinned, which would limit the number of applications to zero since "all have sinned and fallen short of the glory of God." (Romans 3:23)*
>
> *Davis had four options: Issue the license, have someone else issue it, resign, or go to jail. She chose to go to jail, which, unlike Rosa Parks to whom she is being compared, makes her look more like a religious fanatic than a martyr. Removal of her name from the marriage license is a good compromise.[195]*

Thomas's logic (or lack thereof) is fatally misguided. Why assume that a Christian cannot both share the Gospel with others and take a bold, sacrificial stand against objective evil? Why presume that, since there are other evils in the world, one mustn't fight any of them? Isn't that exactly the logical extreme of what Thomas is doing here? While Thomas may not see the urgency in fighting this particular evil, there are many called by God to do so. Rosa Parks wasn't viewed as hero by most when she engaged in civil disobedience to challenge the objective evil that is racism. But she now is. Indeed, it can be argued that history will ultimately, and similarly, count Kim Davis the reluctant hero for her fearless stand against wickedness in much the same way.

Moreover, what evils did Parks fail to fight when she chose to focus on resisting laws forcing her and all other blacks to the back of the bus? Like Davis, she chose her battles. Thomas engages a bit of hypocrisy here when one considers that his entire career has been based on sharing his opinion in written form on moral right vs. moral wrong. If he were to follow his own advice, he should stop finding "common ground" with foul-mouthed extremists like Bob Beckel (a liberal, former Fox News contributor who claims to be a Christian), stop calling out other individuals and organizations on matters he perceives to be wrong or evil, stop arguing politics, stop arguing that homosexuality is disordered (even as he apparently insists that others capitulate to the homosexualist agenda) and focus entirely on, as he describes it, winning people to Christ.[196,197,198,199]

Thomas's column is additionally instructive throughout as he maintains that America was never a Christian nation to begin with. This, since slavery was once legal and women were once denied the privilege to vote alongside men. Using this reasoning, one wonders if Thomas believes the Jews were ever God's chosen people? After all, the Israelites had slaves and they didn't allow women to own property (normally), much less vote. They also had a history of disobeying God and systemically engaging in the vilest of wickedness.

If you, like Cal Thomas, are a Christian who willfully chooses not to resist the evil onslaught under which America now suffers, would you at least be so courteous as to take a step back and stop providing aid and comfort to the enemies of God who seek to destroy those of us who refuse to surrender?

It goes without saying that many folks (Christian and otherwise) are reluctant to fight back against the anti-Christians for sake of their own safety and financial security. Still, others have, rather than standing on the Word of Truth, chosen to, instead, guzzle the progressive Kool Aid altogether. For those who are grounded in truth but remain yet afraid to push back, we must have understanding. God's enemies—particularly the homosexualists—are extremely aggressive and becoming more and more so all the time.

Consider, for instance, this brief transcript of Christian call to the *Rush Limbaugh Show* in August of 2012. The caller relayed to El Rushbo a frightening encounter she had with one such homosexualist:

> CALLER: Hi, Rush. It's so good to be on your program today calling from beautiful Lakeville, Minnesota. And I'm calling because I am a conservative Christian stay-at-home mom who believes in liberty and freedom of speech and freedom of religion. Three nights ago I had a gentleman come knocking at my door wanting me to sign a petition that would be against the voter amendment which will appear on Minnesota ballots in November that defines marriage as one man and one woman and then also the voter ID. And when I told him that I could not sign that petition because I, as a Christian, believe in one man and one woman as the definition of marriage, this young man literally went berserk. He flipped out and got so angry to the point where, even his countenance, I felt like I was just looking at a very evil person. And then he started accusing me that I was for the suppression of women and just going way off the wall. It was profound.
>
> RUSH: What? What? How in the world is that—
>
> CALLER: And then I came back to him and said, "You know, I do support your right and your liberty to express your viewpoint. And then I also have my viewpoint." And then he really went off the wall and started yelling and screaming and shouting and waving his arms. I started to fear for my safety, and I told him promptly that I was gonna have to end this conversation.[200]

Keep in mind that the spirit of homosexuality is exactly that—a spirit. And it's not a pleasant one either. When one is given over to a reprobate mind (as Scripture says of those who continue unrepentant homosexual behavior), deception and anger become central aspects of that individual's life. Hence, anti-Christians frequently lack any real level of fear for potential consequences for intimidating and bullying others. Our culture more frequently berates the victims (in this case Rush's caller) rather than the victimizers (the homosexualist seeking a petition signature).

Evil's aggressive nature, coupled with many Christians' timidity, sets off a vicious cycle: the more aggressive (and outspoken) the anti-Christians, the more timid (and silent) many Christians seem to become. And the more timid Christians become, the more aggressive the anti-Christians become. Christians are feeding the beast by failing to respond with truth, in love. Others have made the same observation.

LifeSiteNews, for example, interviewed Peter Kreeft, a Catholic Boston College professor, in June of 2013. Kreeft noted that Christians seem to be losing the battle for our culture:

> Asked about the simultaneous rise of militant Islam and the homosexual activist movement despite their opposing ideologies, Kreeft replied: "They're the only two movements in Western civilization that will fight and die for their beliefs."

> "It is an amazing paradox that they're opposites in almost every way, and yet they're similar in that they will still fight," added Kreeft. "Christians are supposed to fight too, the notion of spiritual warfare, the true meaning of jihad—a war against sin rather than flesh and blood. This is central to Christianity and we've lost it, and therefore opposite forces are entering the vacuum." ...

Asked specifically about the reason for the rise of the homosexual activist movement, Dr. Kreeft replied:

> Because we became sheep. We said, "Abuse us. We're polite. We'll smile at you. We are tolerant of everything." When people are that way, someone who has principles, bad or good, enters. We so worship equality that we are afraid to be different, to be distinctive, to have a distinctive message. And equality is a good defensive weapon, but it has no offense in it. We need equal rights to protect ourselves, but we need something much deeper than equality: We need distinctiveness, we need identity. And if we abandon that, others will come in and take over.

Kreeft stressed, however, that in confronting homosexuality Christians are being loving, in the truest definition of the word.

> "Love fights. Love cares. Love discriminates. And therefore there is in Scripture, very clearly, a thing called the 'wrath of God'. God hates all enemies of love as the doctor hates the cancer that's killing his beloved patient. If you really love a human being you will hate all the dehumanizing forces that are harmful to that human being," he said.

"If on the other hand you don't really love a human being but just toler-ate a human being, then you will hate nothing," Kreeft added. "So, love and hate go together. Love of a human being, no matter who he is, and hate of a human being, no matter who he is, are exact opposites, they are black and white. But love of all humans and hate of all sins— that goes together."[201]

So, while we must understand why many Christians choose to surrender, and even "tolerate" evil, we must condone neither. American Christians will either continue to forfeit our once-great nation, our temporal future (and, by exten-sion, our children), to the forces of evil, or, as Christ commands, we will stand firm against today's burgeoning culture of institutionalized sin—a culture that seeks to destroy all—even if it means losing everything we have.[202]

Some Christians might answer, "But the Bible told us this would happen in the end times. We shouldn't worry about the culture and, instead, should focus on simply bringing the Gospel message to others." That's a misnomer. The two are not mutually exclusive. They are one and the same. While it is true that we must further the good news of the Gospel, we must also remember that, cen-tral to the Gospel, is the admonition to heed the full counsel of Scripture. Yes, "the good news" is the greatest news ever. But I also have some bad news. The other side will never allow Christians (Satan never has) to retreat within the sanctuary of the Church and privately worship our Lord in peace. The anti-Christians have placed a bead directly over the heart of the Church. They in-tend to take us out unless we fearlessly return a heavy volley of truth artillery.

And it's not just churches. Christian colleges and non-profit organizations are likewise in the enemy's crosshairs.

Think I'm overreacting?

In a July 14, 2015 article in the *Atlantic* headlined, "Gay Marriage and the Fu-ture of Evangelical Colleges," University of Tampa professor David R. Wheeler asks, "Now that same-sex couples have the right to wed, will higher-ed insti-tutions that condemn LGBT students still be eligible for federal funding?"[203]

Wheeler was not alone in asking that. "As cultural evolution on the issue of LGBT rights continues to accelerate, it's inevitable that some Americans will start asking hard questions about whether it makes sense to allocate scarce public resources to institutions that are not only anti-gay, but proud of it," opined anti-Christian bigot Barry Lynn, of Americans United for Separation of Church and State. "For starters, can federally supported educational institu-tions bar married same-sex couples from living together in student housing? I doubt it," he added.[204]

In other words, Christian universities must together embrace and facilitate homosexual sin, or lose, at once, both tax-exempt status and access to all students who choose to fund their education via federal loans and grants (which is most of them).

This presents quite a conundrum. It's also a test. Christian universities must either obey God, disobey man and suffer unsavory temporal consequences, or obey man, sell their souls for mammon and suffer a-little-more-than-unsavory eternal consequence.

This is where faith comes in.

German theologian Dietrich Bonhoeffer was a man who faced the gallows for faithfully opposing the Nazi Holocaust. He once wrote, "For faith is only real when there is obedience, never without it, and faith only becomes faith in the act of obedience."[205]

It's really not that complicated. The Christian university that chooses the path of least resistance and conforms to the world—that is, disobeys God and adopts the world's morally relative (read: unbiblical) standards (or lack thereof) on sex and sexuality—immediately becomes at enmity with God. The Christian university that intentionally turns a blind eye to sexual immorality of any kind, or otherwise allows and recognizes sin-based same-sex "marriage," ceases to be a Christian university and, instead, becomes an apostate university—a university better identified as "Christian in name only."

As Jesus admonished, "Enter through the narrow gate. For wide is the gate and broad is the road that leads to destruction, and many enter through it. But small is the gate and narrow the road that leads to life, and only a few find it." (Matthew 7:13-14 – New International Version)

Indeed, in the context of whether Christian universities will capitulate on sodomy-based "marriage," the path of least resistance is the broad road that stems from the wide gate and leads to destruction.

And right now it looks like many Christian universities will choose that destruction—will choose to surrender yet again.

By way of example, and to its shame, formerly Christian Baylor University, located in Waco, Texas, has chosen the path of least resistance. This hits especially close to home for me. I was born in Waco and my parents both attended Baylor. Two of my uncles graduated from Baylor Law, and my grandfather, J. Dell Barber, was a Baylor benefactor. In fact, he has a room in the law school named after him and, before he died, set up the Bertha J. Barber memorial scholarship fund in honor of my great-grandmother.

Reported Baptist News Global:

Baptist-affiliated Baylor University has quietly removed a ban on "homosexual acts" from its sexual conduct code. ...

Lori Fogleman, assistant vice president for media communications, said the change is part of an ongoing review "to ensure that the university has the necessary policies and processes in place to comply with the many legal and ethical mandates to which universities are subject as institutions." She said a review of the sexual conduct policy was contemplated for a couple of years, because officials didn't believe the language in the old policy "reflected Baylor's caring community."[206]

And so, under Baylor University's new apostasy, it is somehow "caring" to affirm students, faculty and staff in a mortal sin that, in the absence of repentance, will lead them to eternal separation from God—to destruction.

It breaks my heart to be so closely affiliated with a Christian university that has so lost its way.

A colleague of mine once praised yet another for being a person who "applies biblical ethics in ways both faithful and nuanced, both orthodox and relevant." I'm not exactly sure what that means, but, in my experience, and in the context of biblical exegesis, the term "nuanced" is usually invoked to rationalize some unbiblical behavior or otherwise cave on some fixed biblical principle.

"Nuance" is the bucket of dirt used to muddy crystal clear living waters.

And how does the faithful, Bible-believing Christian remain "both orthodox and relevant"? How can a Christian be both in the world and of the world? To the world, biblical orthodoxy is, in every way imaginable, irrelevant. Biblical orthodoxy represents absolute truth, who is Christ, and the world denies that Truth.

It hates Him in fact.

Pastor Brian Houston, founder of the popular Hillsong movement, said in 2014:

It can be challenging for churches to stay relevant. ... Many mainstream churches upheld what they would believe is the long established view of what the Bible says about homosexuality. But the world has changed around and about them. ...

So the world's changing and we want to stay relevant as a church. So that's a vexing thing. You think, "How do we not become a pariah?"[207]

Pastor Houston, respectfully, you have it exactly backwards. We, as Christians, are obliged to become pariahs. We must pick up our cross and follow Christ, the ultimate pariah—the one and only God-man who was such a pariah, in fact, that He was scourged, mocked, spat upon and tortured to death on a tree so that all who are willing to become pariahs right along with him, might have eternal life.

No, to remain faithful, Christian universities should abandon efforts to become "nuanced" and "relevant."

It's a fool's errand otherwise.

If Christian universities wish to remain faithful, they must, instead, become pariahs.

They must obey God.

Still, I'm not about to sprout a wellspring of optimism that they will. Many universities and organizations founded on the rock of Christ have long since become compromised, and many have already surrendered completely.

As bad as Barack Obama, Hillary Clinton and other of God's overt enemies may be, it is the furtive anti-Christians (false prophets and teachers) infiltrating Christian congregations, universities and organizations, and assuming the mantel of "Christian leader," who comprise the even larger threat. They damage the Church and her mission and lead people astray with various and sundry heresies and blasphemies, all while undergirded by false authority.

In a November 2014 post, *Juicy Ecumenism*, a blog of the Institute of Religion & Democracy, provided a salient example of just how much damage these false teachers can do:

> The *"culture war is, finally, at long last, coming to a close,"* declared the male-to-female transgender Baptist minister Allyson Robinson on November 6 in Washington, DC's National City Christian Church (NCCC). West Point graduate Robinson's declaration of Lesbian, Gay, Bisexual, and Transgendered (LGBT) victory, surprising in more ways than one, introduced an astonishingly assertive conference rejecting millennia-old Christian sexual ethics.
>
> Robinson, a former Patriot missile battery commander who made a 2006 *"gender transition"* to *"health and...wholeness,"* opened the November 6-8 conference with about 150 attendees of the *"bible-based, Gospel-centered"* pro-LGBT Reformation Project (RP). Allyson wanted to share *"this historic moment when...that which seemed impossible just a few short years ago looks...inevitable"* concerning same-sex *"marriage"* (SSM) and other LGBT agendas. Why remain in a church that *"still refuses to acknowledge"* LGBT *"truths,"* Robinson questioned, for such churches *"are dying"* and will *"rot in their own graves,"* as if LGBT affirmation had not led to past church decline. ...
>
> In an *"incredible parallel"* praised by Vines, Christian ethicist David Gushee closed the conference on November 8 with an address comparing LGBT individuals and Jews, thereby adding another moral analogy to the

common "homophobia"/racism equation. Each "small minority group... was for almost 2000 years the object of a tragically destructive...unchrist-like body of Christian tradition," Gushee analyzed. LGBT individuals, he however conceded, had not faced genocide.

LGBT "sexual minorities" have faced a "teaching of contempt...grounded in...a relatively small number of biblical texts," now "in the process of being discredited." This teaching "ascribed particular vices to LGBT people, including sexual degeneracy, especially against children," Gushee stated while ignoring documented homosexuality-child abuse links. Gushee, however, somewhat contradictorily noted that this teaching also comes from the "very center of Christianity: scripture, tradition, and the leaders of the church, generation after generation."

"I truly apologize that it took me twenty years to figure out" the "very simple truth" concerning LGBT approval, Gushee stated. Gushee's lesbian sister had recently prompted his abandonment of Christian orthodoxy concerning homosexuality. "Celibacy outside of lifetime covenantal marriage" should apply to all Christians, he now concluded, and "is...essential to the well-being of adults and children." How homosexual couple parenting lacking a biological parent/gender role model or the transgenderism of Robinson, a still-married father of four, affected child "well-being," Gushee did not say.[208]

Juicy Ecumenism published another post in August 2015, which observed that anti-Christians are not merely satisfied with being part of the Church and undermining it from within. They intend to conquer and destroy it altogether. The enemies of God, particularly the homosexualist lobby, will settle for nothing short of totalitarianism:

"We are Coming for the Institution, and like a mighty river, we will sweep it away with the might of our love," said Rev. Sara Thompson Tweedy at the close of her remarks at the "Gather at the River" conference held in San Antonio for progressive United Methodists. The heavily LGTBQ-focused conference was sponsored by Reconciling Ministries Network and the Methodist Federation for Social Action.[209]

The organized Church's ill-advised surrender strategy has been a total disaster for American Christians.

But can we undo the damage done?

Chapter 21

What Exactly Can Christians Do to Recover Lost Ground?

Admittedly, thus far we've focused on many of the negatives. We've covered much of what's wrong with today's America and how the enemies of God have successfully waged war on Christianity in general, and certain Christians in particular.

But breathe easy. There's always hope. As Christians, we always have hope. Our hope lies in Christ and Christ alone. It's all about Him.

Let's now focus on some of what we as Christians can do to change things from the way they are, to the way they should be.

To my fellow American Christians, I say this: We will never win in a vacuum. You—we all—must enter the field of battle if we wish to realize even a semblance of victory. We must fight back if we hope to change the current trajectory—if we want to avoid having our children and grandchildren suffer under the heavy hand of government-sanctioned evil.

No more mealy-mouthed compromise. No more weakness, only meekness, which is restrained strength. Unless you are willing to walk them toward truth, you should avoid having too much fellowship with professing Christians who voice the lie that Christians must focus on helping the poor and winning people to Christ alone. Yes, these are worthy causes and we must engage them, but Christ requires so much more. Fighting for the truth is helping the poor. It *is* winning people to Jesus. It shows the world that we actually believe what we profess—that there is objective Truth and He is Christ our Lord.

Christians, we must enter the culture war. We must address America's rampant spiritual warfare at every opportunity.

If we ignore the battle, we lose the war.

What follows is what we must realize, what our worldview must be, and what we must do in order to win.

It's a War

I had breakfast with the Rev. John Peter Gabriel Muhlenberg back in 2013. Well, not the real Peter Muhlenberg, but a preacher friend of mine named Travis Witt. Travis does a powerful impersonation of the Revolutionary War-time pastor-patriot at churches and other venues around the country.

At breakfast, Travis and I discussed the man Muhlenberg and what he stood for.[210]

One early Sunday morning in January 1776, Rev. Muhlenberg was preaching what seemed his normal weekly sermon. His Scripture for the day focused on Ecclesiastics 3, which observes, in part, "To everything there is a season, a time for every purpose under heaven." Muhlenberg continued: "In the language of the holy writ, there was a time for all things, a time to preach and a time to pray, but those times have passed away."

With his voice reaching a dramatic crescendo and his congregation now captivated, a fiery Pastor Muhlenberg then declared: "There is a time to fight, and that time has now come!" He then tore away his clerical robes, revealing, underneath, the crisply pressed uniform of a Colonial Army officer.

His congregation gasped.

Pastor Muhlenberg then marched to the rear of the church building, turned and shook the walls, declaring, "Who among you is with me?" That very day, 300 brave men from his relatively small church stood with Peter Muhlenberg to become the 8th Virginia Regiment.

Frederick Muhlenberg, the good pastor's brother, questioned, in a letter, whether it was Peter's place to fight. Peter wrote back with words as true today as they were then: "I am a Clergyman, it is true," he wrote, "but I am a member of the Society as well as the poorest Layman, and my Liberty is as dear to me as any man, shall I then sit still and enjoy myself at Home when the best Blood of the Continent is spilling? ... [S]o far am I from thinking that I act wrong, I am convinced it is my duty to do so and duty I owe to God and my country."

I think Peter Muhlenberg set an example for each of us to follow. I think we all owe a duty to God, country and one another to stand up and fight for liberty, regardless of our station in life.

Like then, we find ourselves today in the midst of a revolutionary war. Not a war with guns, but a war of ideals. We battle not against a foreign king, but a man among us who thinks he's king. We struggle not against a tyrannical foreign government, but a government of our own making—a government that tilts toward tyranny.

We desperately need revival in this country—spiritual, cultural and political revival. It's time for the next Great Awakening.

The early colonialists like Muhlenberg came together in meetings and looked to God, not government, to guide public affairs. These boldly committed leaders understood that God has given us certain unalienable rights: life, liberty and the pursuit of happiness, and that any government that transgresses against what God gave us has disqualified itself to lead. It has become tyrannical.

Today we face unprecedented threats to our faith and freedom as the government is forcing religious organizations and businesses to provide abortion drugs through the Obamacare mandate. This is only the tip of the iceberg (as I have shown throughout the book). Our basic liberties and moral foundations are under violent assault.

We have come to a critical crossroads. The future of America will be determined in our lifetime by our actions. What we do now will echo throughout history.

Like Muhlenberg, I ask, "Who among you is with me?" We need an army of citizen activists—peaceful warriors for Christ, ready to take back America. Take a stand for righteousness and justice and join the next American Revolution.

John Adams, our second president, once said, "Our Constitution was made only for a moral and religious people. It is wholly inadequate to the government of any other."[211]

Indeed, in contrast with the deeply held religious and moral values embraced by our Founding Fathers—men like Peter Muhlenberg—today's America is governed by an "immoral" and "irreligious" chief executive. Barack Obama is the King George of secular socialism and Hillary Clinton seeks to become Queen Elizabeth. They seek to undermine—or more precisely, to altogether dismantle—the American exceptionalism that, hitherto, has been fundamentally woven throughout our national fabric. They aspire to the lowest common denominator. They seek to uproot Ronald Reagan's "shining city on a hill" and relocate the "land of the free and the home of the brave" to a much lower altitude, alongside those Euro-Marxist nations they so admire and wistfully desire to emulate.

Yes, for everything there is a season.

Now is the season to fight.

Many American Christians will object to my martial language and the call to fight. These are professing Christians who've already surrendered, so let's ignore them, shall we? Even so, still others might be hesitant to engage in the battle due to fear. Many Christians might especially be afraid to ruffle anti-Christian feathers as our lost friends maintain the lion's share of control over waning culture. We must overcome these fears.

We can, and we shall.

Fear Not the Enemies of God

"For it has been granted to you on behalf of Christ not only to believe in him, but also to suffer for him." (Philippians 1:29 New International Version)

Defense of God's design for natural marriage—along with the God-given, constitutional freedom of conscience to decline participation in and, thereby, endorsement of, its unnatural and sin-based counterfeit, so-called gay "marriage"—is now America's premier civil rights struggle. I know from whence I speak (as previously mentioned), as, over ten years ago, I was fired for taking my own stand.

Rather than rolling over and accepting this injustice, I sued in federal court. God used that situation not only to bless me and my family with a significant monetary settlement, but to place me on the front lines in the fast-escalating war against religious liberty. I share this not to boast, but, rather, to encourage you—to illustrate God's marvelous faithfulness in my own life.

As Christians, we are called to stand our ground, in love, against all wickedness. We do so not because we are righteous—we are not—but because of Christ's righteousness in us. As Christ-followers, we are to follow Christ. We are to stand for His truths. When we do, and while we may face persecution, He will ultimately honor our faithfulness for His own glory and purpose.

It's very ugly out there, and it is constantly getting worse. The cases are piling up. We've now seen dozens of bakers, photographers, florists, innkeepers, magistrates, county clerks and other people involved in various vocations surrounding marriage suffer persecution for merely declining to become complicit in sin. Christians are being financially ruined and have even served jail time for refusing to lend their time, talents, gifts and abilities to sanction unnatural marriage rituals.

Let us be abundantly clear once more. Same-sex "marriage" is evil. It is sin. It bears repeating that all good things come from God the Father, and all wickedness comes from the father of lies. If God designed biblical marriage and natural human sexuality, and He did, then we are left no doubt as to who designed its counterfeit—as to who fabricated counter-biblical gay "marriage" and otherwise perverted God's perfect purposes for human sexuality.

As faithful Christians, we cannot, indeed we must not, endorse or participate in that which God calls evil. "Woe to those who call evil good and good evil" (see Isaiah 5:20). We must reject sin.

There have been a number of good and well-intentioned folks who, rather than participating in these pagan gay "marriage" rituals, have either resigned employment or, if business owners, closed their doors altogether. While this is admirable, I submit that, if and when you, dear Christian, are placed in a situation that compels you to choose between obedience to God's just laws or man's unjust laws, that you not only refuse to obey the unjust laws, but refuse to quit.

Stand your ground.

I suggest that when any Christian business owner, magistrate or county clerk is told that he must participate in a sinful gay "marriage" ceremony, that he not only refuse to do so, but that he refuse to step down. Do not resign your post. Force the government to overtly persecute you—to take punitive action against you for your righteous stand. Even if you face chains.

Pray for courage, and God will provide it.

The Apostle Paul set the example when, while chained to a wall in a Roman prison, he wrote the following to the church in Philippi:

> Now I want you to know, brothers and sisters, that what has happened to me has actually served to advance the gospel. As a result, it has become clear throughout the whole palace guard and to everyone else that I am in chains for Christ. And because of my chains, most of the brothers and sisters have become confident in the Lord and dare all the more to proclaim the gospel without fear. (Philippians 1:12-14 – New International Version)

Not only did Paul supernaturally face anti-Christian persecution without fear. He faced it with great joy:

> Yes, and I will continue to rejoice, for I know that through your prayers and God's provision of the Spirit of Jesus Christ what has happened to me will turn out for my deliverance. I eagerly expect and hope that I will in no way be ashamed, but will have sufficient courage so that now as always Christ will be exalted in my body, whether by life or by death. For to me, to live is Christ and to die is gain. (Philippians 1:18-21 – New International Version)

After several magistrates in North Carolina stepped down rather than being forced to preside over same-sex "marriage" rituals, Mat Staver said the following: "I appreciate the conviction of these magistrates, but rather than resign they should remain at their post. Liberty Counsel will represent them, but once they resign there is not much we can do to help."[212]

Staver noted that in 2004, after the Massachusetts Supreme Judicial Court unconstitutionally "imposed same-sex marriage on the Commonwealth, Catholic Charities ceased its adoption ministry because it refused to place children in same-sex households":

> *"The commitment to Church teachings and conscience is commendable, but Catholic Charities should not have voluntarily ceased its adoption ministry. If the government wants to impose an intolerant agenda on people of faith and trample their religious convictions then let it happen in public for all to see. I cannot believe the American people will long tolerate an intolerant agenda," said Staver.*

> *"Where would the Civil Rights movement be if Dr. Martin Luther King, Jr., voluntarily went home when he faced opposition? Where would we be today if Rosa Parks had voluntarily moved to the back of the bus? The quest for religious freedom was the reason America was born. We cannot voluntarily give up this unalienable right," concluded Staver.* [213]

As Paul concluded:

> *Whatever happens, conduct yourselves in a manner worthy of the gospel of Christ ... without being frightened in any way by those who oppose you. This is a sign to them that they will be destroyed, but that you will be saved—and that by God. For it has been granted to you on behalf of Christ not only to believe in him, but also to suffer for him. ... (Philippians 1:27-29 – New International Version)*

When standing for truth, be not ashamed. Be of great courage and great cheer no matter what trials you may face.

And be blessed for the opportunity.

Indeed, we have nothing to fear in pushing back against the anti-Christians because God is fighting for us. Still, what needless fear remains might be drastically diminished yet if American churches would join the fight, instead of languishing on the sidelines and disseminating the "gospel of nice," over the Gospel of Christ.

Churches Need to Get "Political"

Churches, pastors and priests need to get "political" as a matter of course (and by "get political," we mean engage the culture with grace and truth, as salt and light). It should become second nature. With God's many admonitions to do so, it's no small wonder that many American churches still need persuading.

And when they do get political?

Well, if God is for us, who can be against us?

Consider, for instance, how thousands of pastors across America in 2012 (and thousands more since) have called the left's blind bluff. They have challenged the empty words of "separation of church and state" and have handily defeated the progressives in one particular fight, at least.

Yes, "separation" still applies, but only insofar as it requires the state to remain separate from the Church. That is to say, that government still is not to interfere with the free exercise of either speech or religion.

As we briefly covered earlier, for decades, hard-left anti-Christian groups like the ACLU, People for the American Way (PFAW) and Barry Lynn's Americans United (AU) have employed a cynical disinformation scheme intended to intimidate clergy into silence on issues of morality, culture and Christian civic involvement—issues that are not political so much as they have been politicized, issues that are inherently "religious."

Churches often cave to progressives at the first sign of a threat or intimidation. But in one particular instance a few years back, they didn't clam up at all. The results were (and continue to be) both enlightening and encouraging.

AU sent 60,000 letters to churches across the nation in 2012 warning pastors, priests and rabbis that "[i]f the IRS determines that your house of worship has engaged in unlawful intervention, it can revoke the institution's tax-exempt status."[214]

That was a lie.

Despite hundreds of thousands of threatening letters sent by these liberal outfits (and as many complaints filed with the IRS) not a single church has ever lost tax-exemption for socio-political activity—zip, zero, nada. Not even for endorsing candidates from the pulpit. The left has cried wolf far too many times. No one will come running. Especially not the IRS.

That's because churches, unlike other nonprofit organizations, don't need a letter of tax exemption from the Internal Revenue Service. Churches are constitutionally tax-exempt simply by virtue of existence. It's automatic. The only way the IRS could revoke a church's tax-exempt status would be to disband the Church, which, obviously, the government has no authority to do. It's simple. Pastors, if you get a letter from the ACLU, PFAW or AU, I suggest a singular use for it: bird cage liner.

Keeping all this in mind, something I've long expected has finally occurred. After AU sent out its letters, the IRS ran up the white flag. That bureaucratic bully we all love to hate announced that, for the indefinite future, it is "holding any potential church audits in abeyance," for violating its arbitrary "no politicking" rule.[215]

This rule stems from the blatantly unconstitutional "Johnson Amendment," which, in 1954, was introduced by then-Sen. Lyndon B. Johnson. At the time, Johnson was facing opposition from Christians and anti-communists. He pushed the rule through in an effort to muzzle them.

NBC News later reported that the IRS tried to walk back those remarks after pressure from the media and other anti-Christian forces pressured it to do so:

> *The IRS, however, isn't acknowledging that it has stopped enforcing the ban on candidate endorsements by officials of 501(c)3 charitable organizations.*
>
> *In response to queries from NBC News, the IRS disavowed comments by a regional official of its division overseeing tax-exempt organizations, who said last month that the agency was "holding any potential church audits in abeyance" while it revises its regulations in light of the 2009 ruling.*
>
> *Dean Patterson, a spokesman for the IRS, said the official "misspoke," adding: "The IRS continues to run a balanced program that follows up on potential non-compliance, while ensuring the appropriate oversight and review to determine that compliance activities are necessary and appropriate."*[216]

So, unfortunately, Johnson's scheme has achieved much success and likely will continue to do so—even as it lacks constitutional authority to yank any church's tax exemption for "politicking."

But there is more to the story. Since 2008, the Christian legal organization Alliance Defending Freedom (ADF) has spearheaded a First Amendment exercise called "Pulpit Freedom Sunday." Since then, thousands of pastors across America have boldly exercised their guaranteed constitutional rights by addressing "political" issues from the pulpit. This has included directly endorsing candidates. These pastors have dared the IRS to come after them. And in 2012, the IRS balked.

Essentially, the goal of the ADF initiative was twofold. First, it was hoped that if the IRS tried, somehow, to revoke a church's tax-exempt status, that church could sue and, once and for all, have the Johnson Amendment ruled unconstitutional.

The second possibility was that, rather than having the "no politicking" rule completely thrown out, the IRS would choose, instead, the path of least resistance—that it would simply do nothing. It chose door No. 2 in 2012. Not only did the IRS not do anything, it threw in the towel.

The next step would be to repeal the toothless Johnson Amendment. This would do away with any residual confusion. A Republican-led Congress and president could do just that... especially if churches across America unified and demanded it.

So what will it take to awaken American churches and pastors?

In 1980, Moral Majority leader Jerry Falwell, along with other venerable Christian leaders, was central to placing Ronald Reagan in the White House. Today's socio-political stage is strikingly similar. Pastors can achieve something similar if they unite.

So why aren't they? Where are America's pastors and why are they silent? There are hundreds of thousands of pastors across the U.S. and yet they largely have chosen to muzzle themselves when it comes to cultural and political matters. This isn't an honorable or "civil" thing to do. Rather, it is a unilateral surrender of the battlefield. The enemies of God haven't stopped their fight and thus they now run rampant and unopposed. All of us will stand before God someday and we will be held to account for our actions. How will America's pastors answer for their decision to give up on opposing evil?

So pastors, stand up and be counted. You pulled away the IRS muzzle in 2012. The choice is clear.

You know what to do.

Now go and do it.

Still, fighting back against the anti-Christians requires more than just pastors and churches as a body. It also means taking care of our own houses.

Which means, in large part, raising godly children, full of grace and truth. They are the future.

Make Godly Children

"I do not want to drive across a bridge designed by an engineer who believed the numbers in structural stress models are relative truths." – R.C. Sproul

I was delighted to speak at Faith Christian Center in Arlington, Texas in 2013. I joined that community of believers in celebrating the 25th anniversary of the church's affiliated school, St. Paul's Preparatory Academy. The topic of my discussion was "How to Raise Christian Children in Today's Culture."

As I prepared my remarks it occurred to me that raising children to both love and faithfully serve the Lord and Creator of the universe, Jesus Christ, is not unlike a primary goal of the late Dr. Jerry Falwell, founder of Liberty University, where I am blessed to serve as associate dean of Liberty Law.

In 1971, Dr. Falwell launched LU—now the world's largest Christian university—and quickly got about the business of "training champions for Christ."

I submit that "raising Christian children in today's culture" and "training champions for Christ" are one and the same, and that both fruitful endeavors stem from the same rich soil.

Truth.

But what is today's culture exactly? What is a champion for Christ? And, perhaps most importantly, what—or Who—is Truth?

Merriam-Webster defines "champion" as "someone who fights or speaks publicly in support of a person, belief, cause, etc." It is not merely a passing suggestion that Christian parents and educators train champions for Christ. It's a command given us by God Himself: "Start children off on the way they should go [train them], and even when they are old they will not turn from it." (Proverbs 22:6 – New International Version)

We faithful are additionally tasked with an unambiguous calling on the way we (and our children) should go: "[Jesus] said to them, 'Go into all the world and preach the gospel to all creation. Whoever believes and is baptized will be saved, but whoever does not believe will be condemned.'" (Mark 16:15 – New International Version)

The Apostle Paul admonishes in Romans 1:16 that we should not be "ashamed of the gospel," but, rather, should "[d]o [our] best to present [ourselves] to God as one approved, a worker who does not need to be ashamed and who correctly handles the word of truth." (2 Timothy 2:15 – New International Version)

In addition to leading by example, this means steeping Christian children and young people in the "word of truth"—the Holy Scriptures—and equipping them, in love, to champion (to "fight or speak publicly in support of") the infallible, unchangeable and absolute truths found therein.

This is so even when the absolute truths of Scripture have become unpopular in a world that prefers the absolute lie of relativism.

Indeed, though some may wander the prodigal's path for a time, and still others may remain lost, we can only then—having obeyed the command to train our children in the way they should go—release, hope, pray and have faith that the Holy Spirit will be that eternal light to illuminate temporal life's perilous path—that Christ will be a lamp unto the feet of our beloved.

Jesus commands His followers to be His hands and feet—to be salt and light in a rotting world that loves darkness. (Matthew 5:13-16)

True, salt preserves, but in an open wound, it also burns. Today's relativist culture is an open wound.

True, light's bright glare can be illuminating to those eager to see. But it is also blinding to those whose eyes have become adjusted to darkness.

When the light of Christ is shined, it sends lovers of evil scurrying for the shadows.

For this reason, Christ warned, "You will be hated by everyone because of me, but the one who stands firm to the end will be saved." (Matthew 10:22 – New International Version)

In a culture that slaughters the unborn, mocks purity, celebrates sexual sin and makes a joke out of the institution of marriage by imagining sin-based counterfeits, it remains a daunting task for Christian parents to raise children with both the courage and conviction to stand unashamed for God's truth. From an earthly standpoint, it seems counterintuitive to both welcome and find joy in being hated by the world.

Even more, for young people who might prefer popularity over principle—at least for now—the prospect of being "hated by everyone" lacks a certain level of appeal.

That's OK. Stand strong, parents. Persevere.

Because, ultimately, that's the price of admission.

It boils down to instilling in our children a biblically orthodox Christian worldview—that is to say, absolute truth. Anything else is nothing at all. Anything else is relativism, which holds that there is no absolute truth and imagines, absolutely, that, as theological giant Francis Schaeffer often described, "Man is the measure of all things."

As history has proven, when man is the measure of all things, all things can, and usually do, go horribly wrong. Consider, for example, the hundreds of millions killed under the relativist regimes of Hitler, Stalin, Mao, et al.

Indeed, train your children in "the way they should go, and even when they are old they will not turn from it." They will use God's Word, the true measure of all things, as they endeavor to actually measure all things.

Funny thing, absolute truth. It's absolute. It's like a buoy pulled beneath the lake's surface and fixed tight with rope. With time, and against the tide of Christ's love, that rope—the lie of relativism—eventually rots. It snaps under its own weakness, hurling the buoy, truth, from cold darkness to warm sunlight.

Even if taught Scripture your children, like the prodigal son, may be pulled under and tied down for a time by relativism's glittery allure. But when the relativist rope rots, fear not, for those who have been fastened to "the way, the truth and the life"—who is Christ—will burst back into the light.

And then what champions they will be.

Raising godly children, firmly grounded in the Word of Truth, is not simply critical because it ensures our most precious people will have eternal salvation with Christ, but because it prepares this next generation of Christ-followers to continue the war against the anti-Christ left. The enemies of God will never rest. They continue to relentlessly target our children for conversion to evil and separation from God. This conversion strategy includes using information operations—messaging designed to influence and deceive—to sway our children (and people at large).

This is another area where Christians have failed, an area we don't even understand. Christians need to fight back in the arena of information operations. This necessarily includes correctly identifying the enemies of God, not just as our opponents, but as our spiritual enemies—enemies for whom we continue to pray and love.

Information and Influence Operations

In 2007, and with that same nauseating arrogance that has come to define him, then presidential candidate Barack Obama duplicitously quipped, "I am absolutely convinced that culture wars are just so '90s. Their days are growing dark."[217]

Dark, indeed. America's soon-to-be cultural-Marxist-in-chief would then spend the greater part of a decade waging war against our nation's Judeo-Christian culture and heritage at levels, and in ways, unseen in our storied history. Today, his anti-Christian crusade continues unabated. In fact, and with less than a year left to complete his baleful conspiracy, this neo-pagan extremist has begun to rapidly accelerate his unravelings.

Chief among his targets for destruction are conservative and Christian organizations and individuals who pose a threat to his envisaged "fundamental transformation" of our once-Judeo-Christian nation. The Obama vision? A godless, Euro-socialist dystopia crafted in his own secular humanist self-image.

We're well on our way.

Still, even the president of the United States, alone, cannot destroy an entire nation from within. His sinister (yes, sinister) objective of a Christ-less society

(Jesus is the real target here) is shared by many who, like Obama, labor under the darkest of spiritual deceptions.

To accomplish the larger progressive dream of unmaking America, this man, this cagey figure of whom we still know very little, finds himself flanked by powerful comrades in arms—by hundreds of equally extremist and very well-funded anti-Christian groups.

Thankfully, the SPLC and hundreds more of these anti-Christian organizations are now being called out and held accountable. Understandably, they've begun scrambling for damage control. They're on the defensive.

Like I said, this has been a long time coming. Many American Christians still don't seem to understand how important information and influence operations are. But perhaps we will begin to better understand their import if we start emphasizing their significance.

Controlling the narrative and ensuring that truth prevails is key. And controlling the narrative and spreading truth allows for recognizing new ways to fight back against the anti-Christians. One new way we need to recognize is that the rules the progressives have set for modern America are rules that we shouldn't obey. Specifically, we must refuse to obey the misguided idea that the U.S. Supreme Court is infallible and the supreme authority in the United States of America.

The Supreme Court Is Not Supreme

To vocal opponents of judicial activism, the U.S. Supreme Court's *Obergefell v. Hodges* opinion in 2015 came as little surprise, even as that politically motivated opinion dealt a major credibility blow to the Court. In it, the justices presumed to do the impossible—both redefine the age-old institution of natural marriage and to give this fictional definition precedence over freedoms actually enumerated in the Bill of Rights. According to Rasmussen in July of 2015, only "36 percent of Likely U.S. Voters still think the high court is doing a good or excellent job."[218]

Incredibly, even the *Chicago Tribune* had this scathing assessment of the High Court:

> *We must confess we are shocked at the violence and servility of the Judicial Revolution caused by the decision of the Supreme Court of the United States. We scarcely know how to express our detestation of its inhuman dicta, or to fathom the wicked consequences which may flow from it. ... This decision has sapped the constitution [sic] of its glorious and distinctive features, and seeks to pervert it into a barbarous and*

unchristian channel. ... Jefferson feared this Supreme Court, and fore-told its usurpation of the legislative power of the Federal Government. His prophecy is now reality. The terrible evil he dreaded is upon us.[219]

As many of us warned, this opinion is already being used to crush Americans' constitutionally guaranteed freedoms. This was not lost on the *Tribune*, which added, "To say or suppose, that a Free People can respect or will obey a decision so fraught with disastrous consequences to the People and their Liberties, is to dream of impossibilities. No power can take away their rights. They will permit no power to abridge them."

The New York Tribune was equally dismissive: "The decision, we need hardly say, is entitled to just as much moral weight as would be the majority of those congregated in any Washington bar-room."[220]

OK, I'll come clean. The above quotes are not in reference to Obergefell. But they might as well have been. These quotes addressed the Supreme Court's equally illegitimate 1857 Dred Scott decision. Whereas, in Dred Scott, the justices defied natural law and presumed a "right" for whites to own blacks, the Court's 2015 Obergefell decision likewise defied natural law and presumed to deconstruct and redefine the institution of marriage.

Both decisions are illegitimate, and here's why. For the U.S. Supreme Court to justifiably overturn some law duly passed by the United States Congress, its opinion must be deeply rooted in one or more of the following:

- A clear reading of the U.S. Constitution;
- Some prior court precedent;
- History and the Common Law;
- Our cultural customs or traditions;
- Some other law enacted by Congress.

As the High Court's four dissenting justices rightly observed in Obergefell, the "five attorneys" who invented this newfangled "right" to "gay marriage," failed, abysmally, on each and every requirement.

The same was true of Dred Scott.

And so both opinions should be summarily ignored.

As President Andrew Jackson famously quipped of a Supreme Court opinion he thought usurped his executive authority, "[Chief Justice] John Marshall has made his decision; now let him enforce it!"[221]

After the Dred Scott decision was released, Sen. William Pitt Fessenden, R-Maine, who later served as Abraham Lincoln's Secretary of Treasury, said this: "[It is charged] that I am undermining the institutions of the country by attacking the Supreme Court of the United States! I attack not their decision, for they have made none; it is their opinion."[222]

Over the last few decades, the other two branches of government, the legislative and the executive, have, for some inexplicable reason, acquiesced to the notion of judicial supremacy—a dangerously dominant concept that erroneously regards the United States Supreme Court as the final arbiter of all things public policy. If this is so, then these nine unelected lawyers are ultimately unaccountable to anyone or anything, and the other two branches of government are but toothless figurehead bodies merely spinning their wheels while spending our dollars.

This flies in the face of the framers' intent. It's also the very unfortunate reality under which we live. It is fully within the constitutional authority of the other two branches of government to rein in these judges gone wild.

Article III, Section 2, of the U.S. Constitution gives Congress the authority to "check" judicial activism, up to and including when justices illegitimately legislate from the bench: "[T]he Supreme Court shall have appellate jurisdiction, both as to law and fact, with such exceptions, and under such regulations as the Congress shall make."

Our Republican-led Congress, from a regulatory standpoint, has the absolute constitutional authority to smack down this rogue Supreme Court. Unfortunately, to date, it has either been unwilling or unable to do so.

Still, it's not Republicans alone who must halt this judicial imperialism. Freedom-loving Democrats, to the extent that such animal yet exists, must also join the fight. After the Dred Scott opinion, they did.

"[F]orthwith we are told that the Supreme Court of the United States has become the appointed expounder of Democratic principles. Since when?" asked Sen. George Pugh, D-Ohio. He continued:

> Who constituted the judges of the Supreme Court the makers or expounders of Democratic principle? Certainly not Thomas Jefferson, who pronounced them the sappers and miners of the Constitution; certainly not Andrew Jackson, who told them he would interpret his own oath, as well as his own principles, according to his views of the Constitution. ... When we get to going by courts, it seems to me we have departed from the whole spirit and principle of the Democratic Party.[223]

My, how the Democratic Party has changed.

In the vast majority of their writings the Founding Fathers were explicit that the judicial branch of government is effectively the weakest of the three. Regrettably, such is not the case with today's modern misapplication. Americans currently live under what is, for all intents and purposes, a counter-constitutional judiciocracy led by nine unaccountable, black-robed autocrats.

No, five extremist lawyers don't get to decide "the law of the land." Only the legislature can do that. The High Court merely issues opinions.

And then the other two branches decide what, if anything, to do with them.

The Declaration of Independence acknowledges that true rights are God-given and unalienable.

Religious free exercise is sacrosanct.

"Gay marriage" is pretend.

And the Supreme Court is not the Supreme Being.

So, why should we as Christians comply with illegal, ungodly and unjust opinions from the Supreme Court? We shouldn't. We are commanded by God, in fact, to disobey laws that contradict His own. And why shouldn't we encourage churches, politicians, pundits and others to do the same?

Furthermore, ignoring illegitimate Supreme Court rulings isn't the only thing Christians should be doing.

We should be resisting all ungodly laws.

Ignore Unjust, Ungodly Laws

Christians are sinners and are no less so than the unsaved. We know this. We are saved from eternal torment, self-wrought, by the grace of Christ alone. If you are an unrepentant, "out and proud" homosexual practitioner, then you are not. It is our deepest prayer that you, too, will accept the free gift of eternal salvation, repent and "go and sin no more."

The alternative is a living hell.

Christians are obligated to avoid sin—to "do no evil." "Or do you not know that the unrighteous will not inherit the kingdom of God? Do not be deceived: neither the sexually immoral, nor idolaters, nor adulterers, nor men who practice homosexuality. ..." (1 Corinthians 6:9 – English Standard Version)

It really is that simple. And this is why, as faithful Christians (apostate "Christians" notwithstanding), we will never have anything whatsoever to do with pagan, sin-based same-sex "wedding" rituals regardless of what the law says.

We will not bake fake wedding cakes.
We will not arrange fake wedding flowers.
We will not take fake wedding pictures.
We will not host fake wedding receptions.

We will not do these things because to do these things is to disobey God. It is to aid sin, to cause people to stumble, which, in and of itself, is to layer sin upon sin. "It would be better for him if a millstone were hung around his neck and he were thrown into the sea, than that he would cause one of these little ones to stumble." (Luke 17:2 – New American Standard Bible)

While we all fall short of His glory, the history of God's people has shown that no unjust law presuming to force us to do otherwise, will ever make us disobey God in this or any other regard. I realize that forcing others to affirm that which offends God makes progressives feel better about their sins for a time. I also realize that it infuriates progressives when we refuse to join in as they attempt, ineffectively, to justify their wickedness by calling it "marriage."

This is nothing new. We Christians have been infuriating pagans by refusing to bend on truth for over 2,000 years.

And we will continue to do so until Christ returns.

Children don't like to be told "no." They sometimes throw a fit when we don't give them what they want. Still, when we know that some desire they may have is both wrong and harmful to them, we must tell them no.

We're telling the anti-Christians no because we love them with the love of Christ. But understand this: As we are so commanded, we must, and do, hate the evil conduct by which the anti-Christians define their identity. Sexual immorality—in this case self-destructive and disease-spreading sodomy, which violates the laws of nature and nature's God—is a grave sin that will destroy anyone who engages in it in both body and soul.

If we as parents were to condone, support and even assist our children in the commission of a grave sin, of a wrong, what kind of parents would we be?

So what kind of friend would we be to the enemies of God if we condoned, supported or assisted them in the commission of their grave "gay marriage" sin?

Maybe this will help you to understand. Whereas, and while you may be in denial of this fact, sexual immorality is the central defining characteristic of your temptation-driven "gay" identity, Christ's righteousness and our obedience to Him are, at least in part, central aspects of our Holy Spirit-gifted Christian identity.

I don't care if the anti-Christians financially ruin us, sue us, throw us in jail or even feed us to the lions. We will never, under any circumstances, while empowered by the Holy Spirit, deliberately disobey God to please them or anyone else. "Do not be afraid of those who kill the body but cannot kill the soul. Rather, be afraid of the One who can destroy both soul and body in hell." (Matthew 10:28 – New International Version)

Of late, we Christians are especially inspired by our brothers and sisters who are setting the example of how to disobey ungodly and illegitimate laws—how to engage in civil disobedience.

"If Rob walked in the store today, I would hug him and catch up on his life. The same faith that tells me that I can't be a part of Rob's wedding is the same faith that tells me to love him as Christ does."[224]

And with this gracious, compassionate and very truthful statement, Barronelle Stutzman, the elderly grandmother and floral artist who faces financial ruin at the hands of both homosexual activists and the state of Washington, has at once mirrored the love of Christ and exhibited the heart of a lion.

Because of the tremendous negative publicity that Washington Attorney General Bob Ferguson's and Rob Ingersoll's persecution of Ms. Stutzman has generated, Ferguson offered in 2015, via press release, to quickly settle the case for $2,000—as long as Ms. Stutzman would surrender her Christian freedom and right of conscience and promise, going forward, to sin. That is, to take part in sodomy-based "marriages."[225]

Again, and with characteristic grace and courage, she flatly declined.

"[This conflict] is about freedom, not money," wrote Ms. Stutzman in reply to the offer. She continued:

> I certainly don't relish the idea of losing my business, my home, and everything else that your lawsuit threatens to take from my family, but my freedom to honor God in doing what I do best is more important. Washington's constitution guarantees us "freedom of conscience in all matters of religious sentiment." I cannot sell that precious freedom. You are asking me to walk in the way of a well-known betrayer, one who sold something of infinite worth for 30 pieces of silver. That is something I will not do.[226]

Truth, in love.

The anti-Christians, homosexual and otherwise, will one day realize, hopefully before it becomes too late, that they are not only on the wrong side of history, they are on the wrong side of eternity.

It breaks my heart to know that.

And so, in addition to engaging in civil disobedience when man's laws are at enmity with God's own, we must also refuse to obey these laws in the interest of helping those who remain under the ultimate law—those who perish.

The anti-Christians will most certainly not respond peacefully to this just civil disobedience. But that's to be expected. We must be prepared to accept, joyfully, the persecution that will necessarily follow, and otherwise stand firm in the face of hardships as we hold the line against this progressive onslaught.

Embrace Persecution

The American government's incarceration of Kim Davis marked the first time in modern American history (outside of the incarceration of abortion protesters and slavery abolitionists) that an American citizen was imprisoned by the U.S. government for merely exercising her Christian faith. As we have repeatedly observed: War has been declared by the American government and American progressives on Christ and His followers.

And there is no turning back.

Anti-Christian persecution is the civil rights cause of our time. The cultural Marxists in power have seceded from our constitutional republican form of government, with its Judeo-Christian moorings, and have supplanted, in its place, a secular socialist oligarchy. Like Union troops hunkered at Fort Sumter, faithful Christians are now exiles in our own land. Anti-Christian progressives have demanded unconditional surrender, and federal Judge David Bunning fired the first mortar.

Kim Davis wasn't just a political prisoner of the American government; she was a political prisoner in a spiritual war. Like so many accidental civil rights heroes that came before her, Davis, a Democrat who was overwhelmingly elected as Rowan County Clerk, peacefully and graciously refused to violate her Christian conscience. She declined to sign her name to marriage certificates that defy God's natural design for the timeless institution and requested, as a simple accommodation, that either her name be removed from the marriage licenses, thus eliminating her personalized acquiescence to the Supreme Court's novel attempt to usurp God's authority and redefine this cornerstone institution, or, alternatively, "to allow licenses to be issued by the chief executive of Rowan County or [by] developing a statewide, online marriage license process."

That was it. Simple, reasonable and fair. Our nation has a rich history of respecting the rights of conscientious objectors, and Kim Davis, like tens of millions of her brothers and sisters in Christ, was exactly that.

"There is absolutely no reason that this case has gone so far without reasonable people respecting and accommodating Kim Davis's First Amendment rights," said Mat Staver, Davis's attorney and head of Liberty Counsel, a Christian civil rights organization.[227]

"I've weighed the cost and I'm prepared to go to jail, I sure am," Kim said in an interview with Todd Starnes.

> *"This is a heaven or hell issue for me and for every other Christian that believes," she said. "This is a fight worth fighting."*[228]

And so to jail she went (Republican governor Matt Bevin has since, and thankfully so, signed into law protective accommodations for Kim and other Christian government officials).

Reasonable people can disagree on the propriety of Kim's actions. Some said that she was right in refusing to violate her conscience by signing her name to a legal document that presumed to solemnize that which God condemns. Still others said that she needs to either "do her job" or resign—that she took an oath and was violating that oath.

Nevertheless, all reasonable people must agree that imprisoning this innocent woman for her conscience was both an absolute outrage and gross violation of her constitutional liberties. Even the ACLU thought it was a bridge too far.[229] The fact remains that people don't shed their First Amendment rights when they become government employees. Kim Davis swore to uphold the U.S. Constitution, the Kentucky Constitution and the laws of the Bluegrass State. When she took her oath, United States law, the Kentucky Constitution and the Kentucky Revised Statutes all reflected the millennia-old definition of natural marriage: "Only a marriage between one man and one woman shall be valid or recognized as a marriage in Kentucky."

The Kentucky Legislature has yet to change this law one jot or tittle. Instead, five left-wing extremist lawyers in Washington, D.C. issued an opinion presuming to move the goalposts mid-game. Court opinions are not "the law of the land." Judges don't make laws—only the legislature can do that. Kim Davis was not defying the law; she was upholding it as codified.

Accordingly, she has repeatedly asked, "Under what law am I authorized to issue homosexual couples a marriage license?"

Neither Judge Bunning nor anyone else has ever answered that.

Because no such law exists.

In a statement at the time, Mat Staver made the same point:

> *Not long ago 75 percent of Kentuckians passed the state's marriage amendment. Today a Christian is imprisoned for believing what the voters affirmed: marriage is between a man and a woman. Five people on the Supreme Court imposed their will on 320 million Americans and unleashed a torrent of assaults against people of faith. Kim Davis is the first victim of this tragedy.*[230]

Indeed, many scoffed at our warnings that Christians would someday be forced to either endorse "gay marriage" or go to jail. Well, scoff no more. That day has arrived. The full-on criminalization of Christianity has begun. You must now either bow a knee before the false gods of same-sex "marriage" and "gay rights," or face the fiery "contempt of court" furnace. We have moved from anecdotal instances of anti-Christian discrimination to systemic religious persecution. Those of us who won't obey these illegal and ungodly new laws will be found to be in "contempt of court" when they haul us before a judge.

You're going to hear that term a lot in coming days, weeks, months and years—"contempt of court." It's the straw man charge that will be utilized to imprison not just Christian public officials, but others as well. Christian business owners, lawyers, private sector employees, parents of school-age children who don't want their children indoctrinated by sexual anarchist propaganda and many others will be held in contempt of court, denied due process and incarcerated indefinitely.

The persecution isn't coming.

The persecution has arrived.

And that's what it means to be a Christ-follower.

So pray for a million more like Kim Davis.

Become like Kim Davis.

Is she perfect? Certainly not. None of us are. Indeed, before Kim's transformational Christian rebirth four years ago, she was thrice divorced and "played in the devil's playground" for much of her life.

She was lost.

But now she's found.

God has an amazing way of taking empty, broken vessels, rebuilding their lives and then using them mightily for His glory and honor.

Stand, like Kim, fearlessly, lovingly and boldly for Christ, declaring, as did the apostles when faced with a similar decision, "We must obey God rather than any human authority." (see Acts 5:29 – New Living Translation)

Indeed, as the Bible's Daniel, a "public official," boldly refused to disobey God and commit sin by worshipping a pagan king, so too has Kim Davis honored our Lord by refusing to bow before a pagan court—by refusing to call evil good and good evil.

And as I mentioned, once she did this and the federal government hauled her off to prison in response, she became a martyr. And that persecution has awakened many Americans who previously were not aware of how bad things have become.

So even as we Christians must now prepare for persecution and be ready to accept it as we fight back against progressives' war on our freedoms, we must, all the while, remain strong. God is with us and will work good even out of the most dire of circumstances.

Progressivism Is Communism – And Revolution Is at Hand

A preferred ploy of left-wing change agents is to ridicule critics when they point out the undeniable parallels between the goals of today's "progressive" movement, to include the Democratic Party in general, and the goals of the early, and very much still alive, communist movement.

If, for instance, one mentions the historical fact that nearly every adult who, at any time, was in any position of influence over a young, soon-to-be-radicalized Barry Soetoro was an avowed communist, to include his own parents, then one is immediately mocked and dismissed as a neo-McCarthyite hack pining for the bygone days of the Red Scare. This is an evasive, ad hominem strategy employed by those who are caught, for lack of a better word, red-handed.

To all this I say, if the jackboot fits, wear it. If it quacks like a commie and goose-steps like a commie, then a commie it is.

There are multiple layers within "progressivism's" pseudo-utopian, truly dystopian Marxist philosophy. The left's lust for redistributionist statism is well-known. Less understood, however, is the "progressive" rush toward cultural Marxism.

Cultural Marxism entails, among other things, that secularist aspect of left-wing statist ideology that seeks, within society, to supplant traditional values, norms and mores with postmodern moral relativism. Cultural Marxists endeavor to scrub America of her Judeo-Christian, constitutional republican founding principles, and take, instead, a secular statist Sharpie to our beloved U.S. Constitution.

Historian and U.S. military affairs expert William S. Lind describes cultural Marxism as "a branch of western Marxism, different from the Marxism-Leninism of the old Soviet Union. It is commonly known as 'multiculturalism' or, less formally, Political Correctness. From its beginning, the promoters of cultural Marxism have known they could be more effective if they concealed the Marxist nature of their work, hence the use of terms such as 'multiculturalism.'"

Pastor, attorney and Massachusetts gubernatorial candidate Scott Lively is globally admired by liberty-loving traditionalists. Conversely, he's universally reviled by cultural Marxists. He drills down a bit deeper: "Cultural Marxism is a variation of the Marxist strategy to build a utopian socialist order on the ashes of Christian civilization, but through subversion of the moral culture, especially the elimination of the natural family, rather than solely through destruction of capitalism."

True though this may be, the ideological seeds of contemporary cultural Marxism nonetheless sprout from deep within the dead soil of historical communism. It is not economic redistributionism alone through which "progressives" seek to both "fundamentally transform America" and otherwise conquer the world, but, rather, and perhaps primarily, it is also through victory over the pejoratively tagged "social issues" (i.e., the sanctity of marriage, natural human sexuality and morality, ending the abortion holocaust, religious liberty, the Second Amendment and the like).

This is neither speculative nor hyperbolic. Both the historical record and the U.S. Congressional Record bear out this sinister reality. Regrettably, today's "low-information voters" as Rush Limbaugh calls them—to include the useful idiots within the GOP's "moderate" and libertarian wings—are simply too lazy, shortsighted or both to learn the facts.

"Surrender on the 'social issues'!" demands the GOP's cultural Marxist-enabling kamikazes.

In 1963, U.S. Rep. A.S. Herlong Jr., D-Fla., read into the Congressional Record a list of "Current Communist Goals" as enumerated by Dr. Cleon Skousen in *The Naked Communist*, penned in 1958. I encourage you to read the whole list, but for now let's focus on those goals that most closely align with the seditious agenda of America's "progressive" movement. It's actually most of them. Though Herlong was a Democrat, the list reads like today's Democratic Party Platform.

The party of the jackass has come a long way:

- Develop the illusion that total disarmament [by] the United States would be a demonstration of moral strength.
- Permit free trade between all nations regardless of Communist affiliation and regardless of whether or not items could be used for war.
- Provide American aid to all nations regardless of Communist domination.
- Grant recognition of Red China. Admission of Red China to the U.N.
- Promote the U.N. as the only hope for mankind. If its charter is rewritten, demand that it be set up as a one-world government with its own independent armed forces.
- Resist any attempt to outlaw the Communist Party.

- Do away with all loyalty oaths.
- Capture one or both of the political parties in the United States.
- Use technical decisions of the courts to weaken basic American institutions by claiming their activities violate civil rights.
- Get control of the schools. Use them as transmission belts for socialism and current Communist propaganda. Soften the curriculum. Get control of teachers' associations. Put the party line in textbooks.
- Infiltrate the press. Get control of book-review assignments, editorial writing, policymaking positions.
- Gain control of key positions in radio, TV, and motion pictures.
- Continue discrediting American culture by degrading all forms of artistic expression. (An American Communist cell was told to "eliminate all good sculpture from parks and buildings, substitute shapeless, awkward and meaningless forms.")
- Eliminate all laws governing obscenity by calling them "censorship" and a violation of free speech and free press.
- Break down cultural standards of morality by promoting pornography and obscenity in books, magazines, motion pictures, radio, and TV.
- Present homosexuality, degeneracy and promiscuity as "normal, natural, healthy."
- Infiltrate the churches and replace revealed religion with "social" religion. Discredit the Bible and emphasize the need for intellectual maturity which does not need a "religious crutch."
- Eliminate prayer or any phase of religious expression in the schools on the ground that it violates the principle of "separation of church and state."
- Discredit the American Constitution by calling it inadequate, old-fashioned, out of step with modern needs, a hindrance to cooperation between nations on a worldwide basis.
- Discredit the American Founding Fathers. Present them as selfish aristocrats who had no concern for the "common man."
- Belittle all forms of American culture and discourage the teaching of American history on the ground that it was only a minor part of the "big picture."
- Support any socialist movement to give centralized control over any part of the culture— education, social agencies, welfare programs, mental health clinics, etc.
- Infiltrate and gain control of more unions.
- Infiltrate and gain control of big business.
- Transfer some of the powers of arrest from the police to social agencies. Treat all behavioral problems as psychiatric disorders which no one but psychiatrists can understand [or treat].
- Dominate the psychiatric profession and use mental health laws as a means

of gaining coercive control over those who oppose Communist goals.

- Discredit the family as an institution. Encourage promiscuity and easy divorce. Emphasize the need to raise children away from the negative influence of parents. Attribute prejudices, mental blocks and retarding of children to suppressive influence of parents.
- Create the impression that violence and insurrection are legitimate aspects of the American tradition; that students and special-interest groups should rise up and use ["]united force["] to solve economic, political or social problems.
- Internationalize the Panama Canal.
- Repeal the Connally reservation so the United States cannot prevent the World Court from seizing jurisdiction [over domestic problems. Give the World Court jurisdiction] over nations and individuals alike.

If achieving these specific communist (and decidedly anti-Christian) goals was the final "progressive" step toward the larger goal of securing communist governance in America, then, tragically, "progressives" have realized that larger goal.

Look around. We are no longer the United States of America. We have become The Communist States of America.

Which means, for those who love liberty, revolution is once again at hand.

Still, God remains sovereign and Christ on His throne. We can win. We will win.

Ultimately, in the end, we do win.

Even so, with faith, prayer and action, we can win this war in the here and now. We can have widespread spiritual revival and a return to the Christian principles that made America the greatest nation on earth.

In Christ, all things are possible. It's not just a platitude. It's an eternal truth. And as bad as America might seem today, if it is God's will that we have temporal victory and reverse course, we both can and will—no matter the odds.

Let us pray for His continued strength as we gird our loins for battle.

And then let's get busy.

Will you join the fight?

Notes

1   Mark David Hall (Ph.D.), "Did America Have a Christian Founding?" *Heritage Foundation*, June 7, 2011, accessed October 29, 2015, http://www.heritage.org/research/lecture/2011/06/did-america-have-a-christian-founding.

2   CIA World Factbook – Turkey," *Central Intelligence Agency*, October 15, 2015, accessed October 29, 2015, https://www.cia.gov/library/publications/the-world-factbook/geos/tu.html.

3   Project, "The Barbary Treaties 1786-1816 – Treaty of Peace and Friendship, Signed at Tripoli November 4, 1796," *Lillian Goldman Law Library, Yale University*, n.d., accessed October 29, 2015, http://avalon.law.yale.edu/18th_century/bar1796t.asp.

4   Wars, 1801–1805 and 1815–1816," *Office of the Historian, U.S. Department of State*, n.d., accessed October 29, 2015, https://history.state.gov/milestones/1801-1829/barbary-wars.

5   Project, "The Barbary Treaties 1786-1816 – Treaty of Peace and Amity, Signed at Tripoli June 4, 1805," *Lillian Goldman Law Library, Yale University*, n.d., accessed October 29, 2015, http://avalon.law.yale.edu/19th_century/bar1805t.asp.

6   Schweitzer, "Founding Fathers: We Are Not a Christian Nation," *Huffington Post*, February 26, 2015, accessed October 15, 2015, http://www.huffingtonpost.com/jeff-schweitzer/founding-fathers-we-are-n_b_6761840.html.

7   Edwards, "Was America founded as a Christian nation?" *CNN*, July 4, 2015, accessed October 29, 2015, http://www.cnn.com/2015/07/02/living/america-christian-nation/.

8   Debate Over Same-Sex Marriage in Alabama; Alabama Chief Justice Roy Moore Speaks," *CNN*, February 12, 2015, accessed October 14, 2015. http://transcripts.cnn.com/TRANSCRIPTS/1502/12/nday.06.html.

9   Thomas Jefferson to Benjamin Rush, 23 September 1800," *Founders Online, National Archives*, September 29, 2015, accessed December 26, 2015, http://founders.archives.gov/documents/Jefferson/01-32-02-0102.

10 William Safire, "B.C./A.D. or B.C.E./C.E.?" *New York Times Magazine*, August 17, 1997, accessed October 29, 2015, http://www.nytimes.com/1997/08/17/magazine/bc-ad-or-bce-ce.html.

11 Chris Hastings, "BBC turns its back on year of Our Lord: 2,000 years of Christianity jettisoned for politically correct 'Common Era'," *Daily Mail*, September 24, 2011, accessed October 29, 2015, http://www.dailymail.co.uk/news/article-2041265/BBC-turns-year-Our-Lord-2-000-years-Christianity-jettisoned-politically-correct-Common-Era.html.

12 Mark David Hall (Ph.D.), "Did America Have a Christian Founding?" *Heritage Foundation*, June 7, 2011, accessed October 29, 2015, http://www.heritage.org/research/lecture/2011/06/did-america-have-a-christian-founding.

13 Hall is referencing Massachusetts. Others sources say Massachusetts disestablished the official state church in 1833.

14 Mark David Hall (Ph.D.), "Did America Have a Christian Founding?" *Heritage Foundation*, June 7, 2011, accessed October 29, 2015, http://www.heritage.org/research/lecture/2011/06/did-america-have-a-christian-founding.

15 "Prop. 8 supporters suffer vandalism, violence," *OneNewsNow.com*, November 3, 2008, accessed October 29, 2015, http://www.onenewsnow.com/politics-govt/2008/11/03/

prop-8-supporters-suffer-vandalism-violence. (**NOTE**: The "here" in brackets in the quotation appeared in the original source.)

16 Gerhard Peters and John T. Woolley, "Democratic Party Platform of 2004," *The American Presidency Project*, July 26, 2004, accessed February 1, 2016, http://www.presidency. ucsb.edu/ws/index.php?pid=29613.

17 Gerhard Peters and John T. Woolley, "2008 Democratic Party Platform," *The American Presidency Project*, August 25, 2008, accessed February 1, 2016, http://www.presidency. ucsb.edu/ws/index.php?pid=78283.

18 Gerhard Peters and John T. Woolley, "2012 Democratic National Platform," *The American Presidency Project*, September 3, 2012, accessed February 1, 2016, http://www. presidency.ucsb.edu/ws/index.php?pid=101962.

19 Joel Gehrke, "DNC: 'Government is the only thing that we all belong to'," *Washington Examiner*, September 4, 2012, accessed February 1, 2016, http://www. washingtonexaminer.com/dnc-government-is-the-only-thing-that-we-all-belong-to/ article/2506923.

20 Gerhard Peters and John T. Woolley, "2012 Republican Party Platform," *The American Presidency Project*, August 27, 2012, accessed February 1, 2016, http://www.presidency. ucsb.edu/ws/index.php?pid=101961. (NOTE: The platform refers to God as "God" 10 times and God as "Providence" twice.)

21 Matt Barber, Twitter post, September 4, 2012, 4:00 p.m., accessed February 1, 2016, https://twitter.com/jmattbarber/status/243076032020758530.

22 Zack Ford, Twitter post, September 4, 2012, 4:01 p.m., accessed February 1, 2016, https:// twitter.com/ZackFord/status/243076230096756736.

23 ItIsGoodToBeQueen, Twitter post, September 4, 2012, 4:48 p.m., accessed February 1, 2016, https://twitter.com/redandright/status/243088046189342720.

24 Michael Gryboski, "Court Rules in Favor of 9/11 Cross, Against Atheist Lawsuit," *Christian Post*, July 28, 2014, accessed January 9, 2016, http://www.christianpost.com/news/ court-rules-in-favor-of-9-11-cross-against-atheist-lawsuit-123949/.

25 David French, "Does the Sight of a Cross in a Museum Give You Indigestion?" *American Center for Law and Justice* (blog), July 27, 2011, accessed February 1, 2016, http://aclj.org/ war-on-terror/does-the-sight-of-a-cross-in-a-museum-give-you-indigestion.

26 "World Trade Center Relic Cross Attacked," *Liberty Counsel press release*, September 17, 2012, accessed February 1, 2016, https://www.lc.org/newsroom/details/world-trade-center-relic-cross-attacked-1.

27 "Reasons Against Satirizing Religion – December 13, 1757 Letter from Benjamin Franklin to an Unknown Recipient," *TeachingAmericanHistory.org, A Project of the Ashbrook Center at Ashland University*, n.d., accessed April 24, 2016, http://teachingamericanhistory.org/ library/document/reasons-against-satirizing-religion/..

28 Michael Gryboski, "Court Rules in Favor of 9/11 Cross, Against Atheist Lawsuit," *Christian Post*, July 28, 2014, accessed January 9, 2016, http://www.christianpost.com/news/ court-rules-in-favor-of-9-11-cross-against-atheist-lawsuit-123949/.

29 "US Supreme Court Justice Ruth Bader Ginsburg to Egyptians: Look to the Constitutions of South Africa or Canada, Not to the US Constitution," *Middle East Media Research Institute*, January 30, 2012, accessed February 1, 2016, http://www.memritv.org/clip_ transcript/en/3295.htm.

30 Jody Brown, "Reid vows to counter ruling by 'five white men'," *OneNewsNow.com*, July 9, 2014, accessed February 1, 2016, http://www.onenewsnow.com/politics-govt/2014/07/09/reid-vows-to-counter-ruling-by-five-white-men.

31 Sahil Kapur, "Senate Dems Ready To Unveil Bill Reversing Hobby Lobby Ruling," *Talking Points Memo*, July 8, 2014, accessed February 1, 2016, http://talkingpointsmemo.com/dc/murray-udall-legislation-hobby-lobby.

32 Ed O'Keefe, "Gay rights groups withdraw support of ENDA after Hobby Lobby decision," *Washington Post*, July 8, 2014, accessed February 1, 2016, https://www.washingtonpost.com/news/post-politics/wp/2014/07/08/gay-rights-group-withdrawing-support-of-enda-after-hobby-lobby-decision/.

33 Gary Glenn, e-mail message to author, 2014. (**NOTE**: I do not recall the exact date of the email.)

34 Chris Johnson, "ENDA's religious exemption still concerning as vote nears," *Washington Blade*, November 3, 2013, accessed February 1, 2016, http://www.washingtonblade.com/2013/11/03/enda-religious-exemption/.

35 The Editors, "Ban Gay Discrimination. No Exceptions," *Bloomberg View*, July 10, 2014, accessed October 22, 2015, http://www.bloombergview.com/articles/2014-07-10/ban-gay-discrimination-no-exceptions.

36 "Obama Scolds Fox News Over Welfare, Poverty: "We're Going To Have To Change How The Media Reports On These Issues"," *RealClearPolitics*, May 12, 2015, accessed February 1, 2016, http://www.realclearpolitics.com/video/2015/05/12/obama_scolds_fox_news_over_welfare_poverty_were_going_to_have_to_change_how_the_media_reports_on_these_issues.html.

37 Steven Ertelt, "Hillary Clinton: Force Christians to Change Their Religious Views to Support Abortion," *LifeNews*, April 27, 2015, accessed February 1, 2016, http://www.lifenews.com/2015/04/27/hillary-clinton-force-christians-to-change-their-religious-views-to-support-abortion/.

38 Frank Bruni, "Bigotry, the Bible and the Lessons of Indiana," *New York Times*, April 3, 2015, accessed February 1, 2016, http://www.nytimes.com/2015/04/05/opinion/sunday/frank-bruni-same-sex-sinners.html.

39 "'Painfully dumb tweet!': 'Smug' Chris Cuomo gets schooled on hate speech and the Constitution," *Twitchy*, May 6, 2015, accessed February 1, 2016, http://twitchy.com/2015/05/06/painfully-dumb-tweet-smug-chris-cuomo-gets-schooled-on-hate-speech-and-the-constitution/. (**NOTE**: Mr. Cuomo appears to have deleted his tweet. Therefore, we use this reference instead, which includes a link to the apparently deleted tweet.)

40 Eugene Volokh, "No, there's no "hate speech" exception to the First Amendment," *Washington Post*, The Volokh Conspiracy (blog), May 7, 2015, accessed February 1, 2016, https://www.washingtonpost.com/news/volokh-conspiracy/wp/2015/05/07/no-theres-no-hate-speech-exception-to-the-first-amendment/.

41 Matt Barber, "Why Are They Called 'Homofascists'? Here's Why ...," *BarbWire.com*, April 3, 2014, accessed February 1, 2016, http://barbwire.com/2014/04/03/called-homofascists-heres/.

42 William Saletan, "Purge the Bigots," *Slate*, April 4, 2014, accessed February 1, 2016, http://www.slate.com/articles/news_and_politics/frame_game/2014/04/brendan_

eich_quits_mozilla_let_s_purge_all_the_antigay_donors_to_prop_8.html.

43 William Saletan, "Purge the Bigots," *Slate*, April 4, 2014, accessed February 1, 2016, http://www.slate.com/articles/news_and_politics/frame_game/2014/04/brendan_ eich_quits_mozilla_let_s_purge_all_the_antigay_donors_to_prop_8.html.

44 Doug McKelway, "Software CEO paying for his politics with his job?" [VIDEO], *FoxNews.com*, April 4, 2014, accessed February 1, 2016, http://video.foxnews. com/v/3432043947001/software-ceo-paying-for-his-politics-with-his-job/?#sp=show-clips.

45 Proposition 8: Who gave in the gay marriage battle?" *Los Angeles Times*, n.d., accessed February 1, 2016, http://projects.latimes.com/prop8/.

46 Anonymous, "Mozilla, Mo' Problems – Ritual Sacrifice in Silicon Valley," *First Things*, April 2, 2014, accessed January 10, 2016, http://www.firstthings.com/web-exclusives/2014/04/ mozilla-mo-problems.

47 Steven Nelson, "Chick-fil-A president: Gay marriage is 'inviting God's judgment on our nation'," *Daily Caller*, July 18, 2012, accessed October 21, 2015, http://dailycaller. com/2012/07/18/chick-fil-a-president-gay-marriage-is-inviting-gods-judgment-on-our-nation-audio/.

48 Maegan Vazquez, "Chicago church leaders roast Rahm Emanuel over Chick-fil-A stance," *FoxNews.com*, July 31, 2012, accessed December 31, 2015, http://www.foxnews. com/us/2012/07/31/chicago-religious-leaders-back-chick-fil.html.

49 Ros Krasny, "Boston mayor to anti-gay-marriage Chick-fil-A: stay away," *Reuters*, July 26, 2012, accessed December 31, 2015, http://www.reuters.com/article/us-usa-gaymarriage-chickfila-boston-idUSBRE86P1AT20120726.

50 Aaron Sankin, "Ed Lee: Chick-Fil-A Not Welcome In San Francisco," *Huffington Post*, July 27, 2012, accessed December 31, 2015, http://www.huffingtonpost.com/2012/07/27/ed-lee-chick-fil-a_n_1711721.html.

51 Tim Craig, "Gray opposes Chick-fil-A expansion; calls it 'hate chicken'," *Washington Post*, July 28, 2012, accessed December 31, 2015, https://www.washingtonpost.com/blogs/ dc-wire/post/gray-opposes-chick-fil-a-expansion-calls-it-hate-chicken/2012/07/27/ gJQA8SIREX_blog.html.

52 Daniel Halper, "Chick-fil-A 'Set a World Record'," *Weekly Standard*, August 2, 2012, accessed December 31, 2015, http://www.weeklystandard.com/chick-fil-a-set-a-world-record/article/649217.

53 Michelangelo Signorile, "Chick-fil-A: Were the Protests a Big Fail? And Where Do We Go From Here?" *Huffington Post*, August 6, 2012, accessed October 21, 2015, http://www. huffingtonpost.com/michelangelo-signorile/chick-fil-a-were-the-prot_b_1746382. html.

54 "'Tastes Like Hate': Torrance Chick-Fil-A Vandalized Ahead Of 'Same Sex Kiss Day'," *CBS Los Angeles*, August 3, 2012, accessed December 31, 2015, http://losangeles.cbslocal. com/2012/08/03/tastes-like-hate-torrance-chick-fil-a-vandalized-ahead-of-same-sex-kiss-day/.

55 "Chick-fil-A in Martinsburg re-opens after bomb threat," *Journal*, August 1, 2012, accessed December 31, 2015, http://journal-news.net/page/content.detail/id/582561/ Chick-fil-A-in-Martinsburg-deemed-safe-after-bomb-threat.html?nav=5006.

56   Dana Loesch, "Chick-fil-A'd: Bully Fired after Video Goes Viral," *Breitbart News Network*, August 2, 2012, accessed December 31, 2015, http://www.breitbart.com/big-journalism/2012/08/02/chick-fil-a-drive-thru-bully-fired/.

57   Leon Stafford, "Cathy seeks to put gay marriage flap behind Chick-fil-A," *Atlanta Journal-Constitution*, March 14, 2014, accessed October 29, 2015, http://www.ajc.com/news/business/cathy-seeks-to-put-gay-marriage-flap-behind-chick-/nfCHj/.

58   Paul Duggan and Mary Pat Flaherty, "Family Research Council guard shot by gunman in D.C.," *Washington Post*, August 15, 2012, accessed December 31, 2015, https://www.washingtonpost.com/local/crime/family-research-council-guard-shot-by-gunman-in-dc/2012/08/15/e420527e-e719-11e1-a3d2-2a05679928ef_story.html.

59   "Family Research Council," Southern Poverty Law Center, n.d., accessed January 6, 2016, https://www.splcenter.org/fighting-hate/extremist-files/group/family-research-council.

60   Elizabeth Harrington, "Before Shooting: *Southern Poverty Law Center* Put Family Research Council on 'Hate Map'," CNSNews.com, August 16, 2012, accessed December 31, 2015, http://cnsnews.com/news/article/shooting-southern-poverty-law-center-put-family-research-council-hate-map.

61   Ann E. Marimow, "Family Research Council shooter pleads guilty to three felonies," *Washington Post*, February 6, 2013, accessed October 21, 2015, https://www.washingtonpost.com/local/family-research-council-shooter-pleads-guilty-two-three-felonies-including-terrorism-charge-in-federal-court/2013/02/06/aa2086b2-7075-11e2-ac36-3d8d9dcaa2e2_story.html.

62   J. Matt Barber, "Liberal Violence Rising," *CNSNews.com*, November 21, 2011, accessed December 31, 2015, http://www.cnsnews.com/blog/j-matt-barber/liberal-violence-rising.

63   "Family Research Council," *Southern Poverty Law Center*, n.d., accessed January 6, 2016, https://www.splcenter.org/fighting-hate/extremist-files/group/family-research-council.

64   Erick Erickson, "Southern Poverty Law Center Inspires Floyd Lee Corkins' Attempted Mass Shooting," *RedState*, February 6, 2013, accessed December 31, 2015, http://www.redstate.com/2013/02/06/southern-poverty-law-center-inspires-floyd-lee-corkins-attempted-mass-shooting/.

65   "Southern Poverty Law Center Incited Shooting Spree Against Family Research Council," *Liberty Counsel press release*, February 7, 2013, accessed December 31, 2015, https://www.lc.org/newsroom/details/southern-poverty-law-center-incited-shooting-spree-against-family-research-council-1.

66   Lauretta Brown, "DOJ Official Praises the Southern Poverty Law Center's Work in Combatting Domestic Terrorism," *CNSNews.com*, October 15, 2015, accessed October 22, 2015, http://www.cnsnews.com/news/article/lauretta-brown/doj-official-praises-southern-poverty-law-centers-work-combating.

67   Lee Stranahan, "All In: Democrats Support Black Lives Matter Presidential Town Hall," *Breitbart News Network*, October 21, 2015, accessed October 22, 2015, http://www.breitbart.com/big-government/2015/10/21/democrats-support-black-lives-matter-presidential-town-hall/.

68   Lee Stranahan, "Fail: Obama's Defense of Black Lives Matter Contradicted by BLM Co-

Founder's Own Words," *Breitbart News Network*, October 23, 2015, accessed October 25, 2015, http://www.breitbart.com/big-government/2015/10/23/fail-obamas-defense-black-lives-matter-contradicted-blm-co-founders-words/.

69 Todd Starnes, "Pentagon: Religious Proselytizing is Not Permitted," *Fox News Radio – Todd Starnes*, April 30, 2013, accessed January 7, 2016, http://radio.foxnews.com/toddstarnes/top-stories/pentagon-religious-proselytizing-is-not-permitted.html.

70 Chris Carroll, "Pentagon: OK to talk about faith, but not to push beliefs on others," *Stars and Stripes*, May 2, 2013, accessed January 7, 2016, http://www.stripes.com/pentagon-ok-to-talk-about-faith-but-not-to-push-beliefs-on-others-1.219261.

71 Avalon Project, "Washington's Farewell Address 1796," *Lillian Goldman Law Library, Yale University*, n.d., accessed January 7, 2016, http://avalon.law.yale.edu/18th_century/washing.asp.

72 "Liberty Counsel Will Defend Our Armed Forces Charged With Proselytizing," *Liberty Counsel press release*, May 9, 2013, accessed January 7, 2016, https://www.lc.org/newsroom/details/liberty-counsel-will-defend-our-armed-forces-charged-with-proselytizing-1.

73 Mikey Weinstein, "6/26/15 MIKEY's OP-ED – MRFF Demands Ouster of All Homophobic Military Chaplains," *Military Religious Freedom Foundation*, June 26, 2015, accessed October 23, 2015, http://www.militaryreligiousfreedom.org/2015/06/62615-mikeys-op-ed-mrff-demands-ouster-of-all-homophobic-military-chaplains/.

74 U.S. Congress, House, Armed Services Committee (Subcommittee on Military Personnel), *Religious Accommodations in the Armed Services*, 113th Cong., 2d sess., November 19, 2014, accessed October 23, 2015, http://armedservices.house.gov/index.cfm/2014/11/religious-accommodations-in-the-armed-services.

75 Penny Starr, "Lawmaker Calls Out Witness for Anti-Christian Remarks – 'Fundamentalist Christian Monsters'," *CNSNews.com*, November 20, 2014, accessed October 23, 2015, http://cnsnews.com/news/article/penny-starr/lawmaker-calls-out-witness-anti-christian-remarks-fundamentalist-christian.

76 Lexi Smith, "Gohmert says Obama is tolerating bigotry against Christians in the U.S. military," *Houston Chronicle, Texas on the Potomac* (blog), July 10, 2013, accessed January 7, 2016, http://blog.chron.com/txpotomac/2013/07/gohmert-says-obama-is-tolerating-bigotry-against-christians-in-the-u-s-military/.

77 "Fleming Receives Religious Freedom Award from Military Chaplains – Chaplain Alliance presents first ever Torchbearer for Religious Freedom award," *U.S. Rep. John C. Fleming (LA-4) press release*, September 30, 2014, accessed January 7, 2016, http://fleming.house.gov/news/documentsingle.aspx?DocumentID=394758.

78 U.S. Army War College, Strategic Studies Institute, "About the Strategic Studies Institute," n.d., accessed January 7, 2016, https://www.strategicstudiesinstitute.army.mil/about/strategic-studies-institute.cfm.

79 Dr. Don M. Snider, COL (USA Ret) and Alexander P. Shine, "A Soldier's Morality, Religion, and Our Professional Ethic: Does the Army's Culture Facilitate Integration, Character Development, and Trust in the Profession?" *Professional Military Ethics Monograph Series* 6 (2014): 1-2, accessed January 7, 2016, http://www.strategicstudiesinstitute.army.mil/pubs/download.cfm?q=1203.

80 Maxine Bernstein, "Lesbian couple refused wedding cake files state discrimination

complaint," *Oregonian*, August 14, 2013, accessed January 7, 2016, http://www.oregonlive.com/gresham/index.ssf/2013/08/lesbian_couple_refused_wedding.html.

81 Kelsey Harkness, "State Takes Legal Action to Seize $135K From Bakers Who Refused to Make Cake for Lesbian Couple," *Daily Signal*, October 1, 2015, accessed October 22, 2015, http://dailysignal.com/2015/10/01/state-takes-legal-action-to-seize-135k-from-bakers-who-refused-to-make-cake-for-lesbian-couple/.

82 Valerie Richardson, "Florist refuses attorney general's options to settle lawsuit over same-sex weddings," *Washington Times*, February 22, 2015, accessed January 7, 2016, http://www.washingtontimes.com/news/2015/feb/22/florist-rejects-washington-attorney-generals-deal-/.

83 Barronelle Stutzman, "Why a friend is suing me: the Arlene's Flowers story," *Seattle Times*, November 9, 2015, accessed January 7, 2016, http://www.seattletimes.com/opinion/why-a-good-friend-is-suing-me-the-arlenes-flowers-story/.

84 "Attorney general urges court to uphold decision on Arlene's Flowers case," *Tri-City Herald*, December 24, 2015, accessed January 7, 2016, http://www.tri-cityherald.com/news/local/article51562850.html.

85 Joseph Backholm, "WA Florist Sued for Beliefs About Marriage," *Family Policy Institute of Washington* (blog), April 9, 2013, accessed January 7, 2016, http://www.fpiw.org/blog/2013/04/09/wa-florist-sued-for-beliefs-about-marriage/.

86 Ken Klukowski, "Baker Faces Prison for Refusing to Bake Same-Sex Wedding Cake," *Breitbart News Network*, December 12, 2013, accessed January 7, 2016, http://www.breitbart.com/big-government/2013/12/12/christian-baker-willing-to-go-to-jail-for-declining-gay-wedding-cake/

87 Leonardo Blair, "Order Forcing Christian Colorado Baker to Do Sensitivity Training for Gay Clients 'Vague' and 'Lousy,' Says Lawyer," *Christian Post*, June 4, 2014, accessed January 7, 2016, http://www.christianpost.com/news/order-forcing-christian-colorado-baker-to-do-sensitivity-training-for-gay-clients-vague-and-lousy-says-lawyer-120958/.

88 Leah Jessen, "Baker Who Doesn't Want to Make Wedding Cakes for Same-Sex Couples Takes His Case to Colorado Supreme Court," *Daily Signal*, October 26, 2015, accessed October 26, 2015, http://dailysignal.com/2015/10/26/baker-who-doesnt-want-to-make-wedding-cakes-for-same-sex-couples-takes-his-case-to-colorado-supreme-court/.

89 David Limbaugh, "Fascist Leftists in Houston," *WND.com*, October 16, 2014, accessed January 8, 2016, http://www.wnd.com/2014/10/fascist-leftists-in-houston/.

90 Matt Barber, "'LGBT': The 'T' Is for Tyranny," *BarbWire.com*, October 18, 2014, accessed January 8, 2016, http://barbwire.com/2014/10/18/lgbt-t-tyranny/.

91 Sarah Pulliam Bailey, "Houston subpoenas pastors' sermons in gay rights ordinance case," *Religion News Service*, October 15, 2014, accessed January 7, 2016, https://www.washingtonpost.com/national/religion/houston-subpoenas-pastors-sermons-in-gay-rights-ordinance-case/2014/10/15/9b848ff0-549d-11e4-b86d-184ac281388d_story.html.

92 Michael Gryboski, "Former Astros Star Speaks Out Against Houston's Transgender Bathroom Ordinance," *Christian Post*, October 18, 2015, accessed October 25, 2015, http://www.christianpost.com/news/astros-lance-berkman-transgender-bathroom-houston-147872/.

93 Leonardo Blair, "Houstonians Could Face $5K Fine If They Object to Men in Women's Bathrooms, Ad Campaign Says," *Christian Post*, October 21, 2015, accessed October 25, 2015, http://www.christianpost.com/news/houstonians-could-face-5k-fine-if-they-object-to-men-in-womens-bathrooms-ad-campaign-says-148145/.

94 "Voters reject Houston Equal Rights Ordinance," *KHOU.com*, November 4, 2015, accessed January 8, 2016, http://www.khou.com/story/news/politics/2015/11/03/early-voters-say-no-to-houston-equal-rights-ordinance/75125446/.

95 Mat Staver, "The Criminalization of Christianity," *Liberty Counsel Connect*, September 5, 2015, accessed April 24, 2016, http://libertycounsel.com/the-criminalization-of-christianity/.

96 "Kentucky clerk won't give gay couple marriage license, defying order," *Associated Press*, August 13, 2015, accessed February 1, 2016, http://www.foxnews.com/us/2015/08/13/kentucky-clerk-wont-give-gay-couple-marriage-license-defying-order.html.

97 Ken McIntyre, "County Clerk Appeals Federal Judge's Gay Marriage Mandate," *Daily Signal*, August 13, 2015, accessed April 24, 2016, http://dailysignal.com/2015/08/13/county-clerk-appeals-federal-judges-gay-marriage-mandate.

98 Ariane de Vogue, "Kentucky clerk Kim Davis continues to refuse same-sex marriage licenses," *CNN*, September 1, 2015, accessed April 24, 2016, http://www.cnn.com/2015/08/27/politics/same-sex-marriage-gay-marriage-kentucky/.

99 Brian Beutler, "Throw Kentucky Clerk Kim Davis in Jail," *New Republic*, September 2, 2015, accessed February 1, 2016, https://newrepublic.com/article/122701/put-kentucky-clerk-kim-davis-jail.

100 Michael Brendan Dougherty, "Burn Kim Davis!" *Week*, September 8, 2015, accessed February 1, 2016, https://web.archive.org/web/20160101231405/http://theweek.com/articles/575247/burn-kim-davis.

101 Scott Lively, "My Analysis of the SMUG Lawsuit," *DefendTheFamily.com*, April 25, 2015, accessed February 1, 2016, http://www.defendthefamily.com/pfrc/newsarchives.php?id=4586691.

102 Republic of Uganda, Embassy of the Republic of Uganda and Permanent Mission to the European Commission, *Letter from Ambassador Stephen T.K. Katenta-Apuli to the Hon. Jerzy Buzek, President of the European Parliament (Uganda: Murder of David Kato)*, March 15, 2011, accessed February 1, 2016, http://www.europarl.europa.eu/meetdocs/2009_2014/documents/droi/dv/4_08letterfromuganda_/4_08letterfromuganda_en.pdf.

103 Stephanie Barry, "Judge Michael Ponsor pens "The Hanging Judge," shedding light on the legal system and death penalty," *Springfield Republican*, June 2, 2013, accessed February 1, 2016, http://www.masslive.com/news/index.ssf/2013/06/judge_michael_ponsor_reveals_s.html.

104 Michael Ponsor, "Remarks on Being Sworn in as a United States District Judge," *Western New England Law Review*, 16, Issue 2 (1994): 215, accessed February 1, 2016, http://digitalcommons.law.wne.edu/cgi/viewcontent.cgi?article=1273&context=lawreview.

105 Kirsten Andersen, "U.S. pastor faces 'crimes against humanity' charges for opposing gay agenda as First Circuit refuses to toss suit," *LifeSiteNews.com*, December 11, 2014, accessed February 1, 2016, https://www.lifesitenews.com/news/u.s.-pastor-faces-crimes-against-humanity-charges-for-opposing-gay-agenda-a.

106 Susan K. Livio, "Gay rights advocates hopeful after Christie signs bill banning conversion therapy," *NJ.com,* August 19, 2013, accessed January 8, 2016, http://www.nj.com/politics/index.ssf/2013/08/christie_signs_bill_banning_licensed_therapists_from_using_gay-to-straight_conversion_therapy_on_kid.html.

107 Richard J. Wolitski, Ron Stall, and Ronald O. Valdiserri, *Unequal Opportunity: Health Disparities Affecting Gay and Bisexual Men in the United States* (New York: Oxford University Press, 2008), 81.

108 "Governor Christie Harms New Jersey Children By Signing Change Therapy Ban. Liberty Counsel Will File Suit," *Liberty Counsel press release,* August 17, 2013, accessed February 1, 2016, https://www.lc.org/newsroom/details/governor-christie-harms-new-jersey-children-by-signing-change-therapy-ban-liberty-counsel-will-fil.

109 "Gov. Christie Signs Bill Banning Gay Conversion Therapy On Minors," *State of New Jersey Governor Chris Christie press release,* August 19, 2013, accessed February 1, 2016, http://nj.gov/governor/news/news/552013/approved/20130819a.html.

110 "Gov. Christie Signs Bill Banning Gay Conversion Therapy On Minors," *State of New Jersey Governor Chris Christie* press release, August 19, 2013, accessed February 1, 2016, http://nj.gov/governor/news/news/552013/approved/20130819a.html. (**Note**: Gov. Christie doesn't specifically cite the 2009 APA report but rather cites the APA in general. However, the New Jersey General Assembly bill *does* specifically cite the 2009 APA report, so it can be reasonably assessed the Gov. Christie is referring to the same APA report.)

111 State of New Jersey Legislature, General Assembly, Assembly Bill 3371, 215th Leg., October 15, 2012, accessed February 1, 2016, http://www.njleg.state.nj.us/2012/Bills/A3500/3371_I1.HTM (**Note**: Four of the five sponsors are Democrats. Assemblywoman Holly Schepisi was the only Republican sponsor of the bill.)

112 "Report of the Task Force on Appropriate Therapeutic Responses to Sexual Orientation," *APA Task Force on Appropriate Therapeutic Responses to Sexual Orientation* (2009), accessed April 25, 2016, https://www.apa.org/pi/lgbt/resources/therapeutic-response.pdf. (**Note**: The report uses the terms "feelings" and "self-concept" throughout the report, so no page number is listed in the citation.)

113 "Report of the Task Force on Appropriate Therapeutic Responses to Sexual Orientation," *APA Task Force on Appropriate Therapeutic Responses to Sexual Orientation* (2009): 45, accessed April 25, 2016, https://www.apa.org/pi/lgbt/resources/therapeutic-response.pdf.

114 "Report of the Task Force on Appropriate Therapeutic Responses to Sexual Orientation," *APA Task Force on Appropriate Therapeutic Responses to Sexual Orientation* (2009): 50, accessed April 25, 2016, https://www.apa.org/pi/lgbt/resources/therapeutic-response.pdf.

115 "Report of the Task Force on Appropriate Therapeutic Responses to Sexual Orientation," *APA Task Force on Appropriate Therapeutic Responses to Sexual Orientation* (2009): 53, accessed April 25, 2016, https://www.apa.org/pi/lgbt/resources/therapeutic-response.pdf.

116 "Report of the Task Force on Appropriate Therapeutic Responses to Sexual Orientation," *APA Task Force on Appropriate Therapeutic Responses to Sexual Orientation* (2009): 79, accessed April 25, 2016, https://www.apa.org/pi/lgbt/resources/therapeutic-response.pdf.

117 Nicholas A. Cummings, "Sexual reorientation therapy not unethical: Column," *USA Today*, July 30, 2013, accessed February 1, 2016, http://www.usatoday.com/story/opinion/2013/07/30/sexual-reorientation-therapy-not-unethical-column/2601159/.

118 "NJ Sponsor of Change Therapy Ban Threatens to Remove Children from Parents, Liberty Counsel Files Lawsuit (audio clip)," *Liberty Counsel press release*, August 23, 2013, accessed January 8, 2016, https://www.lc.org/newsroom/details/nj-sponsor-of-change-therapy-ban-threatens-to-remove-children-from-parents-liberty-counsel-files.

119 Alan Ewart, "Leelah Alcorn: Gay Rights Activist Says Parents Should Be Prosecuted," *Inquisitr*, January 1, 2015, accessed January 8, 2016, http://www.inquisitr.com/1720499/leelah-alcorn-gay-rights-activist-says-parents-should-be-prosecuted/.

120 Matt Barber, "Dan Savage: 'Tolerant' bully," *WND.com*, May 1, 2012, accessed January 8, 2016, http://www.wnd.com/2012/05/dan-savage-tolerant-bully/.

121 Katie McHugh, "Dan Savage: 'Abortion should be mandatory for 30 years'," *Daily Caller*, November 6, 2013, accessed January 8, 2016, http://dailycaller.com/2013/11/06/dan-savage-abortion-should-be-mandatory-for-30-years/.

122 Austin Ruse, "LGBT Activists Urge UN to Designate 'Reparative Therapy' a Form of Torture," *Breitbart News Network*, November 10, 2014, accessed January 8, 2016, http://www.breitbart.com/Big-Peace/2014/11/07/Gays-Want-UN-to-Name-Reparative-Therapy-a-Form-of-Torture.

123 Grant Wishard, "Harvard-affiliated hospital dumps Christian doctor because he won't celebrate gay sex," *College Fix*, December 30, 2015, accessed January 8, 2016, http://www.thecollegefix.com/post/25668/.

124 Allum Bokhari, "NYC Will Fine You $250,000 For 'Misgendering' A Transsexual," *Breitbart News Network*, December 27, 2015, accessed January 8, 2016, http://www.breitbart.com/tech/2015/12/27/nyc-will-fine-you-250000-for-misgendering-a-transsexual/.

125 J. Richard Pearcey, "The Revolt of Intelligence Against "Marriage Equality"," *Pearcey Report*, March 18, 2013, accessed January 8, 2016, http://www.pearceyreport.com/archives/2013/01/cupp_cpac_homosexuals_revolt_of_intelligence_against_marriage_equality.php.

126 Austin Ruse, "State Dept. Honors Advocate of Destruction of Marriage," *Breitbart News Network*, June 23, 2014, accessed January 8, 2016, http://www.breitbart.com/big-government/2014/06/23/state-dept-honoree-calls-for-destruction-of-marriage/.

127 Clinton Fein, "The Gay Agenda," *Annoy.com*, June 8, 2005, accessed February 1, 2016, http://www.annoy.com/features/doc.html?DocumentID=100722.

128 Michael Foust, "If gay marriage is legalized, polygamy is next, briefs warn," *Baptist Press*, March 20, 2013, accessed April 25, 2016, http://www.bpnews.net/39916/if-gay-marriage-is-legalized-polygamy-is-next-briefs-warn.

129 Dennis Hollingsworth, et al., Petitiones, vs. Kristin M. Perry, et al., Respondents, On Writ of Certiorari to the United States Court of Appeals for the Ninth Court, No. 12-144 in the Supreme Court of the United States, Brief Addressing the Merits of the States of Indiana, Virginia, Alabama, Alaska, Arizona, Colorado, Georgia, Idaho, Kansas, Montana, Nebraska, North Dakota, Oklahoma, South Carolina, South Dakota, Texas, Utah, West Virginia and Wisconsin as Amici Curiae in Support of the Petitioners, January 29, 2013, accessed February 1, 2016, http://www.americanbar.org/content/dam/aba/

publications/supreme_court_preview/briefs-v2/12-144_pet_amcu_merits_soi-etal.authcheckdam.pdf.

130 Jeremy W. Peters, "The Gayest Place in America?" *New York Times*, November 17, 2013, accessed January 8, 2016, http://www.nytimes.com/2013/11/17/fashion/Washington-DC-has-thriving-gay-lesbian-and-transgender-population.html.

131 Andrew Sullivan, "Andrew Sullivan on Barack Obama's Gay Marriage Evolution," *Newsweek*, May 13, 2012, accessed January 8, 2016, http://www.newsweek.com/andrew-sullivan-barack-obamas-gay-marriage-evolution-65067.

132 Brendan Bordelon, "MSNBC anchor: 'So many people consider President Obama to be the first gay president'," *Daily Caller*, December 16, 2013, accessed January 8, 2016, http://dailycaller.com/2013/12/16/msnbc-anchor-so-many-people-consider-president-obama-to-be-the-first-gay-president/.

133 George E. Condon, Jr., "On Gay Rights, Obama Has Built a Legacy," *National Journal*, June 17, 2014, accessed October 29, 2015, http://www.nationaljournal.com/white-house/on-gay-rights-obama-has-built-a-legacy-20140617.

134 Laurie Higgins, "Obama Chooses Homosexuals over Veterans," *BarbWire.com*, June 1, 2014, accessed October 22, 2015, http://barbwire.com/2014/06/01/obama-chooses-homosexuals-veterans/.

135 L. Brent Bozell III and Tim Graham, "A New Evangelizing Foreign Policy," *CNSNews.com*, July 7, 2014, accessed January 8, 2016, http://cnsnews.com/commentary/l-brent-bozell-iii/new-evangelizing-foreign-policy.

136 Terence P. Jeffrey, "Obama at LGBT Fundraiser: Ban 'Conversion Therapy' for Transgender Minors," *CNSNews.com*, September 28, 2015, accessed January 8, 2016, http://cnsnews.com/news/article/terence-p-jeffrey/obama-lgbt-fundraiser-ban-conversion-therapy-transgender-minors.

137 Charlie Spiering, "Obama Warns Christians: Gay Rights More Important Than Religious Freedom," *Breitbart News Network*, September 28, 2015, accessed January 8, 2016, http://www.breitbart.com/big-government/2015/09/28/obama-warns-christians-gay-rights-important-religious-freedom/.

138 Patrick Goodenough, "Kerry: Foreign Gov'ts Must Accept Same-Sex Spouses of US Personnel Stationed Abroad," *CNSNews.com*, June 19, 2014, accessed January 8, 2016, http://cnsnews.com/news/article/patrick-goodenough/kerry-foreign-gov-ts-must-accept-same-sex-spouses-us-personnel.

139 Austin Ruse, "State Dept. Honors Advocate of Destruction of Marriage," *Breitbart News Network*, June 23, 2014, accessed January 8, 2016, http://www.breitbart.com/Big-Government/2014/06/23/State-Dept-Honoree-Calls-for-Destruction-of-Marriage.

140 Vanessa Gera, "US takes gay rights global, despite unsure welcome," *Associated Press*, June 28, 2014, accessed January 8, 2016, http://cnsnews.com/news/article/us-takes-gay-rights-global-despite-unsure-welcome.

141 Elias Biryabarema, "U.S. cuts aid to Uganda, cancels military exercise over anti-gay law," *Reuters*, June 19, 2014, accessed January 8, 2016, http://www.reuters.com/article/us-usa-uganda-gay-announcement-idUSKBN0EU26N20140619.

142 Olga Dzyubenko, "U.S. raps Kyrgyzstan for proposed 'gay propaganda' law," *Reuters*, October 13, 2014, accessed January 8, 2016, http://www.reuters.com/article/us-rights-kyrgyzstan-gay-idUSKCN0I20HR20141013.

143 Diane Montagna, "US Won't Help Fight Boko Haram Until Nigeria Accepts Homosexuality, Birth Control, Bishop Says," *Aleteia*, February 17, 2015, accessed January 8, 2016, http://www.aleteia.org/en/religion/article/us-wont-help-fight-boko-haram-until-nigeria-accepts-homosexuality-birth-control-bishop-says-5344466437144576.

144 Edith M. Lederer, "US and Chile are putting spotlight on lesbian and gay attacks by Islamic State extremists," *Associated Press*, August 13, 2015, accessed January 8, 2016, http://www.startribune.com/us-chile-put-spotlight-on-extremist-attacks-on-lgbt-people/321825571/.

145 Melanie Hunter, "State Dept to Spend $49,083 to Create a Network to Support the LGBT Community in India," *CNSNews.com*, October 2, 2015, accessed January 8, 2016, http://cnsnews.com/news/article/melanie-hunter/state-dept-spend-49083-create-network-support-lgbt-community-india-0.

146 "Transgender Day of Remembrance," *U.S. Department of State, John Kerry press statement*, November 20, 2014, accessed January 8, 2016, http://www.state.gov/secretary/remarks/2014/11/234297.htm.

147 JamesMichael Nichols, "Matthew Shepard Murdered By Bisexual Lover And Drug Dealer, Stephen Jimenez Claims In New Book," *Huffington Post*, September 12, 2013, accessed January 8, 2016, http://www.huffingtonpost.com/2013/09/12/stephen-jimenez-matthew-shepard_n_3914707.html.

148 Aaron Magid, "US ambassador's visit to LGBT event sparks outrage in Jordan," *Al-Monitor*, June 16, 2015, accessed January 8, 2016, http://www.al-monitor.com/pulse/originals/2015/06/jordan-gay-event-us-ambassador-wells-uproar-lgbt-rights.html.

149 Patrick Goodenough, "Kenyan Politician: If Obama Brings 'Gay Agenda, We Will Tell Him to Shut Up and Go Home'," *CNSNews.com*, July 7, 2015, accessed January 8, 2016, http://cnsnews.com/news/article/patrick-goodenough/kenyan-politician-if-obama-brings-gay-agenda-we-will-tell-him-shut.

150 Patrick Goodenough, "Kenyan President Tells Obama: LGBT Rights 'a Non-Issue' For Kenyans Today," *CNSNews.com*, July 27, 2015, accessed January 8, 2016, http://cnsnews.com/news/article/patrick-goodenough/kenyan-president-tells-obama-lgbt-rights-non-issue-kenyans-today.

151 Michael W. Chapman, "Uganda President to Obama on Gays: 'Respect African Societies and Their Values' – What Gays 'Do is Terrible'," *CNSNews.com* (blog), July 27, 2015, accessed January 8, 2016, http://cnsnews.com/blog/michael-w-chapman/uganda-president-obama-gays-respect-african-societies-and-their-values-what.

152 'Jola Sotubo, "Gay Marriage: 'We'll force Nigeria to legalize same-sex unions,'" US says," *Pulse*, July 15, 2015, accessed October 20, 2015, http://pulse.ng/local/gay-marriage-we-ll-force-nigeria-to-legalize-same-sex-unions-us-says-id3974975.html.

153 Lisa Anderson, "U.S. names first-ever LGBT human rights envoy," *Reuters*, February 23, 2015, accessed January 8, 2016, http://www.reuters.com/article/us-usa-diplomacy-lgbt-idUSKBN0LR23D20150223.

154 Patrick Goodenough, "7 Homosexual U.S. Ambassadors: Trade Deals Should Advance LGBTI Rights," *CNSNews.com*, June 10, 2015, accessed January 8, 2016, http://cnsnews.com/news/article/patrick-goodenough/7-homosexual-us-ambassadors-trade-deals-should-advance-lgbti-rights.

155 Julio Severo, "U.S. Homosexual Envoy Wants Brazil in New International Pro-sodomy

Coalition to Deflect Accusations of US 'Cultural Imperialism'," *BarbWire.com*, June 13, 2015, accessed January 8, 2016, http://barbwire.com/2015/06/13/0635-u-s-homosexual-envoy-wants-brazil-in-new-international-pro-sodomy-coalition-to-deflect-accusations-of-us-cultural-imperialism/.

156 Lisa Schlein, "US Battles Global Discrimination Against LGBTI People," *Voice of America*, June 30, 2015, accessed October 22, 2015, http://www.voanews.com/content/united-states-battles-discrimination-lgbti-people/2843957.html.

157 Austin Ruse, "In Face of Islamist Terror, Senate Bill Makes LGBT U.S. 'Foreign Policy Priority'," *Breitbart News Network*, June 17, 2014, accessed January 8, 2016, http://www.breitbart.com/Big-Peace/2014/06/17/In-Face-of-Increased-Islamist-Terror-Senators-Say-LGBT-is-U-S-Priority.

158 Tatiana Lozano, "Sen. Markey Wants to Establish Special LGBT Envoy at State Department," *CNSNews.com*, June 23, 2014, accessed January 8, 2016, http://cnsnews.com/news/article/tatiana-lozano/sen-markey-wants-establish-special-lgbt-envoy-state-department.

159 Austin Ruse, "In Face of Islamist Terror, Senate Bill Makes LGBT U.S. 'Foreign Policy Priority'," *Breitbart News Network*, June 17, 2014, accessed January 8, 2016, http://www.breitbart.com/Big-Peace/2014/06/17/In-Face-of-Increased-Islamist-Terror-Senators-Say-LGBT-is-U-S-Priority.

160 Jacqueline Klimas, "Bill would allow transgender troops to serve openly," *Washington Times*, June 23, 2015, accessed October 22, 2015, http://www.washingtontimes.com/news/2015/jun/23/bill-would-allow-transgender-troops-serve-openly/.

161 Dominic Holden, "Out Transgender Airman, In Male Uniform, Attends White House Pride Reception," *BuzzFeed*, June 24, 2015, accessed January 8, 2016, http://www.buzzfeed.com/dominicholden/out-transgender-airman-in-male-uniform-attends-white-house-p.

162 "CIA Celebrates LGBT Pride Month in June," *Central Intelligence Agency press release*, June 19, 2014, accessed January 8, 2016, https://www.cia.gov/news-information/featured-story-archive/2014-featured-story-archive/cia-celebrates-lgbt-pride-month-in-june.html.

163 "DIA celebrates Pride Month: 'Be proud of who you are'," *Defense Intelligence Agency press release*, June 20, 2014, accessed January 8, 2016, http://www.dia.mil/News/Articles/ArticleView/tabid/11448/Article/566994/dia-celebrates-pride-month-be-proud-of-who-you-are.aspx.

164 "Fact Sheet: The 2015 National Security Strategy," *White House, Office of the Press Secretary press release*, February 6, 2015, accessed January 8, 2016, https://www.whitehouse.gov/the-press-office/2015/02/06/fact-sheet-2015-national-security-strategy.

165 Barack Obama, "National Security Strategy," *White House, President of the United States*, February 2015, 20, accessed January 8, 2016, https://www.whitehouse.gov/sites/default/files/docs/2015_national_security_strategy_2.pdf.

166 Barack Obama, "National Security Strategy," *White House, President of the United States*, February 2015, 21, accessed January 8, 2016, https://www.whitehouse.gov/sites/default/files/docs/2015_national_security_strategy_2.pdf.

167 Rosa Brooks, "Can Gay Marriage Defeat the Islamic State?" *Foreign Policy*, June 26, 2015, accessed October 20, 2015, http://foreignpolicy.com/2015/06/26/can-gay-marriage-

defeat-the-islamic-state/.

168 John Lloyd, "The coming clash of civilizations over gay rights," *Reuters* (blog), August 12, 2013, accessed October 20, 2015, http://blogs.reuters.com/john-lloyd/2013/08/12/the-coming-clash-of-civilizations-over-gay-rights/.

169 JaneQRepublican, "Obama EEOC Chair Appointee Chai Feldblum In Her Own Words," *YouTube*, October 6, 2009, accessed February 1, 2016, https://www.youtube.com/watch?v=zYt1wYvuxDo. [Suggested Edit: The correct quotes are, "gay sex is morally good," and "want to revolutionize social norms"]

170 Matt Cover, "Obama's EEOC Nominee: Society Should 'Not Tolerate Private Beliefs' That 'Adversely Affect' Homosexuals," *CNSNews.com*, January 18, 2010, accessed February 1, 2016, http://cnsnews.com/news/article/obama-s-eeoc-nominee-society-should-not-tolerate-private-beliefs-adversely-affect.

171 Maggie Gallagher, "Banned in Boston," *Weekly Standard*, May 15, 2006, accessed February 1, 2016, http://www.weeklystandard.com/banned-in-boston/article/13329.

172 Anonymous, e-mail message to author, 2013. (**NOTE**: I do not recall the exact date of the email.)

173 Matt Walsh, "If you want to prove you don't hate gays, all you have to do is worship at their feet," *The Matt Walsh Blog*, July 22, 2014, accessed October 17, 2015, http://themattwalshblog.com/2014/07/22/want-prove-dont-hate-gays-all-you-have-to-do-is-worship-at-their-feet/.

174 Rush Limbaugh, "Two Serious Questions for You to Ponder," *The Rush Limbaugh Show*, July 2, 2015, accessed October 16, 2015, http://www.rushlimbaugh.com/daily/2015/07/02/two_serious_questions_for_you_to_ponder.

175 "Strategies of the Homosexual Movement: 'The Overhauling of Straight America'," *MassResistance*, n.d., accessed October 15, 2015, http://www.massresistance.org/docs/issues/gay_strategies/overhauling.html.

176 Michael Medved, *Hollywood vs. America* (New York: HarperPerennial, 1993), 239-240.

177 Marshall Kirk and Hunter Madsen, *After the Ball: How America Will Conquer Its Fear & Hatred off Gays in the 90s* (New York: Doubleday, 1989).

178 "The homosexual propaganda campaign in America's media – The powerful, sophisticated psychological techniques that the homosexual movement has used to manipulate the public in the media," *MassResistance*, n.d., accessed October 16, 2015, http://www.massresistance.org/docs/issues/gay_strategies/after_the_ball.html.

179 Lorena O'Neil, "Supreme Court Legalizes Gay Marriage in United States: Hollywood Cheers," *Hollywood Reporter*, June 26, 2015, accessed January 10, 2016, http://www.hollywoodreporter.com/news/supreme-court-gay-marriage-ruling-805181.

180 Spencer Kornhaber, "The Modern Family Effect: Pop Culture's Role in the Gay-Marriage Revolution," *Atlantic*, June 26, 2015, accessed January 10, 2016, http://www.theatlantic.com/entertainment/archive/2015/06/gay-marriage-legalized-modern-family-pop-culture/397013/.

181 Scott Collins and Meredith Blake, "Years before court ruling, pop culture shaped same-sex marriage debate," *Los Angeles Times*, June 27, 2015, accessed January 10, 2016, http://www.latimes.com/entertainment/la-et-st-0628-media-gay-marriage-20150628-story.html.

182 Tim Appelo, "THR Poll: 'Glee' and 'Modern Family' Drive Voters to Favor Gay Marriage – Even Many Romney Voters," *Hollywood Reporter*, November 3, 2012, accessed January 10, 2016, http://www.hollywoodreporter.com/news/thr-poll-glee-modern-family-386225.

183 Marco della Cava, "Hollywood: Gay marriage's best man," *USA Today*, June 26, 2013, accessed January 10, 2016, http://www.usatoday.com/story/life/2013/06/26/gay-marriage-hollywood-impact-cultural-shift/2461763/.

184 Ross Douthat, "The Terms of Our Surrender," *New York Times*, March 1, 2014, accessed January 10, 2016, http://www.nytimes.com/2014/03/02/opinion/sunday/the-terms-of-our-surrender.html.

185 Linda Harvey, "Why Are Christians Apologizing to 'LGBT' Activists?" *BarbWire.com*, October 15, 2015, accessed January 10, 2016, http://barbwire.com/2015/10/15/why-are-christians-apologizing-to-lgbt-activists/.

186 Lee Duigon, "Church Leaders Hoist White Flag in Culture War," *BarbWire.com,* August 13, 2014, accessed October 16, 2015, http://barbwire.com/2014/08/13/church-leaders-hoist-white-flag-culture-war/.

187 Michael Brown, "Christian Recording Artist Vicky Beeching Reveals She Is Gay: How Should Christians Respond?" *Christian Post*, August 18, 2014, accessed February 1, 2016, http://www.christianpost.com/news/christian-recording-artist-vicky-beeching-reveals-she-is-gay-how-should-christians-respond-124982/.

188 C. S. Lewis, *The Great Divorce* (San Francisco: HarperSanFrancisco, 2001), 75.

189 tub1, "Jesus calls a Canaanite woman a dog," *Unholy Bible* (blog), January 31, 2007, accessed October 16, 2015, https://unholybible.wordpress.com/2007/01/31/jesus-calls-a-canaanite-woman-a-dog/.

190 Drew Altman, "Behind the Increase in HIV Infections Among Gay and Bisexual Men," *Wall Street Journal*, Washington Wire (blog), September 25, 2014, accessed February 1, 2016, http://blogs.wsj.com/washwire/2014/09/25/behind-the-increase-in-hiv-infections-among-gay-and-bisexual-men/.

191 Ron Stall et al., "Running in Place: Implications of HIV Incidence Estimates among Urban Men Who Have Sex with Men in the United States and Other Industrialized Countries," *AIDS and Behavior*, 13, Issue 4 (2009): 615, accessed February 1, 2016, http://link.springer.com/article/10.1007%2Fs10461-008-9509-7.

192 Steve Inskeep, "The Preacher and the Activist," *NPR*, June 30, 2006, accessed January 10, 2016, http://www.npr.org/templates/story/story.php?storyId=5523909.

193 Kristin Larson, "Evangelical Colleges Inching Toward Affirmation of Homosexuality," *Juicy Ecumenism* (blog), April 3, 2013, accessed January 10, 2016, https://juicyecumenism.com/2013/04/03/evangelical-colleges-inching-toward-affirmation-of-homosexuality/.

194 Janet Mefferd, "Enough with the 'Dialogue,' Already," *Janet Mefferd Today*, June 17, 2015, accessed October 17, 2015, http://janetmefferd.com/2015/06/enough-with-the-dialogue-already/.

195 Cal Thomas, "Two Kingdoms In Conflict," *CalThomas.com*, September 8, 2015, accessed October 17, 2015, http://calthomas.com/columns/two-kingdoms-in-conflict.

196 Bob Beckel and Cal Thomas, "Common Ground with Bob Beckel & Cal Thomas," n.d., accessed October 17, 2015, http://calthomas.com/common-ground.

197 Bob Beckel and Cal Thomas, "Common Ground: Slay the Trump monster," *CalThomas.*

com, September 16, 2015, accessed October 17, 2015, http://calthomas.com/common-ground/gop-debate-round-2.

198 Cal Thomas, "Ben Carson and a Muslim President," *CalThomas.com*, September 23, 2015, accessed October 17, 2015, http://calthomas.com/columns/ben-carson-and-a-muslim-president.

199 Michael W. Chapman, "Cal Thomas: Gay Marriage, 'All the Prophecies' 'Coming True,' The 'End Times' Are 'Right on Schedule,'" *CNSNews.com* (blog), March 5, 2015, accessed October 17, 2015, http://www.cnsnews.com/blog/michael-w-chapman/cal-thomas-gay-marriage-all-prophecies-coming-true-end-times-are-right.

200 Rush Limbaugh, "Caller Intimidated by Door-to-Door Militant Gay Rights Activist," *The Rush Limbaugh Show*, August 3, 2012, accessed October 17, 2015, http://www.rushlimbaugh.com/daily/2012/08/03/caller_intimidated_by_door_to_door_militant_gay_rights_activist.

201 John-Henry Westen, "Why the simultaneous rise of homosexuality and Islam? An interview with Peter Kreeft," *LifeSiteNews.com*, June 26, 2013, accessed October 17, 2015, https://www.lifesitenews.com/news/why-the-simultaneous-rise-of-homosexuality-and-islam-an-interview-with-pete.

202 Matthew 16:26

203 David R. Wheeler, "Gay Marriage and the Future of Evangelical Colleges," *Atlantic*, July 14, 2015, accessed February 1, 2016, http://www.theatlantic.com/education/archive/2015/07/evangelical-colleges-struggle-gay-marriage-ruling/398306/.

204 David R. Wheeler, "Gay Marriage and the Future of Evangelical Colleges," *Atlantic*, July 14, 2015, accessed February 1, 2016, http://www.theatlantic.com/education/archive/2015/07/evangelical-colleges-struggle-gay-marriage-ruling/398306/.

205 Dietrich Bonhoeffer, *The Cost of Discipleship* (New York: Touchstone/Simon & Schuster, 1995), 64.

206 Bob Allen, "Baylor drops language referring to 'homosexual acts'," *Baptist News Global*, July 9, 2015, accessed February 1, 2016, https://baptistnews.com/ministry/organizations/item/30260-baylor-drops-ban-on-homosexual-acts.

207 Jonathan Merritt, "TRANSCRIPT: Hillsong's Brian Houston on same-sex issues," *Religion News Service*, October 16, 2014, accessed February 1, 2016, http://jonathanmerritt.religionnews.com/2014/10/16/transcript-hillsongs-brian-houston-sex-issues/.

208 Andrew E. Harrod, "New LGBT 'Gospel Truth' Appears at Washington, DC, Church Conference," *Juicy Ecumenism* (blog), November 20, 2014, accessed January 10, 2016, https://juicyecumenism.com/2014/11/20/new-lgbt-gospel-truth-appears-washington-dc-church-conference/.

209 Katy Kiser, "Methodist Protest Caucuses: 'We Are Coming For the Institution'," *Juicy Ecumenism* (blog), August 29, 2015, accessed October 17, 2015, https://juicyecumenism.com/2015/08/29/methodist-protest-caucuses-we-are-coming-for-the-institution/.

210 My recreation of what Travis Witt told me about John Peter Gabriel Muhlenberg is based off my recollection of the conversation between Travis and me, and research of Muhlenberg's words. Many of the quotations attributed to Muhlenberg (and those with whom he conversed) that I use in my recreation of the conversation may have originated from the following book: Jim Ryun & Sons, *Heroes Among Us* (Shippensburg, PA: Destiny Image, 2002), 199-214.

211 "From John Adams to Massachusetts Militia, 11 October 1798," *Founders Online, National Archives*, December 30, 2015, accessed February 15, 2016, http://founders.archives.gov/documents/Adams/99-02-02-3102.

212 "Stand Your Ground," *Liberty Counsel press release*, November 3, 2014, accessed February 15, 2016, https://lc.org/newsroom/details/stand-your-ground.

213 "Stand Your Ground," *Liberty Counsel press release*, November 3, 2014, accessed April 25, 2016, http://canadafreepress.com/article/stand-your-ground.

214 "Church Leaders Refuse to be Intimidated Regarding Political Activity," *Liberty Counsel press release*, November 2, 2012, accessed February 15, 2016, https://www.lc.org/newsroom/details/church-leaders-refuse-to-be-intimidated-regarding-political-activity-1.

215 Kimberly Winston, "Atheists sue IRS for failure to monitor church politicking," *Religion News Service*, November 16, 2012, accessed February 15, 2016, https://www.washingtonpost.com/national/on-faith/atheists-sue-irs-for-failure-to-monitor-church-politicking/2012/11/15/39b2bf80-2f66-11e2-af17-67abba0676e2_story.html.

216 M. Alex Johnson, "Pulpit politics: Pastors endorse candidates, thumbing noses at the IRS," *NBC News*, November 4, 2012, accessed February 15, 2016, http://usnews.nbcnews.com/_news/2012/11/04/14703656-pulpit-politics-pastors-endorse-candidates-thumbing-noses-at-the-irs.

217 Carrie Dann, "Obama on judges, Supreme Court," *NBC News*, July 17, 2007, accessed February 15, 2016, http://firstread.nbcnews.com/_news/2007/07/17/4439758-obama-on-judges-supreme-court.

218 "What Do Voters Think of the Supreme Court Now?" *Rasmussen Reports*, July 24, 2015, accessed April 24, 2016, http://www.rasmussenreports.com/public_content/archive/mood_of_america_archive/supreme_court_ratings/what_do_voters_think_of_the_supreme_court_now.

219 As quoted in Stanley I. Kutler, ed., *The Dred Scott Decision: Law or Politics* (Boston: Houghton Mifflin Company, 1967), 59.

220 As quoted in Stanley I. Kutler, ed., *The Dred Scott Decision: Law or Politics* (Boston: Houghton Mifflin Company, 1967), 59.

221 Jeffrey Rosen, "The Supreme Court – The First Hundred Years," *PBS*, December 2006, accessed February 15, 2016, http://www.pbs.org/wnet/supremecourt/antebellum/history2.html.

222 As quoted in Stanley I. Kutler, ed., *The Dred Scott Decision: Law or Politics* (Boston: Houghton Mifflin Company, 1967), 59.

223 As quoted in Stanley I. Kutler, ed., *The Dred Scott Decision: Law or Politics* (Boston: Houghton Mifflin Company, 1967), 59.

224 Diana Chandler, "'I would hug him,' says florist of gay accuser," *Baptist Press*, March 3, 2015, accessed February 15, 2016, http://www.bpnews.net/44312/i-would-hug-him-says-florist-of-gay-accuser.

225 "Statement of Attorney General Bob Ferguson Concerning Arlene's Flowers Same-sex Marriage Discrimination Case," *Washington State Office of the Attorney General press release*, February 19, 2015, accessed February 15, 2016, http://www.atg.wa.gov/news/news-releases/statement-attorney-general-bob-ferguson-concerning-arlene-s-flowers-same-sex.

226 Barronelle Stutzman, *Letter to Washington Attorney General Bob Ferguson*, February 20, 2015, accessed February 15, 2016, http://www.adfmedia.org/files/ArlenesFlowersSettlementOfferResponse.pdf.

227 "Accommodations Would End Rowan County Dispute," *Liberty Counsel press release*, August 31, 2015, accessed February 15, 2016, http://www.lc.org/newsroom/details/accommodations-would-end-rowan-county-dispute-1.

228 Todd Starnes, "EXCLUSIVE: Kentucky Clerk: 'This is a fight worth fighting'," *FoxNews.com*, September 3, 2015, accessed February 15, 2016, http://www.foxnews.com/opinion/2015/09/03/kentucky-clerk-am-prepared-to-go-to-jail.html.

229 Steven Nelson, "Kentucky Clerk Kim Davis Jailed for Contempt," *U.S. News & World Report*, September 3, 2015, accessed February 15, 2016, http://www.usnews.com/news/articles/2015/09/03/kentucky-clerk-kim-davis-jailed-for-contempt.

230 "Supporters to Stage "I'm with Kim" Rally at Jail," *Liberty Counsel press release*, September 4, 2015, accessed February 15, 2016, https://www.lc.org/newsroom/details/supporters-to-stage-im-with-kim-rally-at-jail-1.

CPSIA information can be obtained at www.ICGtesting.com
Printed in the USA
LVOW11s0335010716

494824LV00001B/1/P